WITHDRAWN
HARVARD LIBRARY
WITHDRAWN

Religion in the Americas Series

Edited by

Henri Gooren

(Oakland University, Rochester, MI, USA)

VOLUME 7

Old Colony Mennonites in Argentina and Bolivia

Nation Making, Religious Conflict and Imagination of the Future

by

Lorenzo Cañás Bottos

BRILL

LEIDEN · BOSTON
2008

Cover photograph (c) Jordi Busque / www.jordibusque.com

This book is printed on acid-free paper.

Library of Congress Cataloging-in-Publication Data

A C.I.P. record for this book is available from the Library of Congress.

BX
8129
.O4
C36
2008

ISSN 1542-1279
ISBN 978 90 04 16095 8

Copyright 2008 by Koninklijke Brill NV, Leiden, The Netherlands
Koninklijke Brill NV incorporates the imprints Brill, Hotei Publishing,
IDC Publishers, Martinus Nijhoff Publishers and VSP.

All rights reserved. No part of this publication may be reproduced, translated,
stored in a retrieval system, or transmitted in any form or by any means, electronic,
mechanical, photocopying, recording or otherwise, without prior written permission
from the publisher.

Authorization to photocopy items for internal or personal use is granted by
Koninklijke Brill NV provided that the appropriate fees are paid directly to
The Copyright Clearance Center, 222 Rosewood Drive, Suite 910,
Danvers, MA 01923, USA.
Fees are subject to change.

PRINTED IN THE NETHERLANDS

To Susanne, and our common future.

happened in the intervening years.[2] Regarding the Mennonites, he commented that many had left for Bolivia, and more were in the process of leaving. He continued telling me about his problems with his pick-up truck, which meant that he would not go to the colony that day (he supplied the Mennonites with groceries and other general goods). I then arranged a taxi to take me to the Mennonite colony. As we covered the 35 kilometres long dirt road that connects Guatraché with *La Nueva Esperanza* (lit. 'the new hope' or '*Das Neue Hoffnung*' in the original German name that the Mennonites gave to the old Estancia Remecó) we could see the pampas spreading all around us.[3] The brown and yellow fields with just a few, almost imperceptible, undulations here and there, extended up to the blue sky in all directions while the yellowish dust was coming through the half-opened car windows. Wire fences lined both sides of the road, extending for kilometres until every once and then, a tree lined path leading inwards forced them open. Protected from the wind, and hidden from sight by trees planted around them, the *estancias'* (ranches) locations were given away by the windmills' heads that peered over the trees. After some twenty minutes of small talk, the driver mentioned that there was a new bishop and that there was a court trial going on at that very moment in Santa Rosa (the provincial capital) that involved the Mennonites.

After some forty minutes, we reached the colony, clearly distinguishable from the surrounding estancias by its settlement pattern of linear villages forming a grid. Each linear village formed by a straight road lined with houses some 200 metres apart, with a strip of land of around 2.5 kilometres long extending behind each one of them. I asked the taxi driver to take me to Franz's, who has been one of my usual hosts in the colony. He greeted me with a hug, something very unusual between Mennonites, who prefer acknowledging each other at a distance, but through which we both expressed our affection towards each other, followed by a long lasting handshake. He was wearing the standard male Mennonite attire, a blue *schlaubbekjse* (dungarees), light shirt, and a plain brown baseball cap. While still shaking hands he glanced at my

---

[2] Mate is a typical South-American brew, made out of the leaves of the *Ilex paraguarensis*. A gourd is filled with the cured and dried leaves, hot water poured into it, and drunk through a metal straw with a strainer on its lower end. Drunk usually when in company, people take turns in sipping from the same gourd. The *alfajor* is a traditional Argentine sweet, made of two cookies with sweet stuffing in the middle (usually *dulce de leche*—milk jelly, similar to caramel) and then covered with chocolate or caster sugar.

[3] Unless noted, all translations are my own.

backpack and asked me to come inside and bring my luggage into the house. Katherina and Helena (Franz's wife and daughter) were inside, taking care of a baby. "This is my granddaughter, the sun of my life," remarked Franz. I shook hands and exchanged long lasting smiles with both women who were clad in similar dark dresses (decorated with printed flowers in pink, red, white and green) and black embroidered kerchiefs over their heads. They also seemed glad to see me again. Later, over dinner, and in the dim yellow light of the kerosene lamp, Franz stated that for him, as his father had taught him, visits were like fish: only enjoyable while fresh. He remarked on the fact that all the other families that had received me in the past had gone back to Bolivia, and that he was not very happy with the latest changes in the religious structure of the colony. I knew with this that he was going to be my only host, and that I had to be careful in not overstaying at his place. I had not managed in my previous fieldwork to live on my own within the colonies, I thought this was about to change.

"Satan has planted a bitter root among us," Franz said seriously. By this time, we had finished eating, and the women were in the kitchen washing up the dishes, leaving Franz and I alone in the dining room. I was surprized, since on previous field trips he had made a great effort to conceal internal differences and conflicts from me. "These are things I will not talk to you about, they make me sad and I don't want you to know about them," was a reply he had given me in 1997 when I questioned him on some internal differences and conflicts I was able to discern between colonists coming from Mexico and Bolivia. He also mentioned that he was strongly considering going back to Bolivia by the end of the year. I explained to him that I was hoping to stay in the colony for a year, and he suggested that I rent a small house that had been left vacant by one of the emigrated families. In his opinion, there would be no problem of reaching an arrangement with the owner, since he had received me on my previous visits and knew me well, but before that, and due to the new situation, I would now require permission from the *eltesta*.[4] A few days later, I set out to the *eltesta's* house. He replied that my request would be analysed in the following *donnadach* (a fortnightly meeting of the *Leardeenst*—a collective formed

---

[4] Literally 'the eldest one', it is the highest authority within the colony. The Mennonites translate the position as 'obispo'—bishop. For terms in Plautdietsch I follow the orthography proposed by Abraham Rempel (1995).

by the religious authorities: *eltesta, prädjasch* and *dia'koon*). Until then, I would stay at Franz's.

Franz recognized the existence of conflicts that had induced several families to migrate back to Bolivia, as well as forcing a change of *eltesta* (a lifelong position). In Franz's opinion the new *eltesta* "is too young and does not know of suffering, so he lacks understanding on some things...Things have changed a lot over here, and not in a way I am happy about."[5] As I later learned, some of the conflicts were triggered by my previous presence, but more importantly by Sergio and Silvana, an Argentine couple that attempted to become Mennonite, but who eventually moved to Bolivia. Their main sponsors within the colony had been the same people that supported my work.

A few days later, a big lorry stopped by Franz's house and a Mennonite jumped out from it. We introduced ourselves and learned that his name was Benjamin; although we had never met before, he seemed to know a lot about me. Sergio had been his source, telling him about me and my dissertation (Cañás Bottos 1998; published some years later Cañás Bottos 2005), which he was eager to read. I did not have a copy with me at the time, so I told him I would send him one as soon as I could.

Franz was keeping in storage some of Sergio and Silvana's belongings, which Benjamin was picking up to take with him to Bolivia for delivery to their owners, since he had also decided to leave the colony in Argentina. I learned later that he was leaving the colony because he had been threatened with excommunication by the colony authorities because he had translated and circulated some of Sergio's writings (see Chapter 7). As we said goodbye I told him that if I was denied permission to stay, I would personally bring him the dissertation to Bolivia. He replied I would be very welcome at his house and, after shaking hands, he climbed on to the truck and left.

Two weeks later, I received news that a decision had been reached regarding my request. I immediately dashed to the *eltesta's* house. In the *eltesta's* own words, I was refused permission because: "If we let you stay, then we should also allow many other people who wish to stay with us too." I argued that they were already allowing two taxi drivers to live within the colony's boundaries, to which he replied that

---

[5] The previous *eltesta* was relieved from his duties due to a scandal that will be reviewed in Chapter 3.

"they do business with us." Feelings of frustration and powerlessness threatened to overtake me as I saw my whole research project crumbling before my very eyes. I tried to negotiate, but he repeated that the *Leardeenst* had already taken a unanimous decision and that there was nothing else to be done about it. I headed back to Franz's, who inquired into what had happened. I told him about the refusal, and that I was going to Bolivia to do my work with the people that had moved. Franz ended our conversation with a worried face and tone, "I am ashamed of having such people as my spiritual guides. By the end of this year, as soon as I finish with the standing orders for the silos, I'll move to Bolivia too."

What had happened during my two years' absence? What were the causes of these conflicts? How were they handled in practice? Was conflict something not only inherent, but also something that contributed to their continuity? Could this conflict shed any light on the recurrent schismatic history of Mennonites colonies? These were some of the questions that I left for Bolivia in order to answer, and that this book seeks to address.

I was confronted with a conflictive situation that contrasted with the pictures of cohesion, homogeneity and peacefulness drawn by studies of Mennonites and related groups upon which my fieldwork expectations had been built, and which my previous research experiences had only hinted. Behind a façade of sendentarism and rootedness suggested by the clear-cut geographical limits of the colonies, together with their agricultural practices and their investment on improving the land (building houses, roads, wells, etc.) were lurking strategies that spun not only across individual colonies, but also across countries. The cross-border social space within which the Mennonites acted dawned on me, and my research strategy had to follow suit.

Thus, this book is based on ethnographic fieldwork in several Mennonite colonies in Argentina and Bolivia. I spent the southern hemisphere summers of the years 1996, 1997 and 1998, and the month of August 2000 in La Nueva Esperanza. I spent just under a year in Bolivia, between October 2000 and August 2001, doing fieldwork in the Swift Current, Riva Palacios, and Santa Rita colonies, all located in the department of Santa Cruz. Fieldwork in Argentina consisted of living within the colony and participating in everyday activities (feeding and milking the cows, cleaning stables, attending mass, going to the store, visiting, etc.) while performing a variety of research techniques (open ended interviews, collection of genealogies, construction of cultural

Some of the ideas in this book were previously tested in the form of papers presented to different audiences. A different version of Chapter 1 was presented in April 2004 at the Institute for the Study of Social Change, University College Dublin, under the title "From Religious Principles to Ethnic Identity Markers: Transformations of Old Colony Mennonites." A very early version of Chapter 2 was presented at the Instituto de Postgraduaçao em Filosofia e Ciencias Humanas, Universidade do Estado do Rio de Janeiro in May 2001 under the title "Cisma e Continuidade: Dilemas dos Menonitas na Bolivia e na Argentina." I read a reduced version of Chapter 6 at the Latin-American Seminar at the Department of Anthropology, London School of Economics in February 2004. The core of Chapter 5 was presented at the 2005 Annual Meeting of the American Anthropological Association in Washington DC. The ethnographic material in the last three chapters was used to test different arguments at the Decennial Conference of the Association of Social Anthropologists in Manchester in 2003, at a seminar of the School of History and Anthropology, Queens University Belfast in October 2005, and at the European Association of Social Anthropologists Biannual Conference, Bristol in October 2006. I thank the organizers for their invitations, and the participants for their encouraging comments and lively discussions. Needless to say, any mistakes and omissions are all my own responsibility.

In Buenos Aires, special thanks are due to Sergio Visacovsky, Rosana Guber and Santiago Alvarez, who have formed at IDES (Institute for Economic and Social and Development) a vibrant anthropological community. Their friendship and support in Buenos Aires filled an aching void. Jürgen Riester and the rest of APCOB's (Support for Eastern Bolivia's Indigenous-Peasant) personnel provided initial guidance in Santa Cruz de la Sierra. During fieldwork in Bolivia, I maintained a feeling of home at 'Parrillada Las Leñitas' where Flavio Seco always kept a place for me on his family table.

I am deeply grateful to all my Mennonite friends and informants. They all put their reputations (and livelihoods) at risk for supporting me within the colonies. Omar and his family deserve a special mention for going out of their way, and out of the kindness of their hearts, to ease as much as possible my research in Guatraché and La Nueva Esperanza. Thanks also to Sergio and Silvana, for all those unforgettable evening discussions in Tarija.

Last, but not least, to my parents, Susana and Lorenzo, and my siblings, Manuel, Florencia and Lucila. Without their constant support and encouragement, this work would not have been possible.

INTRODUCTION

The Old Colony is one among the wide variety of self-defined Mennonite groups (Kniss 1997; Toews 1989: 227) that recognize Menno Simons (1496–1561), originally a Dutch Catholic priest, as their founder.[1] They are part of a wider grouping known as Anabaptists (due to their rejection of child baptism, the founders and first generation of these groups had undergone a second baptism during adulthood, hence their name which means 'rebaptizers') which also includes the Amish and Hutterites. Like them, they have gone through long stories of migration and persecution between Europe, Asia and America, and have strived to remain 'separate from the world' by forming religiously exclusive agricultural settlements (colonies).

This book presents a political analysis of Old Colony Mennonites in Bolivia and Argentina. However, the reader will find here no analysis of involvement of Mennonites in party politics, nor an analysis of the processes of election and selection of political leaders.[2] Rather, it is political in the wide sense of the term, about the social dynamics involved in the making of Mennonite polities. For this, I have chosen an unusual and often ignored strategic dimension of analysis: the imagination of the future.

Choosing the imagination of the future as a problem to be addressed through the case of Old Colony Mennonites might sound like an oxymoron. This is because groups like the Old Colony Mennonites, Amish and Hutterites have often been perceived as if they lived in the past due to their rejection or selective appropriation of technological advances. This perception has been consolidated by the mass media through movies like *Witness* (Weir 1985) and more recently reality-TV shows like *Amish in the City*.[3] This perception tells more about the world

---

[1] The first usage of the term "Mennisten" (Mennonites) to refer to quietist and pacifist groups is attributed to Jan Łaski (1499–1560) (Cameron 1991: 327; Williams 1962: 487).

[2] For the Mennonites involvement in Canadian and Russian politics I refer the reader to James Urry's excellent work (2006).

[3] For an analysis of the place of the Amish in the popular imagination in the US see David Weaver-Zercher (2001; cf. Walbert 2002). For an analysis of how the Argentine media has portrayed La Nueva Esperanza see (Cañás Bottos 2005: 103–114; 2006).

of the observer than the observed, revealing the concealed assumption that links the passage of time with technological development and progress. But this is only one possible narrative, one amongst many possibilities of imagining the future. Not all societies or groups need imagine the future in the same way, and the evolutionary narrative of modern western society should be taken as but one among many other possibilities. The starting point of this book is that, although all societies or groups possess some sort of temporal narrative and a way of imagining a future towards which they orient their action, the means and content of such imaginations are variable. The notion of 'imagination of the future' I propose here incorporates the ideals of how life ought to be lived, which constitutes the Mennonites' basic orientations in their reproduction over time. I focus on how this imagination is maintained and transformed through processes of internal enforcement and contestation, appropriation, external impositions, and from the application of abstract ideals into practice. I apply this framework to link historical macro level processes with meso-level processes of articulation and border management, together with a biographical approach to conversion narratives, the religious experience and conflict. I show the transformations in both the Mennonite social organization and in the meaning and social relevance of the religious symbols they use to define themselves against the rest of humanity. I also show that the basis of membership has changed from one based on voluntary faith, to a compulsory and common descent based one that is actually in practice. The analysis of their migrations shows regularities that evidence that in their relationships with nation-states the Mennonites contributed to their territorial consolidation and economic development, accepting citizenship while simultaneously rejecting nationality through the building of a community that spans across state borders.

In this book, I go against the predominant representations of Mennonites in at least one other count. Mennonites are usually portrayed as perfect examples of community, where their selective appropriation of technology and their rejection of modernity, makes them the repositories of morality, cohesion, isolation, immutability and solidarity in the face of the evils of the modern world such as anomie, social disintegration, individualism, and accelerated change. Instead, this book focuses on deviance, conflict, and border maintenance as strategic methodological lines of entry for questioning the Mennonite's process of imagining and constructing their future.

A secondary and intimately linked objective is to enquire into broad macro issues and processes such as the rise of the nation-state and globalization, while at the same time provide with the Mennonite's interpretation of both their history and of such formations, as well as their positioning within the broader world. The Mennonites provide a promising standpoint for producing a decentred analysis of the macro-processes of nation-state formation due to a number of reasons (which I develop further in the text): Their contribution to the subversion of the narratives that legitimized the feudal order; their contribution to the territorial consolidation of states; their rejection to becoming part of the body of the nation; and their negotiation with sovereigns for states of exception (Agamben 2005) where they could freely develop separate from the world, and the state. I will provide a view of the global from the local that might help see things that the sedentary history written from the perspective of the state apparatus does not show, or which it forcefully tries to suppress (Deleuze and Guattari 1987: 23). This marginal perspective is then reproduced in the analysis of the Old Colony. The conflicts that arose from the challenges to the established order, their contestation, enforcement, control and processes of disciplining provided a window from which to explore the limits of the Old Colony's imagination of the future, and how different imaginations were built, challenged the established order, and the measures taken to control them.

The contextualization of cases in cultural areas is an established practice in ethnographic writing which simultaneously constructs a range of problems, discourses and theoretical issues that simultaneously guide and limit new research (Gupta and Ferguson 1997). In this way, certain problems are raised and studied in different places: cargo cults and gift giving in Melanesia, honour, shame and patronage around the Mediterranean, and hierarchy in India, etc. The building of a cultural area assumes a direct relationship between geographical proximity and cultural similarity, reinforcing the localized nature of anthropological objects of study (Clifford 1997: 24). The Mennonites question the basis of this grounded notion of cultural area on two counts. First, due to their particular history of movement and attempts at remaining separate for the world, their cultural similarity ought to follow confessional and 'genealogical' instead of geographical proximity. The range of cases thus formed include Amish and Hutterites, who share their sixteenth-century Anabaptist origin, as well as long histories of migration that lead to the formation of agricultural settlements in the American continent.

Finally, the taxonomical effort in the creation of cultural areas has often been subsumed to the national order of things (Malkki 1995b) and research areas have remained within and below the national level assuming that social processes were delimited by national borders or locality as Liisa Malkki (1995a) and Eric Wolf note (1997: 17). In this way reinforcing that such order ordering is the "natural social and political form of the modern world" (Wimmer and Glick Schiller 2002: 302). The Mennonite's history of constant border crossing and their formation of a territorially fragmented community that spans across national borders requires an approach that is not limited by the naturalization of national borders. An appropriate treatment of this dimension has been lacking, which this book aims to fulfil. Indeed, one of the broader objectives of this book is to provide a decentred analysis of the process of formation and transformation of the national order of things as seen through their relationships with the Mennonite order.

In the remainder of this introduction, I present first, a brief analysis of the ways in which Mennonites, Hutterites and Amish have been represented within the social sciences. I then sketch out my understanding of the problem of the future, finalizing with an outline of this book.

Representations of the Mennonites, Amish and Hutterites

Recurrent topics in sociological and anthropological studies of Amish, Mennonites and Hutterites, include their economic success within a context of selective technological appropriation (Bennett 1967), and the effects and threats that these appropriations pose for the social identities of these groups (Kraybill 1989; Kraybill and Nolt 1995; Umble 1996; Redekop 1969; Hostetler 1974, 1993). For example in Donald Kraybill's description of the Amish we can find the following italicized terms: 'local,' 'multibonded,' 'informal,' 'small-scale,' 'homogeneous,' 'mutual-aid' (2003: 8–9), a collection of tropes that point to the discursive construction of the Amish as the perfect realization of community. These studies emphasize community rather than the individual; cohesion rather than conflict; social control and homogeneity rather than resistance and deviance; fixed essentialized borders rather than in flexible, redefinable ones over time. Fred Kniss, one of the few scholars to have focused on conflict processes among US Mennonites recognizes these pitfalls in popular books about Amish that "are often paeans to the simplicity and order of traditional community, capturing in literary form the romantic nostalgia that underlies the lucrative tourist market in things Amish and Shaker" (Kniss 1997: 1). Although this has not always been the case, for in the *Mennonite Encyclopedia*, a major reference work produced by American and Canadian Mennonites, the Old Colony are characterized as having suffered "cultural and religious deterioration" (Klaassen 1955: 504) and of being culturally retarded (Krahn 1959a: 38). Evidencing that prior to becoming sources of nostalgia, these groups had a very different positioning within the Mennonite field.

Nevertheless, academic works by sociologists, historians and anthropologists have tended to produce localized and romanticized portraits that spring from these groups' rejection or selective appropriation of modern technology and its relationship with the groups' identity, and community customs and religion (Hostetler 1964, 1974, 1993; Hostetler and Huntington 1967; Kraybill 1989, 2003; Kraybill and Bowman 2001; Kraybill and Nolt 1995; Schreiber 1962; Schwieder and Schwieder 1975; Bennett 1967; Umble 1996; Loewen 1993). These views feed the curiosity for otherness while reinforcing, as Fred Kniss (1997: 1–2) would have it, the image of these groups as the solution to the longing for community and lost values of the wider US American audience. John Hostetler, one of the most widely published authors on the field, whose work includes both academic monographs (1964; 1974; 1989; 1993; 1967) as well as general audience books (1983; 1995) concludes that:

> Amish communities have preserved some of the qualities the larger American society once had, and now seeks to regain: intimate family and community relationships, respect for children and grandparents, religion as a way of life, mutual help in times of crisis, the use of restraints to control the influence of technology, and a dignified way of dying without going broke. (1993: 397)

The romantic vision of the Amish comes to the foreground here, appearing as a haven from the dangers of the modern world, a living example of the lost US American past. Although almost forty years earlier Old Colony Mennonites were presented as examples of "what Mennonite life in Russia was like 100 years ago" (Krahn 1959a: 42). In these characterizations, two operations are put in motion. On the one hand, the imposition of the observers' narrative, where technological development and moral decline are linked to the passage of time, and therefore a better world, and less complex technology are always imputed to the past. On the other hand, they set in motion the construction of difference through the inversion of the characteristics of the observer, the classical production of the 'other' (Todorov 1984; Kuper 1997): The Amish therefore become a new incarnation of Rosseau's 'noble savages', or early anthropologists' 'primitives'.

These groups have cast a powerful spell on their observers by presenting a series of riddles (Kraybill 1989; see also Umble 1996) to the modern western observer, which, because they touch upon central issues of its worldview, ask for resolution. These riddles are based on these groups' social and cultural viability while practicing a selective appropriation of technology (which resonates somehow disharmoniously with the dominant narrative of progress) and the core ideological values that legitimate their social order, in turn resonating with the observers' ideals that often fail to materialize in modern western society, the longing for community and solidarity mentioned by Kniss (1997). These in turn lead to a confusion identified by Anthony Cohen as the myth of equality in community life (1985: 33 and ff.). This myth arises from the confusion, on the part of the analyst, of equality as an ideology, rhetoric or pragmatism with equality as an actual quality of social relations. A common feature of studies of Anabaptist groups is precisely this confusion between Mennonites' (or Amish and Hutterites') ideologies, rhetorics, and pragmatism (of separation from the world, biblical foundation of the social system, and social immutability) with their actual empirical occurrence.

A first consequence of this confusion is the assumption, on the part of the researcher, of a direct and unproblematic relationship between openly held values and actual observable behaviour in practice (see for example Hostetler 1993; Kraybill 1989; Redekop 1969). Alternatively, to put in the vocabulary of political anthropology, to take the dominant ideology that legitimates the established order as an accurate empirical description of said order. This is then followed by the imputations that groups have an orthopraxis but lack an orthodoxy, the classical means through which a dominant ideology hides its own origins as ideology and masks itself as reality. For example, whereas Donald Kraybill and Carl Bowman state that "Mennonites had always emphasized the *practice* of faith, not the study of abstract doctrines," (2001: 63, emphasis in original) John Hostetler repeatedly mentions the "silent discourse" of the Amish (Hostetler 1995). Indeed, "hegemony—as Jean and John Comaroff argue—at its most effective, is mute" (1991: 24). On another level, and as we will see later, the Mennonites' obstinacy in dealing with powerful empires and states and succeeding in obtaining their conditions to construct their own future according to their own faith, has been anything but quiet. This lack of doctrinal vocality attributed to Amish and Mennonites also allows these authors to dismiss the colonists' own perspectives (and particularly those of internal dissenters). Since faith is assumed to be expressed directly in practices, it rules out any possibility of discrepancy, tension or contradiction between them. It is precisely by problematizing the relationship between practices, belief and faith, that it is possible to gain a window into the dynamics of social and religious change. Part of the argument I will be making in this book is that we ought to bring those changes to the foreground, since through them and in the handling of their promoters, the Mennonites have re-defined themselves, re-tracing their boundaries in a continuous historical process.

This confusion between ideology and observed behaviour also reflects on the understanding of the history and change of these groups. In these studies, the histories of persecution and migration resulting from these groups' quest for building a community of believers that seeks to remain separate from the world are presented as their charters of legitimation (by highlighting continuity, assuming their biblicality and excluding conflict) as historical churches, rather than as examples of ongoing social processes constitutive of their past, present, and future situation (Hostetler 1983; Redekop 1969; Hostetler 1992; Hostetler 1964, 1993; Kraybill 1989; Kraybill and Bowman 2001; Walbert 2002; Bennett 1967; Hostetler and Huntington 1967). Thus, they portray change as a threat rather than as the result of Mennonites being historical agents, or, if they have been historical agents in the past, they are no longer entitled to be so if they wish to remain Mennonites, or Amish. For example Calvin Wall Redekop, in his ethnography on Old Colony Mennonites in Mexico (1969), differentiates cultural from structural assimilation, showing that although the Mennonites have accepted external cultural influences, they have done so very carefully in order to avoid structural assimilation. The imposition of the narrative of modernity, and understanding the Old Colony solely in terms of technological rejection, while confusing their own ideologies of immutability with their actual situation leads Redekop to remark that:

> The Old Colony as a viable ethnic minority is doomed in our contemporary world because of its intentionally obscurantist position [...] Groups which refuse to accept change and progress cannot survive. (1969: 221)

Nevertheless, his warning that Mennonites will not resist their host societies' much longer, will change structurally, and therefore stop being Mennonites (Redekop 1969: 229–243) evidences that the Mennonites are at the end of their history. In a similar vein, Donald Kraybill and Steven Nolt (1995) analyse how the Amish in Pennsylvania have successfully adapted to conditions of land scarcity via the formation of micro enterprises. They focus on the identification of cultural resources that either hinder or help the Amish in such endeavours. The authors conclude that the dynamics that the Amish have so carefully tried to harness in order to maintain their cultural system will, in the end destroy the total fabric of Amish ways—gender roles, child-rearing practices, attitudes toward leisure, church life, class structure, the distribution of power, traditional values, relations with outsiders, and indeed the Amish worldview itself. (Kraybill and Nolt 1995: 239)

Despite Kraybill and Nolt's (1995) emphasis on analysing processes of change, they see them not as different historical ways of being Amish, but as deviations from the "Amish ways" they construct from their present situation. The adoption of instrumental technological advances are considered autonomous and natural (showing the authors' standing within the narrative of modernity that links technological progress with instrumentality and the passage of time), and their adoption a mere accommodation. As such, these changes are perceived to lie beyond culture (due to their unquestioned and ahistoric perceived instrumentality). However, whenever a change is identified anywhere else in their cultural or social system, it is considered as 'acculturation' or 'integration', a threat to their integrity as Amish. Like Redekop's Mennonites, the Amish have also reached the end of their history; they are on a terminal stage whereby any further change would render them un-Mennonite or un-Amish. These evaluations sound like the colony authorities I have met in their warnings that the adoption of this or that feature will endanger their separation from the world, and that Mennonites ought to continue living in the past. By falling prey to the confusion between these groups' ideologies of immutability, which hide their actual change along history, these authors deny Mennonites and Amish of their self-definition, and their agency in imagining and building their own future. A future where they could continue providing new answers to new challenges, re-defining as it were, the meaning and content of what makes the Amish or the Mennonite ways, as they have done in their passage from sixteenth-century Europe to twentieth-century Latin America. It is therefore through these processes that on the one hand the Mennonites become historical actors, by constantly discussing, arguing, and constructing themselves and their future.

But what do the Mennonite authorities meant by the 'past' which characterizes the ideal order? Is it really the past, or a projection from the present in order to stall any changes towards the future? The Mennonites' history I present below focuses on those historical changes that Mennonites ought to conceal since they are a threat to any revealed order. The past is always a projection of the present, to give the illusion of exchangeability, and which justifies a particular present order and imagination of the future. The success of this operation leads to the provision of supporting proof to the ideology of immutability. It is through this construction of the ideal order, the model of what society ought to be like, that acts as a guiding beacon, that this book focuses on. It is an imagination of the future, but which the Mennonites call the 'past' in order to legitimize their present order. The present study therefore attempts to bring to the foreground not only the Old Colony's ostensive values, but also its changes over time, and the contrasts between them and the actual principles that guide their concrete practices. Rephrasing Karl Marx, Mennonites have not only made their own history, but they have had a considerable influence on the conditions within which they have built it. Furthermore, if there is anything that their history shows, it is their zeal in constructing what they consider appropriate social conditions of existence for forthcoming generations.

The Problem of the Future

We have seen how the Mennonites and other related groups that strive for separation from the world, and attempt to control change, have been represented in the literature as located in 'the past', isolated, and uncritically accepting that these groups' actual livelihood is the direct application of their beliefs based on the biblical text (against this, I show in Chapter 1 that the meaning and social relevance of such separation has changed along Mennonite history). The works reviewed above have failed to acknowledge that the Mennonite, Amish, and Hutterite projects of community are indeed 'future oriented'. These misreadings can be understood as arising from the emphasis that these particular community of contemporaries puts on the community of predecessors as a source of guidance in their construction of a community of successors (see Schutz 1967: 79–92). The Old Colony Mennonites might not embrace the modernist project of progress, but their building of a community of believers in order to attain a transcendental salvation at the end of time is simultaneously the evidence of the existence such orientation (albeit a very particular one), and the very core of its imagination. It is now time to make more explicit of what I understand by the 'imagination of the future'.

This imagination was denied in functionalism, its exclusion expressed in the homeostasis towards which social systems theoretically tended. The future of particular societies lay in their reproduction over time, their future was their present, and members of the community, bound by tradition, could not imagine otherwise. In evolutionism, the future was preordained as a constant technological development. This imagination was left to the social scientist philosopher or literary writer. In this light we can see, following David Harvey (2000), the contributions of Karl Marx and Adam Smith as utopias of social process which also brings to the foreground that such imaginations of the future need not be coherent with each other, and may be one of the sources and loci of conflict. Therefore, the social sciences have attributed to themselves, due to their privileged perspective, the task of providing recipes and prognoses for the future of society. Furthermore, although some sociologists like Max Weber argued that the definition of the desirable objectives towards which action should be oriented was to be left to the politician while the social scientist became the provider of the know how for achieving said objectives (1946). For Weber's interpretive sociology, the finding out of different types of 'orientations' that guide individual action has been one of the centres of social analysis. Nevertheless, his interest was not the place of the orientations in the building of a project, but on their unintended consequences (for example, the role of predestination in explaining the rise of capitalism) (1991). Here I propose a shift towards making the empirical ways in which societies imagine their future the object of study, instead of the product of social inquiry.

In recent contributions, a similar situation prevails. Pierre Bourdieu's notion of 'habitus' does not ask about the construction of the final objectives towards which the natives orient the transmission of the habitus (1977; 1990). That is, to take one of his examples, why the Kabyle insist on transmitting the sense of honour. Agency is present in the application of the habitus, but not in its transmission, embodiment and reproduction. To be fair, it is so only as the application in practice of another habitus, which leads to an infinite loop of habitus explaining habitus. Thus, the argument that the habitus tends to reproduce its conditions of creation becomes a black box and 'agents' mere puppets of a self-reproducing habitus. Therefore, the criticism of functionalist theories, viz. that natives are unknowingly duped into contributing to the maintenance of their societies, becomes applicable here too. It should nevertheless be noted that Bourdieu has not neglected the issue of agency, although he considers it *within* the habitus, which is what allows strategy, but in this way the final objectives of action still remain under the aegis of the habitus. In Anthony Giddens' structuration theory (1979; 1986), the process of socially determining which consequences of action should be considered desirable is left untackled. Furthermore, in considering structures as both resources and constraints, Giddens leaves to tradition and considers as unproblematic, the question of why certain resources (structures) are privileged over others. The imagination of the future, as I understand it, encompasses an array of values that are used as a legitimating charter for the guidance of action through their transformation into norms. It is the social-moral equivalent of an architect's blueprints for a building, a 'model for' the temporal-moral constitution of society. In this way, the imagination of the future takes as its point of departure the assumption that every social group has some notions of how life should/ought to be lived that act as guidance in its reproduction and continuity (this however does not mean that these notions are immutable, coherent, or that they are unproblematically reflected in practice).

My understanding of the imagination of the future stems from Edmund Morgan's notion of 'fiction' (1988). Although Morgan does not fully develop the idea of 'fiction' in a theoretical manner, but rather focuses on the historical fictions created in England and the US as means of legitimizing government, and their transformation from the King's body politic who reigns by Grace of God, into the ideas of 'the people,' and 'representation' that lie behind notions of popular sovereignty. What Morgan identifies in these fictions is a suspension of disbelief in order to allow the construction of the legitimation of a particular and imagined social order. In the imagination of the future I foreground the temporal and normative dimensions embedded in these imaginations, without limiting them to the sphere of the legitimacy of sovereignty, but as encompassing a particular society's own projects for its own reproduction. In this sense, the imagination of the future contains within it a particular moral order, a state of the community "not yet realized but demanding to be integrally carried out" (Taylor

2004: 7). What I find suggestive is this process of historical creation of a social (and moral) order on an ideal level that acts as a guiding beacon in the historical reproduction of society, presenting itself as a moral prescription. It is not an unattainable ideal, but rather its claims to its possibility for realization that differentiate it from utopias. Nicolas Shumway applied Morgan's ideas to analyse the *Invention of Argentina* (1991), but in his application, these guiding fictions became reified, the product of the country's elite who constructed a plan for how the nation ought to be. In the 'imagination of the future' I propose a more grounded conceptualization, more flexible in its constitution, and the product not only of 'great thinkers' and 'politicians' but including aspects of everyday life of everyday people. A founding text authored by an exemplar authority might provide a background, and even concrete guidelines, but even these are eventually required to be put into practice, consciously or through the creation of an appropriate habitus that will display and then reproduce them. How abstract imaginations of the future are attempted to be realized in practice, and the dilemmas this entails, are a centrepiece of the analysis presented here. This book therefore deals with the structuration process involved in the Old Colony's imagination of the future. That is, it shows on different levels how this imagination is simultaneously a means and outcome of action, guiding it on the one hand, but simultaneously being constantly transformed through practice.

These imaginations of the future operate on different levels and require different resources. They establish not only a point of reference that guides action, but impose also the means through which they ought to be achieved. They are not only central in providing the necessary 'fictions' that bind the community together and that allow it to become a distinct grouping, but also provide (and require) individuals to display certain conducts, beliefs, notions of self, even to bodily characteristics. They operate on different temporal horizons, from the prescription of daily, weekly and yearly routines, to providing guidelines for its intergenerational transmission reaching all the way to a cosmological future. This book is therefore about the Mennonite construction of this temporal horizon that acts as simultaneously the context, means and outcome of action.

We need now to release ourselves from the original metaphor of the architect's blueprint if we are to understand the continuous process of the imagination of the future. Although useful for introducing the aspects of intentionality and temporality involved in the problem of the future, we need now to open up the model and subject it to a constant application and redefinition. The blueprint becomes a palimpsest, the product of collective authorship, and subject to changes as the building is built, previous lines still there, some allowing new configurations, while others restrict them and yet others get erased, leaving but a smudge behind. Likewise, the imagination of the future is not given once and for all, it is found not only in a constant state of flux through its process of redefinition and application, but also being challenged by other, competing imaginations. An established imagination needs to be enforced and reproduced, alternative visions need to be controlled, deactivated, or externalized. In this way, this construction becomes a legitimation charter for the present (Yamba 1992). As such, the imagination of the future becomes a fundamental aspect for the self-definition of a social group that strives for continuity over time. Its exploration, a promising line of enquiry into the processes of community making, one which opens up the field of vision as to how different projects compete, are imposed and contested, how they are transformed and applied in practice, and how this transformation contributes to a further reworking of these projects.

I suggest here, following the Mexican anthropologist Guillermo Bonfil Batalla (1991; 1992), that by opening up to scrutiny the process by which these structures come to being, tracing their origins, usages, appropriations, and transformations over time, that we are better able to examine the processes by which different imaginations of the future are built and contested in practice. This will provide as well a means through which to explore the relationships between group formation and definition, interaction and individual agency.

More concretely, this approach entails a series of procedures. First, to question the origin of the structures: how they came into being; were they the result of impositions, appropriations, extirpation or internal creativity? Are they being considered by the group as their own? If so, how did they come to be so? In this way, inter-group relationships and macro processes can be traced and related to the transformations of the groups and its culture, as well as incorporating individual agency and the definition of the actual social world of interaction at work. The second step is to enquire into the constraining and enabling aspects of those structures. What do they facilitate and what do they impede? In this way, we can have a clearer view of the relationships between norms and actual practices. The last step would be to question how these structures interact with each other over time, and what are the consequences of the actual practices, how do they transform other structures over time, how is continuity and change achieved and, therefore, which new project emerges as a result. In this way, structures that form the imagination of the future become threads in a sort of Wittgenstein's rope (1967) where none of them necessarily runs along the full length, but in a continuous superposition. The relevance of each thread, changing over time, is dependent on the relationships with other threads at any particular point in the rope. It is the constant superposition and change that gives the rope and the group their continuity along time and space.

Book Overview

In this study I aim to overcome the problems identified in the previous section by focusing on both the ideological and socio-structural levels of analysis at work in the ways the Mennonites imagine their future; a process which they call the "building of a community of believers" or the building of the "Church of Christ on earth." In the first chapter, I focus on the transformation the Mennonites have gone through, from their origins as a persecuted religious movement in sixteenth-century Europe to becoming recipients of Privilegia that allowed the settlement and construction of their first colonies in the Ukraine.

After an analysis of some of the Mennonite foundational texts, and of the internal contemporary organization of the colonies, I show that the colony way of life was the result of external impositions and was only later appropriated and incorporated into a new imagination of the future. I focus on the building and transformation of the Mennonite symbolic and moral order, bringing to the foreground the continuity of the symbols that bind the community together, and which constitute the core of the dominant imagination of the future. These are then contrasted with the variations in both their meaning and social relevance due to the change of the social formation within which they take place. I argue this social transformation carried with it a process of reconfiguration of what once were religious symbols and practices of voluntary adhesion into compulsory markers of group belonging. In other words, unveiling the process of absorption of the political by the religious, that has previously been concealed through its ostensive discursive externalization.

In Chapter 2 I highlight the intimate relationship between the establishment of the Mennonite settlements with the processes of nation-state formation. It provides an insight into macro processes of nation and state formation from a marginal perspective discussing issues of nationality, citizenship and territoriality. This history points to the separateness of the future imagined by the Old Colony from that of nations. I argue that while Mennonites contributed to different state's processes of territorialisation and consolidation of sovereignty, they rejected to become part of nations.

Chapter 3 systematizes the processes of schism and colony formation. I outline the place of schism and migration as ways of coping with problems of state imposition, internal dissent and demographic growth. I also focus on the deployment of cross-border strategies, and inter-colony relationships as a means to out-manoeuvre states in a world where all territories are under the aegis of nation-states, and as a central component in their imagination of the future as a separate people.

Chapter 4 presents an analysis of the processes by which the Old Colony establishes social relations with non-Mennonites, together with some conflicts that have sprung as a consequence of such contacts. I analyse the role of social articulators, highlighting their isolatory aspects. By the end of this chapter I switch to a different level of analysis where the concrete actions and life stories of individuals take the foreground for exploring their agency in dealing with the contradictions and tensions between the necessity of establishing relationships, and the values of separation from the world espoused by the Old Colony. In short, this chapter deals with the dilemmas the Old Colony faces when attempting to maintain the needed relations with the outside world while maintaining separation from it and how they impinge on the daily lives of its members.

Any collective imagination of the future involves a particular imagination of the self for individuals who take part in it. More concretely, the imagination of the future of the Old Colony incorporates a particular notion of the Christian self. Chapter 5 therefore resumes a biographical perspective, where I focus on Sergio and Abraham, two individuals who attempted to cross the boundaries of the Old Colony. This provides an opportunity for the discussion of the experience of conversion, the relationship between individual agents and institutions and macro processes, as well as the principles that regulate membership in the Old Colony; pointing to a shift from the openly held norm of faith-based membership towards the one based on common descent actually in practice. By looking at cases of individuals who were either expelled or refused incorporation, I outline the limits of how the Old Colony imagines and defines its membership.

In Chapter 6 I analyse the writings of Sergio and Abraham, and contrast the place of reading and writing among the Mennonites. I focus on writing as a tool for inducing social change, through the proposal of alternative futures to the Old Colony. Furthermore, I argue that the emphasis on reading tends to consolidate orthodoxy, whereas those oriented towards writing challenge it. I also analyse the author's strategies for convincing their readership, including its incorporation within the biblical narrative, and especially within the Book of Revelation. This chapter therefore deals with the explicit usage of imaginations of the future in order to promote change, and what are the characteristics that alternative imaginations must display in order to be conceived worthy of following.

Chapter 7 deals with the conflicts triggered by the dissemination of Sergio's ideas. I do so by concentrating on the life stories and experiences of conflict of two individuals who have contributed to their dissemination. In bringing to the foreground the contrasts between the norms that are supposed to rule the excommunication process with its manipulation on the part of those in charge of enforcing them, I uncover a strategy of silencing dissenters in order to maintain doctrinal continuity in the face of individual interpretation of scripture. In other words, it shows the processes by which an imagination of the future is enforced, and the ways in which alternatives are treated in order to maintain the status quo.

Finally, in the conclusion, I bring together some general arguments that draw from evidence revealed across the different chapters: the Mennonites becoming a nation, the *Leardeenst* becoming something similar to a state, and the relationship between the sacred, the profane, the natural and the supernatural within the Old Colony and the modern world.

CHAPTER ONE

THE TRANSFORMATIONS OF COMMUNITY

Introduction

This chapter deals with the genesis and transformation of the ideological and social framework that, in the Mennonites' own view, defines, and makes them *Christenvolk* (the people of Christ). I show the transformation of the Mennonite imagination of the future from an alternative project of voluntary adhesion, into a normative one. This transformation, I argue, is inseparable from the transformation in the quality and type of social relations through which the Mennonites have gone through. From a persecuted fragmented religious movement into the constitution of a system of religiously exclusive agricultural settlements, in turn a product of their relation with the different states with which they interacted. Central to understanding these transformations is Anthony Cohen's (1985) insight on the centrality of symbols for defining community, which rests on their versatility for allowing a multiplicity of meaning to be attached to them while generating an apparent implicit consensus which allows to sustain the idea of continuity through time and space. Therefore tenets like 'separation of the world', 'baptism of adults', 'church of believers', etc. ought to be treated as a system of "symbols of faith" (Stromberg 1986: 49 and ff.). As such, I argue that while these symbols have retained their outward appearance of similarity over time, their meaning and social relevance has changed as a consequence of their application in concrete and changing contexts. Furthermore, I show that this system has been transformed from a system of voluntary adhesion and cohesion into one of compulsory concrete diacritics that define the community versus the rest of humanity. This system of diacritics that mark the synchronic relationship of difference with the rest of humanity is complemented by genealogical relations (both diachronic, linking them with their predecessors and successors and synchronic, relating colonies located in different countries), all of them superimposed by an overarching layer of principles that give the symbolic illusion of continuity. In addition, I argue that despite their discursive opposition to both politics and the state, their system of religious organization has been undergoing a process of transformation that, through various processes of monopolization (most notably of violence and symbolic order), has resulted in the absorption and concealment of the political by the religious.

In order to understand the historical making of the Mennonite social and moral orders, which are simultaneously the means and outcome of their imagination of the future, we have to start with an overview of the Europe of the reformation, and a group of reformers and groups that are labelled as Anabaptist (due to their rejection of infant baptism as performed by both Lutherans and Catholics, and their practice of adult baptism). They have also been called 'radical' to differentiate them from the 'magisterial' of Luther and Calvin among others, due to their claim for separation of church and state. Indeed, strictly speaking, Menno Simons was not the initiator of Anabaptism, but joins (Cameron 1991: 326; Williams 1962: 287) the movement that sprung some years before his conversion, and to which we now turn.

Persecutions, migration, and settlement

During the Reformation, the European feudal system was beginning a process of reorganization and centralization known as Absolutism (Anderson 1974; Elias 1982) which became the predecessor of the modern capitalist nation-state (see also Elton 1966). The absolutist state weakened vassal relationships, transformed the nobility into a bureaucracy and attempted administrative, political, juridical, military and tributary centralization (Anderson 1974, Elias 1982). An exemplary product of the usage of matrimonial strategies for territorial consolidation, Charles V was born to Joanna the Mad (daughter of Ferdinand V of Aragon and Isabella I of Castille) and Philip The Handsome (son of the Holy Roman Emperor Maximilian I). Therefore, Charles V inherited Aragon, Castille (and their colonies in America and Africa), the Netherlands, Naples, Sicily, Sardinia, and the Habsburg lands. Charles V became Emperor of the Holy Roman Empire just one year after Luther published his theses, and the battle against the spread of the reformation would become a central task during his reign. A task his successor, Philip II would inherit (Anderson 1974: 70).

The bourgeoisie was undergoing a process of consolidation, and independent cities abounded along the Holy Roman Empire. At the same time peasants were seeing their conditions deteriorate considerably (Elton 1966) triggering the Peasants' War (1524–1526). Therefore, keeping the peasant masses in their traditional place became one of the Absolutist State's main concerns (Anderson 1974).

On the one hand, the proliferation of reformers was an inevitable consequence of Luther's attack on the Catholic Church's claims to the interpretive monopoly of the Bible (O'Leary 1994). On the other, the spread of some of the more extreme religious views was due, according to several scholars (Cohn 1957; Mullet 1980: 60; Hobsbawm 1971), to the general context of extreme change that heightened the uncertainty for many people (peasants and especially the new urban populations) regarding where the world was going. Meanwhile, the Catholic Church was being challenged in both its spiritual and secular functions. As a consequence, as Reinhart Koselleck observes until this period:

> the history of Christianity is a history of expectations, or more exactly, the constant anticipation of the End of the World on the one hand and the continual deferment of the End on the other. (2004: 11)

Indeed, the discourses of the reformers (especially of those "paranoiac megalomaniacs"—as Norman Cohn (1957) repeatedly characterizes them) tended to resolve the theodicies of time, evil, and authority (O'Leary 1994), recovering meaning and providing a *telos* out of chaos (Cohn 1993).

In 1518, Ulrich Zwingli was working in Zurich's cathedral, from where he started the Swiss reformation under the influence of the writings of Luther and Erasmus, abandoning the Catholic Church. Zwingli upheld that salvation was not a consequence of works, but exclusively of faith (*sola fides*), and only reached those chosen by God. He attacked the ideas of purgatory, monasticism, celibacy, papal authority, usage of Latin, aural confession, the invocation of saints, and tried to abolish the mass and put the City Council in charge of the church, therefore promoting a state-church. In 1525, Zwingli confronted two of his earliest followers, Conrad Grebel and Felix Manz, in a public dispute on the issue of paedobaptism. As a result, the Council decreed the exile of Anabaptists. Defiantly, Grebel started baptizing in Manz's house that very same day. Death by drowning for Anabaptists was decreed in March the following year as part of a series of measures to stop their growth, since their influence was spreading beyond Zurich. Grebel and Manz, therefore, became the founders of the later known Swiss Brethren and are considered as both the first Anabaptists and the starters of pacifist Anabaptism (Cameron 1991; Bender 1950; Williams 1962). A violent and apocalyptic branch soon spread in Munster.[1] Eric Hobsbawm claims that these movements were pre-political because they were still looking for the "specific language in which to voice their aspirations about the world" (1971: 2). Although in a world where political domination was religiously legitimized, the channelling in religious terms of political discontent is only coherent with the prevailing system. As I will suggest later following Edmund Morgan (1988), 'the people' as the secular principle of legitimation behind popular sovereignty, inherited the religious logic of its predecessor, 'divine right.' Even more, following Hobsbawm's categories—but disagreeing with his findings—we can consider them revolutionaries on a political level, because they were attempting to go at the very core of the legitimacy of the political order, its religious Papal backing. Whereas on a religious level they were indeed rebels or more correctly heretics (from the Catholic perspective, or simply true Christians from their own) since the legitimacy of the Bible was not questioned, but its interpreters, interpretations and the institutions built on it (see Goody 1986: 6–10).

Both Luther and Zwingli managed to ally with the dominant groups and imposed their churches as official ones.[2] Zwingli's project included the religious homogenization of the Swiss Confederation, which was to be backed by the State. The Reformation also had effects on a wider political level, as Michael Mullet (1980) argues, it was also a process through which the overarching European Christianity was fragmented into local, national churches (see also Zagorin 2003: 47; for the case of Spain see Anderson 1974: 65). The subordination of these national churches to the needs of those states made churchmen national subjects, starting the process of strengthening of proto-nationalisms (Mullet 1980: xii), which eventually led to the legitimation of those states in secular terms by the invention and political activation of the people: nationalism (Habermas 1996: 284; Morgan 1988).

---

[1] Jan Matthys and Jan Bockelson (also known as Beuckels and as Jan van Leyden) were the leaders of a millenarist and violent Anabaptism that was unleashed between 1533 and 1535 in Munster. They persecuted Catholics and Lutherans, and instated communality of goods, polygamy and theocracy (Cohn 1957; Scribner 1994: 757–758; Zagorin 2003: 83). Luz María Martínez Montiel and Araceli Reynoso Medina (1993: 386) erroneously locate Menno Simons as a founder of this movement in this time and place.

[2] Robert Wuthnow provides a detailed analysis of the process of institutionalization of the Reformation (1989) but he gives very little attention to Anabaptism and those reformers and movements which either did not seek, or did not succeed in establishing as official, state backed churches.

The Swiss Brethren, on the contrary, were claiming an immediate reform which included the separation of the church from earthly powers and therefore, to build a 'church of believers' formed by dynamic conventicles that would spread through the constant flow of preachers. One of them was Wilhelm Reublin (c. 1483–1559), who went to Strasbourg where Melchior Hoffman (d. 1543) had a group of followers among which were Obbe Philips of Leeuwarden and Jan Matthys of Haarlem (see footnote 1 above) (Cameron 1991: 320–325; Williams 1962: 357–360). Followers of the Anabaptist message (mainly rejection of paedobaptism, separation of church and state, and pacifism) were varied and heterogeneous, with supporters coming "from all classes and estates" (Stayer quoted in Waite 1992: 459) including urban artisans, peasants, disaffected clerics, university graduates, restive members of landed gentries and other skilled workers (Mullet 1980: 17, 65; Waite 1987).

Menno Simons was born in 1496 in Witmarsum, East Frisia. After his ordination in 1524 he was assigned to a parish in neighbouring Pingjum. It is Simons himself who tells the story of his conversion, a process starting in 1525, although published originally in 1554 (Simons 1983a: 3–7). Together with two other preachers in the parish, they spent their time playing and drinking. Simons had not read the Bible until 1525 (the same time that Grebel and Manz were starting their reformed church), when doubts regarding the presence of Christ in the Eucharist drove him to do so, dissenting from Luther (as Zwingli did) regarding the transubstantiation of the Eucharist. Despite this disagreement, he still explicitly recognized Luther's influence on the impossibility of human authority for binding to eternal death, the doctrine of the separation of church and state, which Euan Cameron explains as follows:

> God had instituted two orders of being, with two regimes or forms of government on earth. One, 'the realm of the spirit', dealt only with the relationship between Christ and the believer's soul. This (spiritual) realm operated through the Word, not through any institution. The second, 'the realm of the World', was the order of secular society, operating by visible structures, published rules, and coercive force. (1991: 152)

This separation of church and state implies the reverse of what republican theorists would promote later, that is, it was aimed towards the exclusion of influence of worldly powers over spiritual matters, and towards the restriction of religious authorities from being associated with the usage of violence. Paraphrasing Bruno Latour who argues that the fourth guarantee of the constitution of the modern is the "crossing out of God" (1993: 32), the Mennonites, in their attempt at 'crossing out the sword' embarked in a process of purification of domains: of restriction of worldly authorities to worldly issues, and of dis-arming of religious structures. We have here an interesting example of a process of separation of domains, and of secularization being promoted from within the religious sphere (see Gauchet for a general argument of the Christian foundation of the disenchantment of the world 1997). An initial step, although short lived and unintended, in the process of the constitution of the political. It was short lived because it was misrecognized and this development remained marginal from mainstream politico/religious thought, although it continued through the Dutch Patriot Movement and the Collegiants (Fix 1987; Israel 2001; Urry 2006: 55 & ff.).

Simons focused on the Scriptural study of the issue of baptism upon hearing about the beheading of Sicke Snyder (or Snijder) at Leeuwarden for being rebaptized. Simons claimed he "could find nothing in them concerning infant baptism [...] and found that it made baptism take the place of the blood of Christ" (1983a: 3–4). Simons' conclusion was that baptism is instead an individual commitment of renouncing sin and worldly life, a conscious manifestation of faith. It is in this way that it liberates the person from his own sins. Adult baptism therefore requires an individual under conditions of free will, and a combination of doctrinal knowledge or spiritual awareness and experience, to produce a voluntary submission to the rules and regulations of the group he was joining. As such, it is another facet in the religiously driven process of secularization, by the transference of the religious from the public to the private sphere, while simultaneously displaying features of the modern notion of the individual.

Despite his doubts, Simons still accepted his promotion in the Catholic Church's hierarchy and continued as a parish preacher in Witmarsum until 1536, when he decided to break with the Catholic Church in order to lead a group of pacifist Melchiorites (followers of Melchior Hoffman) who had not followed Matthys and Bockelson's ideas, taking care over Obbe Philips' group (Stayer 1978: 58–59; Williams 1962: 390–394).

> The hallmark of this sect was adult, or believer's, baptism and hence rebaptism, in itself a crime since the legislation of the Christian Roman emperors of the fourth century. In addition, many of the early Anabaptists favored community of property and were opposed to war and the use of arms, the taking of oaths, and civil magistracy, all of which they

considered un-Christian. These convictions caused them to be widely regarded as rebels against secular authority and fomenters of disorder. (Zagorin 2003: 65)

The decree following the diet of Speyer of 1528 included both the minting of the term 'Protestant' to refer to the adherents of Luther's reforms, and death penalty to any Anabaptist, without the need for the intervention of trial by the Inquisition (Williams 1962: 238). The Spanish administration was located in Brussels. George Huntston Williams (1962: 765) supports a figure of almost three thousand Belgian martyrs for the years between 1550 and 1576, the majority of whom were Anabaptists. None of the new established churches recognized for others the freedom of scriptural interpretation that they demanded for themselves, and therefore, Lutheran, Zwinglian, Anglican and Calvinists churches reproduced over the Anabaptists the persecutions they were once themselves subject to (Zagorin 2003: 81 & ff.).

Simons' head was prized and led an errant life, escaping from persecution while continuing in his preaching, baptizing, and building churches wherever he went, the persecution therefore had the unintended consequence of contributing to the spread and dispersion of the Anabaptist message (Williams 1962: 393). One of the effects of their persecution and constant movement was that many congregations from different origins excommunicated each other on seeing their differences, although rivalries between leaders seemed to have had their part too. During Menno Simons life, the Emden and Franeker congregations were split into rigorists and laxists (waterlanders) excommunicating each other. The same occurred among central and south German congregations (Williams 1962: 495–7; Cameron 1991: 327). Between 1536 and 1543, Simons' field of action was between East and West Frisia. By 1541, he started evangelizing in the south of Amsterdam. By the end of 1543 Simons had gone to northwest Germany, Cologne, and he spent his last fifteen years of life in Holstein and the Baltic Coast. Simons died of natural causes in Westphalia in 1561. After his death Simons was succeeded by Dirk Philips (brother of Obbe), under whom Frisian and Flemish groups mutually excommunicated each other (Cameron 1991: 327; Urry 1978: 25 and ff.; Williams 1962: 499).[3]

---

[3] The Amish were formed under the leadership of Jakob Amman between the years 1693–97. Amman had a stricter consideration of excommunication than other central-european Anabaptists (Hostetler 1992: 5).

Persecution made most of the Mennonites flee to areas such as the Rhine Valley, the delta of the Vistula, East Frisia, and the estuary of the Elbe. They joined pre-existing populations, taking advantage of the wider liberties they had in cities such as Emden, Hamburg, Lubeck, Friedrichstadt, Crefeld, Cologne, Danzig, etc. (Williams 1962; Bender 1957: 685; Hoerder 2002: 296–297; Urry 2006).

> The Netherlandish Anabaptists extensively colonized the marshy delta of the Vistula and surrounding territory in Poland, where in a war-devastated area they were welcomed because of their experience with dikes, canals, and the cultivation of swampy ground (...) The economic motivation in extending toleration to dissenters is clearest in these two areas. In Poland even the bishop of Culm seems to have winked at the concessions in the interest of the common welfare. (Williams 1962: 404)

They settled both in cities and rural areas and by 1770 the total Mennonite population in West Prussia is estimated at around 13,000 people (Urry 1978: 40 and ff.). Beyond agricultural work and drainage of the deltas, a number of Mennonites were successfully undertaking handcrafting, manufacturing and commercial activities (Kirchner 1974; Myovich 1996; Mullet 1980: 38, 39; Francis 1948: 103). Urry claims that later on, the sense of enemy without was diluted when persecution was eased in the Netherlands. Therefore, many of the congregations who remained there "took to seeking the 'enemy within' and the resulting schisms and legalistic rules made converts difficult to find, and the movement soon began to shrink" (1978: 37). Indeed, Williams (1962: 485) proposes the pun "Anabanism" to characterize the period of the second generation of Anabaptists due to their increased use of the ban (excommunication).

This situation continued while in West Prussia, where the Mennonites enjoyed a degree of religious freedom and the absence of overt and bloody persecution, although suffered limitations on the amount of land they could work. Changes in religious ideas and practices as well as their meanings occurred during this period, especially a shift towards a change in the definition of borders by a sense of traditionalism. This also affected their internal organization (Urry 1978: 44), their relationship to others and their attitude towards time and the world. On the one hand, group boundary markers such as dress, language, architecture, and the refusal to wear wigs were being constructed in order to differentiate themselves from the rest of the population with whom they were living (Urry 1978: 45 and ff.). Rural Mennonite populations were also deploying their distinctive Hollandischer, or linear village layout of settlement (see Krahn 1959c).[4] By the end of the eighteenth century, German took over as their written and liturgical language due to the wider availability of books, while Plautdietsch became their everyday language (Urry 1978: 46; Francis 1948: 103). The *Catechism* grew in importance over the *Confession of Faith*. This is significant, because confessions of faith tend to be systematizations of belief, oriented towards defining a religious group in relationship to others, whereas catechisms are usually written in question and answer form, tending to be didactic, and oriented towards the teaching of beliefs to children (see Urry 2006: 30–38). The shift from movement growth due to evangelization to one based generationally (Urry 1978; Myovich 1996) is a clear indicator that the shift from sect to denomination was taking place, and with it shifted the attitude of the group towards time and its position in the world (Wilson 1981: 231 and ff.; Weber 1978: 56). The Mennonites therefore had increased their stakes on their worldly temporal continuity through their generations. If the future community of believers was originally imagined to be built by fellow believers who heard and decided to follow the message, this imagination of the future was now shifting, towards one built by the descendents of the believers. Their temporal investment on their continuity was also expressed on their adoption of institutions such as the *weisenaumt* (financial manager of orphan's and widow's assets), and the *brauntschult* (fire insurance system). Meanwhile, or probably even because of this increased engagement with the world, a different way of enacting the separation from the world was found in the development of rules to forbid objects and practices because they were deemed worldly (Urry 1978: 56). This tension of remaining separate from the world while living on it would be one which they will continue working through along their history. The growth of the group in generational terms, its immigrant origin, and the impossibility of marriage with people from other faiths, made a set of distinctive patronyms, which also acted to mark their belonging to a community distinct from the rest (Urry 1978: 51).

In 1772, Poland suffered the first of several partitions and the reforms implemented affected the Mennonites directly, impeding their agricultural expansion. In 1774, an Edikt forbade the offspring of

---

[4] A detailed distribution of Mennonite settlements in this region and during this period can be found in Urry (1978: 40–43) and in a somewhat schematic fashion in Myovich (1996).

mixed religious marriages to be brought up as Mennonites (Myovich 1996: 231; Urry 1978: 59; 1983: 308; Krahn 1959b: 382). Walther Kirchner (1974) argues that the limitations put on Anabaptists were due to the non-religious effects of some of their religious tenets, such as a) rebelliousness through the questioning of the established order that stemmed from the separation of spiritual and temporal authorities, viz. church and state; b) the refusal of child baptism and to hold marriages in the official churches, therefore not appearing in parish records, and making the state lose one of its tools for the control of the population; c) the refusal to bear arms and to take civil duties, which freed them of time and duties and eventually to the refusal of paying war taxes and therefore gave them economic advantages over the rest of the population. Finally, it was changes in the conscription service in the late decades of the eighteenth century which made the Mennonites feel that the state was against them, that the situation was intolerable, and that their faith and customs were being threatened (Derksen 1988; Kirchner 1974; Urry 1978; 1983: 308; Longhofer 1993: 388; Bender 1957: 685; Francis 1948: 104).

In 1786, George van Trappe (a colonizing agent under the orders of Potemkin, who was put in charge of New Russia by Catherine II) arrived in Danzig with orders to find settlers for the newly conquered territories in the Ukraine. He offered the Mennonites a series of concessions, which would be later confirmed and referred to as the Privilegium, which included, among other points: religious freedom, land, and exemption from taxes and military service (translations of the Privilegium can be found in Urry 1978: 765–767; Krahn 1959b: 381; Huebert 1999: 1).

The Mennonites sent a commission to inspect the land and conditions, returning more than a year later (Huebert 1999). Mennonite migration started in 1788 forming Chortitza in 1789. Simultaneously concealing and making use of the situation, the Mennonites seized this opportunity to attempt making a reality of the 'separation of the world' and the founding of the 'community of believers', which they continued to replicate along their history. Two points that have been systematically overlooked among scholars are that, in the 1863 edict (Urry 1978: 763–764), immigrants were explicitly forbidden to evangelize and proselytize among the local Christian populations (they were free to Christianize Moslems), and to settle within already established populations. They nevertheless expanded, through new waves of migrants as well as through natural growth, forming several other colonies. It is now clear how the already declining proselytism was given its shot of grace at the time of moving to Russia, and that the 'colony way of life' was more the result of an external imposition than an internal development. Their relative isolation in the Ukraine contributed to exacerbate the separatist dynamics developed in Prussia.

Pre-existing and other immigrant populations from both other parts of the Empire and from outside of it, Imperial officials and passing armies, preachers and evangelizers, were all to leave their imprint in Mennonite life. These interacted with internal dynamics and conflicts regarding innovations, new economic opportunities and developments and new theological interpretations (among notable events, an evangelical revitalization led by Eduard Wüst [1818–59], a German pietistic preacher; another one who, through his millenarian prophecies, drove some Mennonites out to central Asia in search of the new Jerusalem; and the founding of the Kleine Gemeinde—the little community, a new community of believers within the colonies) (Urry 1978, 1983; Krahn 1959d; Huebert 1999). By 1801, an edict was issued which had implications in the internal affairs of the colonies by ordaining the formation of an administrative structure separate from the religious one. To the religious offices of *prädjasch* and *eltestasch* were imposed the administrative ones of *schult* and *fäaschta*, in charge of liaising with the Russian State (Urry 1978: 142 and ff.). Meanwhile, each colony developed its own particular characteristics due to the different background of the migration waves that formed them and their own different development, some seeking progress, while others wished to contain social and economic change (Urry 1983; Krahn 1959a). Having reached the point of the historical formation, consolidation, and differentiation of the Mennonite colonies, let us now turn to examine the contemporary organization of Mennonite colonies in South America.

Contemporary Organization of the Church of Christ

The colonies where I did fieldwork belong to the Altkolonier Reinlaender Menonniten Gemeinde (Old Colony Mennonite Community of Reinland, normally referred to by both themselves and others as 'Old Colony'), founded after a schism in Canada in the early twentieth century. Mennonite colonies are geographically and politically divided in *darpa* (sing. *darp*), which is a linear village formed by a number of *wirtschofte* (sing. *wirtschoft*) that lie to each side of a main road.[5] A *wirtschoft* consists of a main house building together with additional outbuildings such as a workshop, barn and stable and a strip of land behind. A nuclear family usually owns, inhabits and exploits each *wirtschoft*. The division of work within the household follows gender and age divisions. Women take care of the house and the vegetable and fruit gardens, whereas men take care of the arable land and any workshops. Cows are milked and taken care of by the whole family. Children follow their same sex parent in their duties and, as they grow up, are awarded increasing responsibilities.

Each *darp* also has its own one-roomed school and teacher, which the children of the *darp* attend. National governments do not officially recognize these schools and they do not follow official curricula. The subjects taught are basic arithmetic and German; all classes are conducted in Plautdietsch. Attendance is restricted to Mennonite children. Schooling age is between seven and twelve for girls, while the boys do a further year. Mennonites argue that girls will not need the mathematics taught to the boys during that extra year. Classes are given six days a week during six months of the year. At school the children are taught German, which is used as both written and liturgical language, whereas Plautdietsch remains strictly within the secular and oral spheres. German, or *Hüagdietsch* ('High-German' in Plautdietsch) is, within the colonies, somehow akin to Latin in medieval Western Europe where "it was the *only language taught*" (Marc Bloch, quoted in Anderson 1990: 24; Anderson's emphasis) because it was the only one worth teaching, as Benedict Anderson comments. Books used include the *Fibel*, a primer with which they are taught language basics. They then move on to the *Katechismus* (Catechism) and lastly the *Neue Testament* (New Testament). After finishing school, children can attend mass, since they can now understand the written and liturgical language. School teachers do not have any special training and receive a small payment in cash, alongside being granted a small house and the rights to till a small plot of land that lie behind every school. The payment comes from contributions of the families from the *darp*. Depending on the colony, the contribution is

---

[5] John Warkentin (1959) provides one of the best analyses of the settlement patterns of the Mennonites in Manitoba, which, in broad lines, was also applied in all the new colonies. Despite the changes he traces in its usage, size, and distribution, the basic pattern remained a grid.

calculated by the number of children being sent to school, the amount of land owned, or a combination of these two principles.

The authority structure of the colony has two branches, which can be loosely termed 'religious' and 'administrative', to follow the Old Colony preferences, since they consider that there is no politics within the colonies. On the one hand there is the *Leardeenst*, the religious structure, formed by various *prädjasch* (preachers, sing. *prädja*), one *dia'koon* (deacon) and one *eltesta*. Members of the *Leardeenst* do not have any specialized training, and can be easily identified by their distinctive clothes: all of black or very dark colours, including collarless shirts, knee high boots, and a black flat cap. The *eltesta* is supposed to have the last word on any issue raised. He also administers baptism and the Lord's Supper and ordains *prädjasch* and other colonies' *eltestasch*. The *eltesta* and the different *prädjasch* take turns for giving mass, and whoever is preaching at the time of a marriage will perform the marriage rites after the mass is over. The marriage rite within the church consists of a reminder on the part of the *prädja* towards the bride and groom of their new obligations, rights and duties, and asks for a verbal confirmation of their decision to marry each other. The *Leardeenst* meets every other Thursday to discuss current issues, which range from the economic situation, problems with their surrounding social context, to the spiritual situation of the colony, and any problematic cases.[6]

The *Leardeenst*'s main duty is to care for the spiritual welfare of the colony. This is achieved through a combination of different processes of socialization and social control. Beyond the political aspects of the administration of sacraments (especially through baptism, Lord's Supper, and especially excommunication as explored below), on the one hand they oversee schoolwork and what is taught to the children. On the other, a continuous process is carried out at the weekly masses, which can last anywhere between two to four hours, and where the sermons continuously remind the attendees of how life should be led following the teachings and examples of Christ, the Apostles and the martyrs. Sermons are seldom the original work of the *prädja* at the pulpit, instead, they rely on past sermons, which are passed down and copied. To this corpus of sermons a *prädja* may add a few of his own

---

[6] The meeting is called the *Donnadach* (day of thunder) (Redekop 1969: 66–67) during my fieldwork Mennonites referred to it in Spanish as *la reunion de los ministros* (minister's meeting) or *la reunion de los jueves* (the Thursday meetings).

during his career (although this is rare), which will, in turn, be adopted by future *prädjasch*. During the mass, the *prädja* reads aloud the sermon, after which he might try to relate it to current issues and problems.

One of the ways in which the *Leardeenst* cares for the spiritual welfare of the *Je'meent* (community, church) is through the definition and enforcement of the *Ordninj*. Strictly speaking, it is the *eltestasch* of the different colonies brought together in a general meeting, the ones who discuss and define the *Ordninj*. The *Leardeenst* possess a powerful tool for enforcing the *Ordninj* and obtaining repentance and compliance: the *Kjoakjebaun* (excommunication). It is a strong and drastic measure, and, following Mt. 18:15–19 a number of intermediary steps need to be taken before applying it. On the discovering of a breach of conduct, a *prädja* or two visit the culprit to indicate the offence and ask for an explanation, repentance and, if applicable, abandonment of the reproachable behaviour or object. If this fails, the offender will be summoned to the *donnadach* (the bi-weekly meeting of the *Leardeenst*) where he would, again, be admonished, but this time by the full *Leardeenst*. The wrongdoer would be reminded that on keeping his attitude, the *Kjoakjebaun* (excommunication) would follow. Upon this failing, again, the offender's case would be raised during mass, in front of the full congregation. Repentance and compliance would again be asked, and if the answer fails to satisfy the *Leardeenst*, the *Kjoakjebaun* is decreed. From that moment, the culprit is no longer a member of the community. The apostate is banned from attending church, and excluded from social activities, although he or she can remain living within the colony, and his property respected (although excommunicants who sell their land in order to leave the colony are usually paid well below market value). All social contact with him or her is forbidden unless it is directed towards the repentance of the apostate.

On the other hand, there is the secular and administrative structure, formed by two *fäaschta* (in charge of representing the colony to the non-Mennonite world) and several *schulte* (one per *darp*, in charge of the administration of the public areas such as the road and school, solving intra-*darp* disputes as well as liaising with the *fäaschta*). All positions are elective, but whereas religious ones are held for life, administrative ones are held in periods that range from one year (*schult*) to two (*fäaschta*). The reader might remember that this administrative structure was in fact an imposition of the Russian State, which was then appropriated, reproduced and considered as their own by the Mennonites. In practice, where a particular *fäaschta* has performed satisfactorily, he is continuously re-elected until he expresses his unwillingness to continue in office (Sawatzky 1971: 267). In La Nueva Esperanza, Johann has maintained his position as *fäaschta* for more than ten years, until he refused to be nominated. By contrast, the *schult* cannot be re-elected. Only the two *fäaschta* are paid for their services, but such an income is of negligible importance and is meant only to cover the expenses that these positions involve—mainly trips to different cities and towns to represent the colony as a whole in front of government officials. They are also in charge of collecting any taxes due and they even charge their own taxes as in La Nueva Esperanza, where a levy of 5% is applied on any products or services sold to non-Mennonites.

Other institutions include the *senja* (singers) which lead the singing in church and get to choose new members; the *brauntschult*, an internal fire insurance system; the *weisenaumt*, who is in charge of administering the assets of widows and orphans, and uses them to give credit to fellow colonists; and the administrators of the different cooperative cheese factories and stores. In La Nueva Esperanza there is also a local accountant who is in charge of consolidating and preparing the paperwork to be handed in to the external chartered accountant. This is a requirement of the Argentine state in order to maintain their status as a religious, non-profit organization.

Only married men can hold these positions. They argue, following 1 Cor. 11:3 that as Christ is the head of man, so is man the head of the woman. Thus, women should submit to men, and only men can have authority.[7] For the election of members of the *Leardeenst*, members are encouraged to pray, fast, and ask the Holy Spirit for guidance. One of the signs searched for, which marks the suitability of a candidate for properly guiding the community, is the way he has raised his children.

A private property regime operates within the colonies. Each member has to buy his own land from the colony or other colonist. The colony as a collective (through a number of representatives, the *eltesta* usually being one of them) legally owns the land in the eyes of the state, and the property of individual plots is recognized only by the colony. In such a way, they insure against non-Mennonites buying land within the boundaries of the colony, as well as making it impossible for members

---

[7] This is a common feature within Anabaptism; see Harrison (1992) for an analysis of the place of women within Hutterite communities.

to use their land as warranty for bank credits—which would open up ownership to non-Mennonites in case of repossession. They adopted this system when they moved to Mexico after their experience in Canada, where land was bought by non-Mennonites and thereby breaking down both their separation and internal homogeneity in religious and ethnic terms (see Warkentin 1959: 362 and ff.). This system also allows the avoidance of state intervention regarding the paying of inheritance taxes and in the division of inheritance. On the other hand, this arrangement also gives the colony authorities an extra potential source of coercive power, since it is a standard practice to underpay for land and goods being sold by excommunicated individuals.

The main economic activities in the colonies are farming or farming-related. There are three main areas of production: Cash crops, cheese, and small manufactures (some of their products include: wooden furniture, silos, and small farm equipment), but due to the social and ecological conditions in different countries and regions, a number of contrasts arise. In Bolivia, the main cash crops are soybeans and cotton, whereas in Argentina emphasis is put upon wheat. The sale of milk to the local Mennonite cheese factories provides most of the families with their everyday cash needs. In Argentina, mozzarella base paste is the main product, which they sell to cheese factories. In Bolivia, the main product is ready-to-eat cheese, sold to shops in nearby towns. In both countries, the production of cash crops is undertaken only when there is surplus land after the expected cows' need for fodder has been satisfied. The production of silos, carpentry, and of small agricultural equipment has experienced a recent boom in Argentina. Some of the factors for this include, on the one hand, the failure to acquire new land for newlyweds, therefore forcing some Mennonites into an economic conversion towards activities that would secure an income without the need for more land. On the other hand, contextual social conditions that contrast with those in Bolivia have made such a conversion profitable. The usage of child and 'black market' labour within the colony contributes to the Mennonites' lower cost of production of goods. Mennonites have three main economic advantages over 'Argentine' labour: first labour's reproduction cost is lower due to the non-monetized and domestic-unit origin of most foodstuffs. Second, by being outside the gaze of the state it is not taxed and third, they benefit, in comparison with commercial enterprises, from the tax reduction and exemption due to being registered as a non-profit religious organization. In contrast, since the Bolivian State is less powerful in terms of enforcing legislation, their situation does not give Mennonites the comparative advantage regarding labour taxation that they have in Argentina. Therefore, Mennonite labour is more expensive than Bolivian, but less than Argentine. Consequently, in Argentina they succeeded in selling manufactured goods, whereas in Bolivia Mennonites hired the local workforce. Or, in more concrete words, Bolivians are often seen working Mennonite fields in Bolivia, whereas Mennonite made silos and furniture can be found in estancias and dealers in La Pampa.

Authoritative Texts

The Mennonites claim that life on earth should be led solely according to the Bible. Rules and regulations, prescriptions and prohibitions are all supposed to be based on the Scripture, or to follow biblical principles and values, therefore not recognizing the modernist structural differentiation between morality and legality. They do, however, recognize and abide to nation-state imposed laws as long as they do not contradict their moral order, in which case they usually migrate. In the eyes of the Old Colonists, religion remains a "fait sociaux totaux" (total social fact) (Mauss 1950: 274) where the moral, legal, political, economical, etc. threads have not been disentangled. Furthermore, I argue, it is precisely the refusal to produce such disentanglement, which has allowed the *Leardeenst* to burn stages in its process of transformation towards becoming a state. Pierre Bourdieu argues that the state "is the culmination of a process of concentration of different species of capital" (1998: 41; emphasis in original), which goes hand in hand with the modern structural differentiation of domains, in order to constitute itself as the "holder of a sort of metacapital granting power over other species of capital and over their holders" (1998: 41) and the rates of exchange among them. It is through the avoidance of the emergence of differentiated types of capital, by subsuming them all to biblical authority, and by claiming the monopoly of its interpretation, that the *Leardeenst* attempts to achieve the "monopoly of the universal" (1998: 59). In other words, in the Old Colony, the religious has absorbed and internalized the political, while simultaneously concealing this fact through the discursive exclusion of politics from the colony. Therefore, the grammar of religion within the Old Colony are different from those of religion in the modern secularized world (Asad 2003).

A number of other sources are used as moral and legal guidelines. These works include Menno Simons' writings (1983b, 1983a), a *Catechism* and *Confession of Faith*, a *Hymnal*, the *Martyrs' Mirror* by Thieleman van

Braght (1982) as well as German translations of John Bunyan's *Pilgrim's Progress*. These texts are not only widespread among Mennonites, but usually for sale in their stores. In addition to this corpus of unchanging texts, a more malleable one exists. Although it is not publicly available in written form, but read once a year during the mass: the *Ordninj*.

From the Mennonites' perspective, this corpus is hierarchically ordered, with the Bible at the apex as the revealed word of God, followed by Simons' works and then the rest. Nevertheless, as I will show later, this hierarchical ordering is not always respected. In practice, Menno Simons' works are used as an exegetical guideline for the Bible and the other texts are mainly used as mediums that help relate the Bible to the predicaments of everyday life. I will not examine these works for themselves, but in relationship to the contexts of reading, writing and interpretation. Indeed, as Chris Fuller (1992) notes in his analysis of popular Hinduism, the practices and beliefs of believers should be given primacy over the tendencies of focusing solely on the sacred texts. This leads to a number of points that should be noted before continuing: First, there is the distance between abstract principles and concrete practices. As Jack Goody argues, it is a requirement of the 'religions of the book' to achieve a certain degree of abstraction if they are to gain applicability across time and space; it is this feature that has allowed them to become world religions (1986: 12–13). Therefore, the relationship between coded morality and the practice of such morality cannot be assumed to be direct, coherent and unproblematic. We have seen in the analysis of previous studies of Mennonites and Amish the results of assuming practice to be a direct expression of belief. Second, and in relation to this, is the interpretation of texts, since the text as inscribed discourse presents the problem of the need of interpretation in order to recover the meaning of the inscribed word of God:

> The subjective intention of the speaking subject and the meaning of the discourse overlap each other in such a way that it is the same thing to understand what the speaker means and what his discourse means (...) With written discourse, the author's intention and the meaning of the text cease to coincide. (Ricoeur 1991: 148)

Therefore, all texts require interpretation in order to grasp the intention of the author. The social relevance of these texts lies not in themselves, but in what Mennonites interpret from them; and their exegetical apparatus is what allows the translation of abstract principles into practice. Thirdly, although the texts may remain the same, the exegesis is susceptible to change over time and space (Goody and Watt 1963: 6). This allows for an image of continuity to be sustained through the maintenance of the unchanged printed word, hiding exegetical, contextual and contingent variations. These variations, which exploit the symbolic potentialities of the word as a symbol (Cohen 1985), also constitute a locus for the insertion of politics through the dynamics of the processes of establishing, enforcing, and the contestation of different interpretations, and therefore of competing imaginations of the future.

In the following section, I will be focusing mainly on the historical and contextual variations of the interpretation of the main symbols and ideas that have led to the Old Colony's contemporary situation. This will then form the necessary background for understanding the enforcement, contestation and conflict between different interpretations, which form the core of chapters 5, 6, and 7.

Identifying the Church of Christ

I had just received a phone call from Benjamin, a member of the Old Colony Mennonites whom I first met in La Nueva Esperanza while he was preparing his move back to Bolivia. He had come to Santa Cruz de la Sierra (the departmental capital of Santa Cruz, Bolivia) with his wife and newborn baby to take them to the hospital for a check up. I went to pick them up at the 6 de Agosto street, a major meeting point for Mennonites when in town. After lunch together, we went to my apartment where we could comfortably talk outside the other Mennonites' controlling gaze. He was surprized when he saw an English language copy of Menno Simons' *Complete Works* on the shelf (1983a, 1983b). Benjamin picked it up and opened it, ignoring the small volume next to it, reading 'Katechismus' [Catechism] on its spine, in bright, bold, silver lettering (Sommerfeld Mennonite Church of Manitoba 1995).[8] I asked him if he knew it and Benjamin said: "Of course I do, it is, after the Bible, the best food for the spirit." I then asked him to point out to me to what he believed to be the most important part of the book, and replied: "I don't know where it is on your book, but on the German

---

[8] The Catechism was a bilingual German-English edition, by the Sommerfeld Mennonite Church in Manitoba. It also includes a bilingual confession of faith authored by Johannes Wiebe (1881), the founder of the Old Colony Mennonites.

version it is around page 82 of the second volume." I went to the table of contents, and translated it into Spanish until I reached the "Reply to Gellius Faber" (Simons 1983b: 77) when he stopped me and grabbed the book from my hands, "there you have, the signs that differentiate the Church of Christ from the Church of the Antichrist." A three-hour long session of translation and discussion ensued, where Benjamin gave me his evaluation of the current state of affairs in the colonies, which, in his opinion, did not precisely follow Simons' directives.

Benjamin had been reading Menno Simons' writings, as many other Mennonites did, but before delving into some of these individual interpretations, it is first necessary to explore the conditions within which these exegetical practices exist. This means analysing not only the ideological background from which individual interpreters nurture themselves (and feed their interpretations back into) but also, the social and historical contexts with which such texts and interpretations interact and obtain social relevance (see Asad 1983: 251). This analysis becomes all the more relevant, since the very content of these interpretations refers not only to the group's self-definition, but also to the constant reconstruction of its imagination of the future that acts as a guiding beacon in their concrete, historical social reproduction.

I will start with some of Menno Simons' signs for identifying the Church of Christ and compare their social significance in his time with their social significance today, since they form the core of their imagination of the future. Then I will continue with the main theological tenets, which are highlighted by both the historical literature as well as by the Old Colony Mennonites themselves.

The first sign is an "unadulterated pure doctrine" (Simons 1983b: 81). Simons does not concretely show how this is differentiated from an adulterated one. He just declares that it should be according to the word of God, and not according to what the audience wants to hear. Simons also calls for the spreading of the word of God as a Christian duty, but, as shown above, Old Colony Mennonites do not evangelize among those not born within the community.

Mennonitism belongs to a wider group of religious groupings called Anabaptists, the name referring to their practice of rebaptizing. This aspect falls within Simons' second sign, the "scriptural use of the sacramental signs" (1983b: 81). Here Simons argues that only those who "by faith, are born of God, sincerely repent, who bury their sins in Christ's death, and arise with him in newness of life" can be baptized (1983b: 81).

The Mennonites argue that the Catholic practice of paedobaptism as a means of liberating the child from original sin is a violent act against Christ's crucifixion. If Christ's crucifixion cleansed humanity of all sins, the original sin is also forgiven and therefore any further action towards it denies Christ's passion.[9] Instead, they consider baptism as a public confession of faith, a conscious decision that can only be made by adults because it implies knowledge and faith in the creed adopted by the congregation.

In the Old Colony, baptism is administered once a year (at Pentecost) by the colony's *eltesta*. Candidates who wish to receive the sacrament prepare themselves by memorizing the questions and answers in the Catechism. Before the service, the *eltesta* asks the congregation if there are any objections against any candidate becoming part of the *Je'meent*. In order to avoid being publicly shamed, candidates go around the colony during the weeks before the ceremony asking for forgiveness for their past actions to people they know they have wronged. All candidates (though segregated by gender) sit on the church's front pews. The *eltesta* asks them a few questions from the Catechism and their voluntary adherence to the colony's belief and acceptance of its regulations and authorities. The candidates answer collectively in unison to each of the questions, after which the *eltesta*, pitcher in hand, pours some water over the head of each of the now kneeling candidates. After pouring the water, the *eltesta* takes the hand of the candidate, and while helping him or her to stand up, welcomes him or her to the *Je'meent*. This is followed by a church service.

When submitting to baptism, individuals commit to abide by the rules and regulations of the colony, publicly manifesting their compliance to the creed, and becoming fully responsible towards the colony as a whole (until then, it is their parents' authority to which they must respond). In this way, they become members of the church and obtain all adulthood rights and duties, most importantly the possibility of getting married and owning land. Some of my informants were conscious of that situation, regretting the current lack of spirituality of the event and claiming that nowadays "young people only baptize just to get married."

---

[9] A similar argument is provided by African-Caribbean Pentecostals in England (see Toulis 1997: 146–7).

Although the seeming compulsoriness of baptism was not recognized, the fact that almost the totality of youngsters 'choose' to be baptized was rather interpreted as an achievement, a sign of the fulfilment of one of their obligations towards God: the passing on of the faith to their descendants. Unlike the Amish, who allow their youth a period of systematic deviance in order to "select out those who would not be fit to be adult Amish people" (Reiling 2002: 148). As one colonist explained:

> We want our children to learn the religion, and then, when they grow up, they will see with their hearts that it is the right religion. They are not obliged; baptism is of their own choosing. But once they are baptized, they are obliged to follow this law, this religion. Because it is not only for us, it is for the one above...We do not baptize children; we only do it when they are able to understand the word of God, the real truth.

The context and significance of baptism has changed from that of sixteenth-century Netherlands.[10] Baptism in the Catholic Church was compulsory, and therefore the incorporation of a new member in a dissenting Anabaptist congregation would have required a new baptism to be undertaken, and be subject to persecution for doing so. Nowadays baptism is almost compulsory within the Old Colony; member's sons and daughters are expected to baptize, marry and die within a colony, and the decision does not lie whether to baptize or not, but in the timing of such an event. Youngsters are therefore being forced into a balancing act between their desire of acquiring full rights, and the burden of the duties involved in being full members of the church. Baptism has therefore been routinized and transformed into a coming of age ritual; even more, it is a true social contract due to

---

[10] Although baptism is one of the central rituals in Christianity the usage of the same label belies the variety of meanings and practices associated with it in different groups, times and places. Whereas for Catholics it is performed by sprinkling on children, and is related to name giving, for Pentecostal groups such as those studied by David Lehmann (1996: 121) in Brazil, baptism is not performed by a preacher on the believer, but by the Holy Spirit, and therefore seems to lie beyond human agency and confers to the baptized the 'nine Charismatic gifts'. For American Catholic Charismatics, this baptism in the spirit can be performed by human agency, and is required for participating in certain activities (Csordas 1997: 166). Among African Jamaican Pentecostalists in Britain, baptism is performed by immersion and there is no specified annual regularity, and it is not considered an incorporation rite: "In this act of obedience individuals publicly express, in word (through testimonies) and deed (by submitting to immersion), their acceptance of salvation and their acknowledgement of Christ as their saviour" (Toulis 1997: 147).

its explicit requirement to learn and accept the rules and regulations of the community for becoming a fully responsible adult towards the community. This is a stark contrast with most western societies where despite their social imaginary being based on the notion of the social contract (Taylor 2004), individuals are made full members of society by the automatic fiat of reaching a certain age (be it at sixteen, seventeen, eighteen or twenty-one).

The other sacrament Simons mentions is the Lord's Supper, which, within the colonies, is held twice a year:

> The dispensing of the Lord's holy Supper to the penitent, who are flesh of Christ's flesh, who seek grace, reconciliation and the remission of their sins in the merits of the death and blood of the Lord, who walk with their brethren in love, peace and unity, who are led by the Spirit of the Lord, into all truth and righteousness, and who prove, by their fruits, that they are the church and people of Christ. (Simons 1983b: 81)

Through baptism, a person becomes a full member of the community, and through the Lord's Supper, he or she periodically confirms his or her belonging to the people of Christ. This reaffirmation of community was well exemplified by Abraham:

> We all get together in the church, and the *eltesta* asks us if we are all in peace with each other. If there is anybody who has a problem with another member of the community, has to stand up and say what the problems are. Things cannot continue until they get sorted. When we are all in peace, we then have communion, and share the Holy Supper.

The same question is asked to the members of the community at the time of baptism: to set the record straight before admitting the aspiring members into the community. This demand of public voicing of the status of the community acts as a double-edged sword since once made public, conflicts would either be defused by the acceptance of peace, or would require immediate action (either redressive or repressive, possibly leading to schism). Other instances like the *broodashoft* (meeting of brothers) where members are called for collective discussion of current issues also play the same role as catalysts for triggering conflicts (see also Redekop 1969: 67; Kniss 1997). Gillian Feeley-Harnik (1994) argues that the Last Supper was an inversion of the Jewish Passover, bringing down sectarian boundaries through the explicit non-observance of dietary restrictions (which were so far used as diacritics). "Jesus' passover, was therefore a rejection of familial and national separatism. His new covenant included all humanity" (Feeley-Harnik 1994: 166). Among the Mennonites, the Lords' Supper acts as a confirmation of the continuity of community by reasserting its exclusiveness and separateness, evidenced by their strict observance in allowing only members of the church. This exclusiveness reinforces the restrictive approach to baptism, where only those born to members are eligible to take part of. Therefore, the Lord's Supper as contemporary practiced by the Old Colony, reverts Jesus' inversion back into familial and national separatism where the Mennonites see themselves as *Christenvolk* (people of Christ) as the elect people of God, formed by direct blood-related descendants of Abraham (I return to this issue in Chapters 5, 6, and 7).

Simons' third sign is "obedience to the word," leading a holy life, being a light in the world, and conforming to Christ's teachings (1983b: 81). The attitude to be held towards the world by such a community is one of rejection. In an earlier writing, Simons gives an inventory of practices the community re-born of Christian baptism must reject:

> avarice, pride, unchastity, pomp, drunkenness, fornication, adultery, hatred, envy, backbiting, lying, defrauding, quarrelling, bloodshedding and idolatry, all impure, carnal works, and forsake the world with all its lusts (…) (1983a: 170)

A separation from the world is necessary since the world represents all that is corruptible, and Christians should be separate from it, thereby rejecting sin, and keeping the unfaithful outside the church. During the sixteenth century this meant the abandonment of sinful conducts, and to keep sinners outside of the church (see Zagorin 2003: 84). Indeed, the community of saints has to be protected from human fallibility and therefore rules of exclusion, such as the *Kjoakjebaun* (excommunication, lit. 'church-ban'), need to be applied to church members who embark on sin and misbehaviour. Therefore, as baptism marks the entry into the community, excommunication marks the exit from it, and the *Leardeenst* holds the key to both of them.

Again, differences arise from Menno Simons' context and that of today's Old Colony Mennonites. Because the converted members would be a persecuted religious minority, there was not much temporal power to be exerted by the religious authorities beyond their immediate realm, the congregation. Within Old Colony Mennonites, the practical limits of the social unit within which the greatest part of social interaction occurs are coterminous with the religious community and subject to the *Leardeenst*. This means that the exertion of power (especially through excommunication) by colony authorities has very concrete and practical implications that range from imposing internal social ostracism, the leaving of the colony and, sometimes, even the loss of means of survival. Whereas sixteenth-century reformers denounced the usage of the sword for religious purposes, today the *Leardeenst* has established itself as a legitimately recognized user of force for internal compliance. The *Leardeenst*, despite lacking a war machine, have nevertheless succeeded in legitimizing their use of violence within the colonies (albeit in a concealed fashion). A claim they cannot make openly since internally it would undermine their own legitimacy while externally it could be considered a challenge to the state on whose territory they have settled.

"Unfeigned, brotherly love of one's neighbour" (Simons 1983b: 82) is the fourth sign. Instead of showing how the biblical mandates can be seen concretely, Simons quotes them and then shows examples of what characterizes the absence of love, including hatred, defamation, dishonour, defilement of women, egoism, faithlessness, robbery, etc. This, together with the sixth sign, the "oppression and tribulation for the sake of the Lord's word" (Simons 1983b: 82) and carrying "the pressing Cross of Christ" are the foundations of non-resistance and the leading a life of poverty and suffering. True Christians should be meek and take Jesus' statement of turning the other cheek, giving the cloak when asked for the purse, and forbidding the use of the sword "which the Lord commanded Peter to put up in the sheath" (Simons 1983a: 4). This meant refusing to bear arms (myth has it that sixteenth-century Mennonites carried only a knife for cutting their bread), and supported the separation of church and state since the association would involve shared responsibility of the force used by the latter (Yoder 2003: 23–31). Nowadays, together with the separation of church and state, it is also understood as a rejection of initiating legal litigation, holding public offices, voting, and undertaking military service. However, the externalization of explicitly political institutions has not eliminated the political, but rather, has been an attempt to conceal the fact of the absorption of the political by the religious within the colonies. The public transcript (see Scott 1990) of recognizing the state as a God given, contributes to consolidate the idea that the political, hence the world, has been externalized from the colony. However, this is a created illusion. In addition to the recognition of the *Leardeenst*'s use of (certain types of) violence as legitimate, the hidden transcript of the proviso of recognizing its authority as long as it does not contradict the Bible, which is a veritable claim to ruling over the exception and hence of sovereignty

(Schmitt 2005), reveals the depth of the appropriation of the political by the religious (the consequences of this will be explored through the handling of conflict and dissenters in chapters 5, 6, and 7).

> The fifth sign is, that the name, will, word and ordinance of Christ, are unreservedly confessed, in spite of all the cruelty, tyranny, uproar, fire, sword and violence of the world, and that they are upheld unto the end (Simons 1983b: 83)

That is, to uphold and publicly manifest their faith under every circumstance, including persecution, suffering and torture. The renouncing of Christ under any circumstance would be reciprocated by Him on Judgement day. Within Menno Simons' context, this is an explicit call to hold on to the faith in the face of persecution. The narratives in the *Martyrs' Mirror* (Braght 1982) are seen today as a clear example of how the confession of faith should be upheld. This is a book actively read within the colonies, especially in times of suffering and persecution. Indeed, oppression and tribulation are to fall on those who follow Christ (sixth sign, already mentioned). This forms the core of their dormant millenarism, which can be awakened at any moment by a wide array of perceived threats from the outside. These threats can be construed as attacks on religion, and the millenarist narrative in the Book of Revelation provides a ready-made role for both persecutors and the persecuted: the abhorrent underlings of the Devil and the much suffering and faithful Church of Christ.

Regulating the Church of Christ: the Ordninj

In everyday life and discourse, Simons' signs are not mentioned in an explicit way, but they have been condensed and translated. In common conversations and explanations, the recurrent theme when talking about prohibitions, morality, religion and how to lead life, were the notions of narrow path, suffering, and poverty. The Mennonites recognize two paths for living life on earth: a narrow, difficult and painful one, and a broad, easy and joyful one. The first leads to salvation while the second to damnation. This dualism is extended into a long series of oppositions including God/Devil, soul/body, salvation/damnation, Christ/antichrist, *Christenvolk* (people of Christ)/*Weltmensch* (men of the world), heaven-earth, etc. Thus, in order to attain salvation, one has to tread the narrow path, bringing suffering and discomfort to the body in a double means to both imitate Christ, and to embody the separation from the world. The worldliness of the body, attested by its corruptible nature (in opposition to the immortal soul), is also the Devil's preferred means of exerting influence on humans through the stimulation of the senses and desires. Thus, the keeping in control of fleshly desires and impulses becomes an internal battle of separation from the world. The reduction and control of elements that add comfort to the body is one of the strategies in this battle. This strategy goes further than achieving an internal separation of the world (while simultaneously becoming external markers of belonging and identity), it is a constant reminder of being ready to suffer (and sometimes the very carrying of these marks becomes an active way of attracting such suffering) on the keeping of the faith. Like for the martyrs, whose letters and histories are eagerly read from the *Martyrs' Mirror* (Braght 1982) as exemplars to emulate, openness to pain is part of their structure of agency as Christians, and are symbols of victory over society's power (Asad 2003: 85). The low value attributed to the body is evidenced by their mortuary practices. Unlike many other Christians, Mennonites are buried in tombs that bear no identification of the deceased, and that are never visited. "Follow me, and let the dead bury their own dead," (Mt. 8:22) was the answer I got when asking about this non-practice. In short, the notion of narrow path, and dualism it entails, becomes a key in understanding the rulings of the *Ordninj* as one particular means of making a Christian habitus.

The *Ordninj* contains a set of concrete rules that regulate a broad range of aspects of everyday life. This text is the most malleable and recent one, since changes to it can be made over time and is susceptible of revision. Such revision is required if it is to continue to provide the translation of abstract principles into concrete, applicable rules. Furthermore, the enforcement of the *Ordninj* transforms the abstract tenets from symbols of adhesion into means of coercion and compulsory identity markers.

It has been impossible for me to obtain a copy of the *Ordninj* in its written form, but references to it were constantly made when Mennonites were explaining why certain things were forbidden, compulsory, or desirable. Again, my interest here lies not on the text itself but on its social consequences. Laypeople do not have copies of the Ordninj either, but rather rely on their memories (and in their internalized habitus, Bible reading etc) of what is read in church once a year for guiding their actions and evaluating them in moral terms, makes these memories more relevant in their social consequences than the letter of the text itself. Granted, in case of conflict, the memory of the individual would be contrasted with the letter of the hidden text, but this need not concern us now. Although the verbal reference used in most cases was *la religión* (the religion), a simple act of speech which shows how the concrete rules have been included as part of the belief system and the success in establishing their legitimacy. In the very few cases where the reference was to the *Ordninj*, informants were quick to differentiate it from the Bible, claiming its man-made nature (in contrast with the Bible's divine inspiration). This is not a minor point, since through this recognition, dissent can be channelled without affecting the Bible itself, but its interpretations and applications (see chapters 5, 6 and 7).

I will not attempt to cover the totality of the *Ordninj*, but concentrate on a few concrete rules that unveil its internal logic and the principles behind them. One of such rules is the prohibition to use rubber tyres on tractors. When tractor usage in Mexico became generalized, a general meeting of *eltestasch* was organized. The issue at stake was that tractors were being used to travel to nearby towns, undermining the literal separation of the world. In a creative compromise to retain tractors' agriculturally productive powers while eliminating its potential for undermining the physical separation from the world, the *eltestasch* decided to ban rubber tyre usage. These had to be replaced by steel tyres since these make them unusable on main roads while their usage for tilling the land remains largely unaffected.

Colony members are forbidden to own and drive cars and pick up trucks. They claim that owning a car is not sinful in itself, but it is an element which facilitates the breaching of the separation of the world. This is applicable on different levels. First, by facilitating travel to nearby towns where many temptations can be found (most notably alcohol and sex). Second, their ownership can be understood as a way of expressing wealth, individuality and competition, which are at odds with the qualities that must be present and developed by true Christians such as poverty, humility and humbleness. A Mennonite summarized for me the consequences of car ownership, both for the spirit and for the purse:

> If we had cars, then the youths would be using them for going out, and visiting their girlfriends, and would be beyond our control...travels to town are expensive when hiring a taxi or a pick-up truck, and they would be cheaper if I had my own car. But this makes me think if going to town is really worth it. If I had a car I would be going every day, and maybe on holidays to know the world, and instead of working I would

be travelling. It might also break down, causing me a greater expense. In the end, owning a car would be too expensive.

The same logic that forbids cars is applied to motorbikes, and bicycles are not allowed because it would be too difficult to draw a line with motorbikes. Furthermore, taking into account their ingenuity for building machinery and their workshop skills, it would be no problem for a youngster to fit a small engine on a bicycle. I was surprized when I discovered that what looked like a mini Ford tractor (10 hp) was indeed a working reduced replica made by Franz's teenage sons. They simply bought a free-standing Honda engine, and built the rest around it out of scrap metal.

Tractors also have to be stripped of their cabins, heating and air conditioning appliances (where present). The removal of the cabin is to avoid the temporary fitting of a glass enclosure. This is to avoid 'unnecessary' comfort of the body. A temporary shade is allowed to avoid the scorching sun. Lights should also be removed, since they break the Godly temporal order of night and day, which translates into working and resting time.

Electricity is allowed as long as it is not used within the house. Permanent wiring in the houses is forbidden, to avoid the temptation of easily plugging in appliances that would provide comfort. Battery operated torches are allowed, as are electric drills, welding equipment and other workshop tools, but no hard-wired light bulbs. Therefore, it is common to see workshops operating a vast array of electrical tools, but lit only with kerosene lamps.

Musical instruments, radios, and music playing equipment in general are also forbidden. Again, Mennonites repeatedly stated that music in itself was not sinful, but that it inevitably leads to dancing, which whets sensual appetites and therefore allows sin to creep in. Music is to be used for the Glory of God, and the lyrics to be "food for the spirit" and not for the delight of the body. Therefore, singing is to be done a capella and following the *Gesangbuch* (hymnal). The rhythm is extremely slow, literally taking minutes for the singing of a single verse, and often hymns are left unfinished. Singing is widely used in mass, during marriage parties, to welcome a guest, or to accompany work.

The body is also directly subject to regulations. Men should wear their hair well trimmed and women should not cut it at all (1 Cor. 11:15). Women's hair is worn plaited, rolled and attached to the sides of the head, and should be covered with a *düak*. The *düak* is a carefully embroidered kerchief used by women to cover their heads whenever they are in the presence of non-family members, or when they are leaving the house. It is also a mark of civil status; white for singles, while black for married women, widows, and spinsters who do not wish to marry. The attire is regulated, in terms of both the type of clothes and the colours and designs allowed. Rings, belts, make-up, perfumes, wrist-watches, jewellery, and other items that are taken as means of ostentation and of self-enhancement are strictly forbidden. Of course, the barrier between what constitutes a clothing necessity, and an attempt at self-enhancement is hard to lay in writing, therefore there are always differences in the way the *Leardeenst* of each colony interprets and enforces the same Ordninj.

When discussing these regulations, and the seeming arbitrariness of some of them (why trousers should be black or blue but not green, for example), a principle was brought up: "In some cases it is not a matter that one is better than the other, but that we all do the same thing." It is therefore the quenching of the quest for individual differentiation that is behind these rules. All these rules are supposed to discourage arrogance and individualism, while encouraging humbleness, meekness, and surrender of the individual to the Divine Will, expressed in compliance with the community. That is, to minimize and subsume individuality to the exalted community of which it forms part. In this way, the negation of the self becomes the price to be paid for the participation in the "body of Christ," for becoming members of the true church who would eventually be saved, of those who have been chosen by Him to be His people, the *Christenvolk*, in opposition to the rest of humanity, the *Weltmensch*.[11] These prescriptions and prohibitions are, in everyday life, transformed into the visible diacritics that mark the definition of group boundaries and membership.

Conclusion: Mennonite Transformations

The historical analysis has also shown how the institutions and the colony way of life that is present today was initially the result of outside impositions rather than from their own projects, which they later

---

[11] On the effects on identity and belonging produced by the usage of regulation attire, among American Mennonite women, see Graybill and Arthur (1999), and, on the Amish attire, Hostetler (1964).

appropriated, considered as their own and reproduced as such. Indeed, one of these appropriations have been the formation of a social order that is coterminous with their religious organization, and where religious authority reigns supreme. The have also transformed the meaning of 'separation of the world' from spiritual into geographical terms, and said separation is marked by ethnic diacritics that have become sacralized. These processes of appropriation have been so effective to the degree that they have become compulsory identity markers, and not abiding to them is considered apostasy and non-Mennonite.

They have also transformed the meaning and practice of separation of church and state. We have seen how Radical Reformers displayed a very modern attitude in their process of separation of domains, especially in attempting to exclude the political from its influence on religious matters. However, the transformation from religious movement interspersed with the rest of the population into religiously exclusive colonies made the social order coterminous with the religiously defined community. This had important political consequences: the *Leardeenst* absorbed the political, internalizing it and concealed this fact through the denial of the existence of politics within the colony. The *Leardeenst*, despite lacking a war machine, acquired in this transformation a practical legitimate monopoly over the use of power within the colonies (while simultaneously denying it and discursively accepting the authority of the state on whose territory they settled). Holding the keys of entry and exit into the community gives the *Leardeenst* material power over the means of survival (as I will show in the last three chapters). By holding the monopoly on the control of the education of children, the interpretation of the Scripture and other authoritative texts, the *Leardeenst* controls the constitution of the moral and political order. In short, the *Leardeenst* is a privileged actor in the definition and enforcement of the Mennonites own 'imagination of the future'. Despite their claims to immutability and calls to avoid change, the future they now imagine as the guiding, realizable community on earth has also been under constant transformation and change with the transformations of their social order since sixteenth-century Europe.

Processes of internal change include the formation of a persecuted, highly proselytist religious group, whose heterogeneous members lived intermingled with the rest of the population, and whose membership was voluntary (and real life risk involved) and its transformation into one where the bulk of the social interactions are held with fellow members, who have been homogenized in their practices and self-presentation, and that grows only generationally. It does not incorporate those not born within the community, but for those born within, membership is almost compulsory. In other words, whereas in sixteenth-century Europe, a Mennonite was someone who voluntarily chose to join the movement at the expense of risking being burned at the stake, most likely living in urban centres (they provided greater anonymity and freedom) without carrying outside visible marks that would show his confession. Today it is someone born into a Menonnite family, who is expected to be baptized (indeed if he or she wants to get married or acquire land needs to do so), who wears a particular set of clothes, who refrains from the usage of certain modern equipment and who lives in a Mennonite colony. In addition, instead of being persecuted by worldly governments, it is someone who is given special privileges for belonging to such a group (at least until the colonists refuse their incorporation into the nation). Not only are they not a materialization of their ancestors' imagination of the future, but also their imagination of the future is different from that of their ancestors. The notable thing is they still claim allegiance to the same symbols, which are perceived as immutable, concealing from themselves and to others, their past and future history.

CHAPTER TWO

NEGOTIATING STATES, REJECTING NATIONS

Introduction

Franz surprized me when he said: "My grandchildren are Argentine, my children are Bolivian, I am Mexican, my parents were Canadian, and my great grandparents Russian." Later he added: "our fatherland is not of this world, our fatherland is heaven." My surprized and amused face had triggered this response. He had just finished telling me how he used his different documents according to which borders he had to cross. Having residence documents for both Bolivia and Argentina (in addition to his Mexican nationality due to his birth), Franz would leave Bolivian immigration with his Bolivian documents, swap them while crossing the bridge, and enter Argentina as a resident.

This vignette can be read on different levels: temporal, physical, and political. Temporally, it is a statement of how Franz locates himself within a historical narrative: a historical narrative, which is not only about the past but one that includes the present and the future, and occurs both on worldly and other worldly levels. Indeed, it is much more than that, as Franz is at the same time explaining and incorporating his life within Paul's words in Phil. 3:20 "Our citizenship, however, is in heaven, and it is from there that we eagerly wait for a Savior, the Lord Jesus Christ."[1] In this sense, history of the past and scriptural narrative become one, joined together through the community of the present. Within this framework, movement is permanent whereas worldly localizations are bound to be temporary. As Ghassan Hage argues for the case of migrant Lebanese, migration ought not to be considered as an automatic source of cultural dislocation, but rather a means of constructing a viable future (2005). The Old Colony case brings to the foreground a critique of the common assumption that "uprootedness" and "nomadism" are automatic threats to cultural identities, an assumption that stems from the sedentary-centric perspective favoured by states (Deleuze and Guattari 1987; Scott 1998). On the political

---

[1] All Bible quotations are from the International Standard Version.

level, the succession of citizenships as a constitutive part of a genealogy, together with Franz's pragmatic usage of documentation indicate that citizenships, as well as locales, are circumstantial and a temporary aspect of a perdurable (although not necessarily impermeable and unchanging) self-definition. Franz is therefore providing a key for the understanding of Mennonite history and community identity in terms of the relationships between Holy Scripture, territoriality, nationality, citizenship, and the state.

As we have seen in the previous chapter, the Mennonites provided central political concepts that lie at the core of the modern nation-state (separation of church and state, the privatization of belief, and the construction of an autonomous individual accountable for his or her own acts). The "purification" of these concepts from their religious origins as Bruno Latour (1993: 10) would have it (on the theological origin of political concepts see Schmitt 2005), was not recognized as such at the time, and the modern notion of social order had to be reinvented, not much later by the likes of Grotius and Locke (Taylor 2004; see also Fix 1987; 1989).

This chapter examines the relationships that Mennonites have forged with the nation-states on whose territories they settled. I demonstrate that the relationships with the different states have been more intense and significant than what can be openly and unproblematically acknowledged by either side. Whereas the Mennonites claim separation between church and state, they have always had a main interlocutor in the different states that claimed sovereignty on the territories they occupied. Not only have the Mennonites been instrumental for the nation-states in the consolidation of suzerainty over the territories where they settled, but also many of the features of their own social system, which they believe to be divinely ordained, are the product of the interaction with nation-states, as we have seen in the previous chapter. The open recognition of these features by the Mennonites would subvert their own narratives of constitution as the people of Christ, who separate themselves from the world and the state (for a related Amish perspective see Yoder 2003). This separation, I show here, has now taken the form of a rejection to take part in the nation. Although in order to imagine their future as separate from the nation, the Mennonites require to secure certain resources and to perpetuate that particular imagination. The central resource has been schooling, which has set them at loggerheads with states' nation-building projects triggering repeated international migrations.

On the other hand, as I have suggested somewhere else, (Cañás Bottos 2006) the fact that territorial consolidation has been achieved thanks to the contribution of a group that afterwards rejects its place within the imagination of the nation, is a potential disruptor of the state's attempt to naturalize the association between nation, territory, and state through the creation of a common history, tradition, mythology, culture, and language. A naturalization central to the constitution of the modern nation-state, as many modern historians and social scientists have argued (Anderson 1990; Brow 1990: 3; Gellner 1983: 48–49; Smith 1997; Habermas 1996; Malkki 1992; Ferguson and Gupta 1992; Borneman 1992).

Therefore, Mennonites and states are involved in a relationship they both ought to conceal: how can the official imagination of the nation reserve a place within its narrative of constitution to a group that refuses a place within its nation? In addition, how can a group that claims separation from the state acknowledge their territorializing contributions? This chapter provides, on the one hand, a decentred perspective on nation-making processes afforded by focusing on their historical relationships with Mennonites. On the other hand, it explores the Mennonites' dynamics of schism and migration as resulting from their relationships with different states.

Invitations, impositions, schisms and migrations

A manifesto in 1762 supported and expanded by an edict in 1763 formed the legal background of an offer made to the Mennonites in Prussia in order to lure them to form part of Potemkin's plans to populate the recently conquered territories of the Ukraine (Urry 1978: 63–65; 2006: 39 & ff.). The Mennonites were not the only targets of said policies to attract immigrants. This was the product of a wider populating policy put in practice by Catherine II, to consolidate Russia's territorial control (1978: 63; see also Anderson 1974: 342–343; Hoerder 2002: 286, 311). Dirk Hoerder paints the following picture of the immigration into the Ukraine:

> the privileged foreign settlers, including Swedes and Jews, were placed in compact settlements along the Volga, in southern Ukraine, and later in Volhynia between Kiev in the east and the Bug River in the west. From the German territories about 11,000 families (41,600 individuals) came. Thus an arc of culturally heterogeneous German-language colonies,

> divided into Protestant, Catholic, and Mennonite groupings stretched from the Baltic-German towns through Volhynia, southwestern Ukraine and the Crimean Black Sea-Germans to the Stavropol—(North Caucasus) Germans and Volga-Germans around Saratov. (2002: 312)

These policies provided the empire with an array of political, economic and military benefits (see Hoerder 2002: 311). Politically, the settling populations would contribute to recognize the legitimacy of the state over a marginal area with uncertain or contested sovereignty. Indeed, the area is reported to have been under a constant flow of hordes, raiders and pillagers (Anderson 1974: 201). Economically, they would contribute to the national economy through their production, consumption and taxation. Militarily, the settlement of agricultural colonies meant that they could easily be used to station and provide supplies to armies on the borders as the Mennonites did during the Crimean War (see Longhofer 1993: 404 note 19; Huebert 1999), as well as constituting a buffer zone for foreigner's incursions.

> It was with the final closure of the Ukrainian and Siberian frontiers in the late 18th century, after Potemkin's colonization schemes were completed, that the Russian peasantry was finally beaten into sullen quiescence. (Anderson 1974: 211–212)

Mennonite migration started in 1788.[2] The first settlement, Chortitza (sometimes also spelled Khortitza) was founded in 1789 by Flemish families coming from Danzig, and would later be referred to as the 'Old Colony'. (Urry 1978: 78; 1983: 309; Krahn 1959a; 1959b: 381). The Mennonites expanded, formed new colonies and prospered economically; soon followed the foundation of Molochna (also spelled Molotschna or Molochnaia) with new waves of migrants.

> The region [...] was incorporated into a systematically well ordered part of the Russian Empire. From the very start the administration applied rules and regulations, it directed and controlled, and gave through its directives a meaning to the region. (Urry 1978: 84)

The Mennonites had indeed become an agent of the Russian State for the incorporation of the territories. This incorporation and meaning of territories was obtained through the sedentarization of the nomadic space (Deleuze and Guattari 1987: 353). That is, the transformation

---

[2] There are discrepancies regarding the size of the contingent: Redekop (1969: 5) claims there were 462 families, whereas Myovich claims only 270 (1996: 232).

of an indistinct territory into one that the state can properly simplify, read, understand, measure, and tax (Scott 1998; see also Deleuze and Guattari 1987). The Mennonites provided the Russian State (and the ones who claimed sovereignty over the territories where they settled afterwards) with a settling pattern that is the epitome of state legibility: the grid. Indeed, this layout is very similar to the one used in Hutu refugee camps in Tanzania (Malkki 1995a) and in high modernist planning (Scott 1998). Through a combination of the recognition of the sovereign, and by providing such legible territorialization, the state effectively captured the territory through the Mennonites (Deleuze and Guattari 1987: 440 and ff.). While the Mennonites had become a tool for the territorialization of the Russian State, the latter facilitated the conditions for the Mennonites to become a religiously exclusive community. Simultaneously concealing and making use of the situation, the Mennonites seized this opportunity to attempt making a reality of the 'separation of the world' and the founding of the 'community of true believers', which they would strive to replicate along their history, although suffering a change in both meaning and function due to the change in social conditions.

After a long process, in which Catherine the Great had played a decisive role, the Russian State was effectively consolidating itself (through the centralization of taxes, armed forces, administrative bureaucracy, and religion). Having successfully achieved territorial consolidation, and administrative centralization, the traditional dynastic legitimation principles of the Czar were being challenged (Hobsbawm 1992: 80–84). The Absolutist state was being transformed into a nation-state through the changing of the principles of legitimation (see Hobsbawm 1992: 80 and 84) having to invent the people (Morgan 1988) and to build and activate its supporting ideology: nationalism (Habermas 1996: 284). Concretely, these policies of Russification were the brainchild of Count Uvarov who stressed orthodoxy, autocracy and nationality as the principles of legitimation behind the Czar (Urry 1978: 378; cf. Anderson 1990: 83,87; Anderson 1974: 347). Alexander II's reforms in the 1860s eventually led to the revocation, in 1871, of their Privilegium and their status changed from 'Foreign Colonist' to 'Settler Proprietors' (for a detailed discussion on the use of land in Russia see Longhofer 1993: 399). The new reforms involved the limitation of land subdivision upon inheritance (leaving a great number of landless Mennonites), the introduction of Russian in the schools, and were soon followed by compulsory military conscription. The measures were of a clear nationalist tone, whereby the inhabitants of the territory were stripped from particular privilegia in order to promote their cultural homogenization and assimilation to the body of the nation (Hoerder 2002: 325).

A number of delegations were sent to carry out negotiations with the Russian government to have their Privilegium recognized. At first, they were offered alternatives but the Mennonites refused, and negotiations continued. Some members of the delegation sent to negotiate with the Minister of State Domains, Count Zelenoi, did not speak Russian:

> Zelenoi was not at all pleased at this failure to comprehend the Russian language and stated in no uncertain terms that he considered it was a sin (cto greshno) that the colonists, after living in Russia seventy years did not understand the language of the fatherland. (Urry 1978: 661).

That a 'sin' could be committed for not speaking the fatherland's language is very significant as it reveals the underlying religious dynamic that from the perspective of the state underlies the relationship between citizen and sovereign; unfortunately, Urry does not tell us what the delegation interpreted out of this usage of religious vocabulary for qualifying political relations. However, the Mennonites must have at least felt uneasy in this apotheosis of the nation and its own Holy Trinity of state, territory, and nation, manifested in this context as the Czar, fatherland, and language:

> The realisation that they were not just Mennonites, or colonists any more, but Russian citizens, subject to wider laws and a broader identity was not a fact many Mennonites liked to face. But events increasingly forced them to confront these problems, to contemplate the great division between being Mennonites and citizens of a state like Russia. (Urry 1978: 649)

In 1873 they started analysing the possibilities of migrating to the US or Canada, but the refusal of the US to grant collective acceptance (they insisted on an individual analysis of cases) forced the decision towards the latter country (Redekop 1969: 5). In a recent work, Urry (2006: 162) mentions that the Mennonites mistrusted governments based on popular sovereignty (like the US) because of their perceived lack of continuity that an autocratic regime seemed to be able to provide. This mistrust had its origins in having been "endlessly warned against the dangers of republicanism and popular government" by ministers of the Russian state (Urry 2006: 162). Regardless of the existence of such propaganda, an autocrat whose authority is legitimized by divine right fits better the Mennonite biblical understanding of the world than one based on notions of popular sovereignty, which replaces God as the ultimate source of legitimacy with a worldly 'people' (Kantorowicz 1957; Morgan 1988). 'Divine right' as a principle for legitimation denotes a political system overtly based on theological concepts and arguments that the Mennonites must have grasped very well (Schmitt 2005). However in spite of secularists, a system of popular sovereignty does not eliminate the religious, but rather, absorbs and conceals it, placing the nation (or the people) in the place of the ultimate principle of legitimation, a concealed apotheosis.

In 1873, the Canadian government invited the Mennonites to settle in their country. As in the case of the Ukraine, territorial consolidation was behind the invitation. Having signed the Oregon treaty in 1844, which established the border on the 49° parallel (although the US claimed up to 54°40') the Canadian government was eager to achieve effective territorial settlement of its territories (Sawatzky 1971: 8; Janzen 1990). The Mennonites were promised their requested privileges such as exemption from military service and from the pronouncement of oaths, free land and transportation, religious freedom, the right to keep their language and to run their own schools (Klaassen 1955; Redekop 1969: 5 and ff.). A delegation was sent and, after an inspection, two tracts were selected; one at the West and the other at the East of the Red River, south of Winnipeg, in Manitoba; from 1873 to 1880 around 7000 Mennonites migrated to Canada (Urry 1978: table 10a; see also Sawatzky 1971: 10; Warkentin 1959: 342).[3]

The Mennonites were divided into two camps: those who accepted the new conditions, and those who wanted to leave. Although, for the latter, the reasons for leaving were varied: the maintenance of tradition and the faith; to re-found the closed order that had been "opened" by their fellow Mennonites in their quest for knowledge and modernization; to avoid Russification; to seize an opportunity for development and for furthering their family's fortunes; and to find the land they were lacking (Urry 1978, 2006).

The first colonists arrived to the East Reserve in 1874. They were coming from Bergthal (4202 people), together with a few families from Chortitza. In 1875, a group of 3240 people led by an *eltesta* named Johann Wiebe arrived; two thirds were from Chortitza, and the rest

---

[3] Janzen (1990: 18 and ff.) provides a detailed analysis of the process of settlement and negotiation between Mennonites and the Canadian government, arguing that the liberties granted to the colonists were due to both the way they led negotiations, and to their usefulness to the government in their population of the west.

from Furstenland. This last group settled in the West Reserve. By 1880, some 300 families left the East Reserve (because its land was low and flooded easily) towards the West Reserve (Warkentin 1959: 346–347; Krahn 1957a; 1957b: 927; Klaassen 1955). The move made evident that each one of the groups had their own peculiarities. These differences included the melodies sung in church, together with the wider acceptance in the East Reserve of public schooling and of the Canadian administrative system. These were the main reasons that prompted the schism that created the Altkolonier Reinlaender Mennoniten Gemeinde, constituted by those in the West Reserve (Redekop 1969: 8–10; Krahn 1957a: 462; Warkentin 1959: 365; Sawatzky 1971: 10–17; Krahn 1957b). The Old Colony became the custodians of tradition while the Bergthalers became champions of progress and of the adaptation to the new environment (Krahn 1957a: 461).

In 1890 the Manitoba Public Schools Act was passed, which establishing a single, secular educational system under the direction of the state, created uneasiness among the Old Colony on the prospect of losing control of their schools (Redekop 1969: 12). Later, within the context of the First World War, the existence of this German speaking population generated a controversy that led to School Attendance Act of 1916. Increasing nationalism became a source of concern to the Old Colonists:

> Roblin [Premier of Manitoba], determined to make all ethnic groups assimilate with the Canadian people, declared in the legislature: 'While we welcome all, our duty to British subjects is to see that the children are taught the principles of the British constitution...What we need is to get the youth filled with traditions of the British flag and then, when they are men...they will be able to defend it.' (Redekop 1969: 13).[4]

Note the similarities between the place of education for nation building purposes as expressed by nationalists in terms of instilling the love for the country and its symbols with the Mennonite transcendental objectives of the teaching of the faith to their children expressed in the previous chapter. The only change is in the orientation towards which affection is oriented, in both cases it is towards a transcendental entity (God, flag, fatherland, etc.). However, this transcendental entity is none other than the groups' own 'self-image' that it is being simultaneously

---

[4] Similar quotations from government officials can be found in Janzen (1990: 93, 103–105).

constructed and inculcated in order to act as a guiding beacon in the reproduction of society.[5] Note also that in the usage of the term 'defend' there is the implicit distinction of friend and enemy, that according to Carl Schmitt defines the sphere of the political (1996). In other words, it is about the socialization of children with the explicit objective of the reproduction of society through their transformation into adults with full membership in a politically defined community, in this case, becoming British subjects. That is, to be inculcated the notion that in the face of the enemy, their state can demand both their death and that they kill others. Schmitt (1996) explicitly denies the comparability between dying for one's country and a martyr's death on the basis that the former implies the collective good, whereas the latter promises only individual salvation. But the denial of this comparison is based on a flawed, restricted and individualized view of religious martyrdom that ignores its collective ramifications as well as empirical manifestations: from becoming exemplars to be followed, to the possibility of different underlying theological interpretations of the martyrdom-salvation relationship. The imposition of national curricula therefore evidences the process not only of competition for the inculcation of the loyalty of forthcoming generations (and the broad spectrum consequences that this entails), but the core means through which the reality of these entities (God, the nation) are constructed.

English was made the sole language of education; school attendance was compulsory at public schools or state-approved private ones. The Mennonites carried out negotiations with the Canadian State in order to maintain their own schooling system, but they all failed. Although exempt from military service, the Canadian State was expecting them to contribute to the WWII effort through the buying of bonds, and the cooperation with the Red Cross; an expectation which some Mennonite groups bluntly refused to satisfy (Redekop 1969: 13; Klaassen 1955).

It seemed that again, land and freedom had to be sought somewhere else. The Mennonites formed new settlements in Alberta, as well as sending emissaries to the US, Brazil, Argentina, Uruguay and Mexico to evaluate the respective situations (Sawatzky 1971: 27, 32; Krahn 1959a:

---

[5] For the case of the Mennonites we should keep in mind Emile Durkheim's observation that it is through God that societies worship themselves (Durkheim 2001). See Bourdieu (1998: 46) for the case of nations and the inculcation of the "national self-image."

40; 1957a: 463). In February 1921 they met with the then President of Mexico, Alvaro Obregón, and returned to Canada with the good news that their requests had been granted.[6] A new division occurred, some decided to stay, accepting the new rules and regulations imposed by the State, while others emigrated to Mexico. Of the 4526 members of the Old Colony that were in Manitoba in 1922, 3340 had gone to Mexico by 1926. Nevertheless, many were to return to Canada unsatisfied with the situation (Krahn 1959a: 41).

The Mexico that received the Mennonites had just come out of the revolution. A land reform had been implemented and, somewhat paradoxically, the Mennonites acquired the land of former *latifundistas* (large landowners) who, through this transaction, found a way of avoiding expropriation (Will 1997). President Obregón, who had a farming background, expected the Mennonites to become a positive development influence, and an example for the rest of the population. Indeed, the Mennonite work ethic is highlighted in the 'Letter of Special Concessions to the Old Colony Church', which was the basis of their Privilegium. As in Ukraine and Canada before, the first years in Mexico were hard. The Mennonites had to adapt their farming practices to the new climates and soil (for an analysis of the agricultural adaptations see Sawatzky 1971). Initially a number of colonies were established in the states of Chihuahua and Durango. Soon they grew in number and had to expand their land base, forming new colonies in the states of Zacatecas, Campeche and Tamaulipas. In addition to the Old Colonists, other denominations also founded settlements in Mexico: Sommerfelders (another Canadian Mennonite branch) built Santa Clara in 1948 and Kleine Gemeinde Mennonites built Los Jagueyes (or Quellen Colony—the Source Colony) (Warkentin 1987: 7–8).

According to some of my informants, it was during this Mexican period that several processes of economic modernization took place in order to both keep labour occupied and increase productivity. Cheese factories were developed, which soon made milk the main source of household income, entailing a reorientation of agriculture from cash crops to fodder for dairy cattle, requiring more labour and providing

---

[6] The "Letter of Special Concessions to the Old Colony Church" signed by the Secretary of Agriculture and Economic Affairs of Mexico, A.I. Villareal and the President of Mexico, Alvaro Obregón gives the Mennonites similar privileges to those obtained previously. Translations of this can be found in Redekop (1969: 251) and in Sawatzky (1971: 40).

increased incomes. At the same time, tractors were introduced in the colonies. Their conspicuous usage as means of transportation to the cities prompted the introduction of a regulation to forbid rubber tyres on them, which were to be replaced with steel ones in order to restrict their usage to agricultural labour.[7] In this way, the Mennonites attempted to maintain their separation from the world while at the same time keeping and consolidating their positioning in the wider economy.

Scarcity of land in Mexico prompted some further migratory movements to Bolivia from the mid-60s onward, as well as to British Honduras (1958), Argentina (1986) and Paraguay (Sawatzky 1971: 189–190). Redekop (1969: 24–25) argues for the following causes for these movements: the fear of an eventual curtailing of the school freedom in Mexico, as well as the end of the military service exemption; a desire for new experiences and adventure, and an opportunity for dissident elements to separate from the strong discipline and restrictions. However, my informants who migrated from Mexico to Bolivia contested this last cause. They claimed that in La Honda colony (in Zacatecas), an important number of Mennonites had accommodated and modernized themselves, loosened the rules and become more worldly—using electricity within houses, owning cars and pickup trucks. Therefore, those wishing to continue being *Christenvolk* (people of Christ) had to enact a new separation from the world that had penetrated into their colonies. That is, the *Christenvolk* had to leave in order to remain separate from the colonists who had become part of the world (see also Wessel and Wessel 1967: 14). This process has continued to the present day and, in December 1999, I was told that there were no longer any Old Colonies in Mexico because of their modernization. In addition, (as was the case with rubber-tyre tractors) these vehicles facilitated access to the world, and therefore to sin. They also claim that it was the lack of land and the economical inviability of pumping water to the surface in order to irrigate land that prompted the new migrations from the colonies in Chihuahua. A colonist in Argentina, who came from Nuevo Casas Grandes, explained to me:

> Where our parents, who came from Canada, established themselves, there was a land shortage, and the territory ended up being small. They then went to Chihuahua, which is an irrigation zone. In 1965 everything was cheap, diesel, fertilizers, etc. By 1985 everything had changed. Everything

---

[7] Although Lanning (1971: 96) claims this change occurred in Bolivia.

went up. If you didn't go well with the harvest, then you could not recover the expenses. The land was not enough, and it was impossible to continue on land that needed irrigation. So we started to look for wide areas that did not need irrigation. Because irrigation expenses were large, in the first years we did well, but not afterwards.

The oil price rise following the Iranian revolution in 1979 and the ensuing Iran-Iraq war together with the fall of soft commodity prices in the 1980s left them at the short end of the bargain, paying more for their supplies, and receiving less for their products. Despite their attempts at remaining separate from the world, global market trends affected them deeply, pushing them towards developing further strategies for survival, including schisms and migrations that drove them to Bolivia and Argentina.

We need to go back in time a few decades in order to properly contextualize the arrival of the Mennonites in Bolivia. From the 1930s a number of important changes were occurring in Bolivia: it is considered by Gustavo Fernandez Saavedra (1999: 98 and ff.) as the start of the nationalistic period. After being left landlocked as a consequence of the War of the Pacific (1879–1883), Bolivia searched for a new oceanic access through the Atlantic. This made them look again at a region that had been forgotten, the Chaco. As Father Julio Murillo described:

> In the administrative plan adopted by the Republic, the occupation of the territories inhabited by savage tribes and the encouragement of immigration for the colonization of these territories were left entirely to the hazards of the future. In the Chaco, while the civilized population diminished instead of increasing, the indigenous population defied for three centuries the authority of the conquistadors and continually flouted the Republic. (Father Julio Murillo quoted in Secretary General to the Council 1934: 153)

The Chaco provided an access to the Atlantic through the Paraguay River, but it become a precious prize when it was discovered that oil was present in important quantities, triggering the Chaco War (1932–1935) between Bolivia and Paraguay.

Until then, the department of Santa Cruz had been an isolated and secessionist prone region (Lanning 1971: 18). After the Chaco War, roads were built and railroad tracks laid (see also Fifer 1967, 1982). Miguel Urquiola (1999: 194) shows how the participation in the total population of the country has steadily increased for the lowlands (on comparison with the valleys and the Andean region) from the 1950s onwards. The former north-south axis (La Paz, Cochabamba, Potosi) was replaced by a west-east one (La Paz, Cochabamba, Santa Cruz). Both internal migration from the Andes, as well as international immigration were directed to the area and Santa Cruz became the second largest city in the country by 1976 (Urquiola 1999).[8]

Legislation promoting the agrarian reform, universal suffrage and the nationalization of the tin mines was passed during Paz Estenssoro's first presidency (1952–1956). In 1954 the Bolivian and Japanese governments organized the formation of agricultural colonies with settlers from Okinawa, leading to the founding of Okinawa 1, 2, and 3, and San Juan de Yapacaní (Suzuki 2006; Consejo Nacional de Población—Fondo de Naciones Unidas para Actividades en Población 1986). In the 1970s Russian Old Believers founded three colonies: Toborichi Rio Grande, Cachuela Esperanza and Nueva Ichoa (Consejo Nacional de Población—Fondo de Naciones Unidas para Actividades en Población 1986; Fifer 1982: 430).[9] In this context of colonization, nationalization, and agrarian restructuring, Mennonites from Mexico were granted their sought for privileges in the Decreto Supremo 06030 of the 16th of March 1962 (signed by Paz Estenssoro during his second presidency) (Consejo Nacional de Población—Fondo de Naciones Unidas para Actividades en Población 1986).[10]

It is therefore within a context of newly obtained territories in need of being populated that the Mennonite delegation is received in Bolivia. As Father Murillo noted (Father Julio Murillo quoted in Secretary General to the Council 1934: 153) the Chaco was far from unpopulated but its indigenous inhabitants continually flouted the republic. The Mennonites seemed to provide several benefits from the perspective of the state. First, they would recognize the legitimacy of the Bolivian State. Second, their sedentary character and pattern of territorialization are more legible to states (see Scott 1998) than the

---

[8] Although the immigration legislation is considered as lacking a consistent policy and highly opportunistic (Consejo Nacional de Población—Fondo de Naciones Unidas para Actividades en Población 1986: 31–32).

[9] They rejected the reformations of Patriarch Nikon through which he established the Russian Orthodox Church as a State religion (see Hosking 1997; Janzen 1990; Crummey 1991) and left Russia in 1933 for China on the hope of reproducing their pre-revolutionary way of life but had to leave that country in 1949, from where they went to Brazil and started to migrate to Bolivia from 1979 (Consejo Nacional de Población—Fondo de Naciones Unidas para Actividades en Población 1986: 162–164).

[10] Wessel and Wessel (1967: 17) mention the existence of a Privilegium offered by the Bolivian Government to a group of Paraguayan Mennonites in 1926 and in 1930. This is the only mention I found regarding such early offer, and no sources are provided.

indigenous population, and in addition, it was expected that the former would have an influence on the latter to settle and eventually develop and practice large-scale agriculture. Third, their contribution to the economic development of the area through the putting into production of previously 'unused' land.

The first Mennonite colony (although not belonging to the Old Colony) to become established in Bolivia was Tres Palmas. Formed by a small group of colonists from Fernheim (a colony in the Paraguayan Chaco) who migrated under the auspices of an agreement with the Bolivian Cotton Company for putting in production of land (Warkentin 1987: 260; Wessel and Wessel 1967: 17). Mennonites of different church affiliations took advantage of the privileges; they settled in Bolivia and grew, developing into several daughter colonies, reaching forty colonies and an approximate 40.000 inhabitants by the year 2000. During the 1980s, the military dictatorship suspended the Mennonites' Privilegium. Worried about the possibilities of continuing in the country, the Old Colony sent a commission to evaluate conditions for immigration in Argentina. They found suitable land and informal assurances of freedom of religion, but in Bolivia the suspension of the Privilegium was lifted and the enterprise abandoned. Soon, Old Colonists from Mexico started looking for alternative countries, fearing the suspension of their own Privilegium, and experiencing shortage of land, they resumed the negotiations from where their Bolivian brethren had left them. Before moving into the formation of La Nueva Esperanza, a few words need to be said about the new country where they were about to move to.

Argentina is usually self-defined as a country of immigrants. Although initial immigratory policies in the nineteenth century were aimed at the population of the vast countryside, most of it ended up in urban centres such as Buenos Aires, Córdoba and Rosario. Settling in the countryside involved either joining pre-existing populations or building their own settlements (locally referred to as colonies) such as Santa Cecilia (Archetti and Stølen 1975; Stølen 1996) formed by Italians from the Friuli; Apostoles (Bartolomé 1990) built by Polish and Ukrainians; and a number of Jewish colonies of diverse origins (Bargman 1992; Bargman et al. 1992; Freidenberg 2005) to mention just a few who have attracted the gaze of anthropologists.[11] In the area where the Mennonites settled, there were numerous colonies formed by Volga Germans which formed Santa Teresa (which is in the same department

---

[11] Jefferson (1926) provides a vivid account of the earlier colonising process.

as La Nueva Esperanza) and San Miguel Arcángel, on the neighbouring province of Buenos Aires, which are now towns indistinct from the rest (for a brief analysis of land ownership in the province of La Pampa and the impact of these migrations see Gaignard 1966). A quick look at any detailed map of the area will bear reference to this process of colonization by the conspicuous use of the term 'Cnia.' (abbreviation for *colonia* [colony]) preceding the names of towns.

Unlike the Mennonites, a process of integration and argentinization (the adoption of the Argentine nationality not only 'in paper'—citizenship—but as part of their identity) has occurred in all of them—usually through public schooling and military service. In the cases where a differentiated identity remains, it is subsumed to the national one, and activated only in front of other Argentines. References to these colonies were constant in talks with the local inhabitants of Guatraché when remembering their own forefathers, as Ana once told me when we were discussing the Mennonites:

> That is exactly the way my grandparents used to live, just arrived from the ships, living from the land, with no electricity nor TV, but they did send us to school so that we could become Argentines and integrate.

Old Colony Mennonites formed La Nueva Esperanza in 1986. The colony occupies an area of 10,000 ha in what used to be 'Estancia Remecó'. Its inhabitants come mainly from the Nuevo Casas Grandes and La Honda colonies in Mexico, and a few families from different colonies in Bolivia. They did not manage to obtain a written Privilegium prior to their immigration, but government officials promised them that they would not be coerced into military service (it was at the time of negotiation in the process of being transformed into a voluntary system) and that they could retain their schooling system. They also consulted lawyers who made a report for them regarding the legislation on the points they were interested in. The report states (from point 3 onwards):

> 3. The thoughts in our Constitution can be summarized saying that everything that the laws do not forbid, is allowed.
> 4. In Argentina there is a wide and total freedom of religion.
> 5. The military service is nowadays compulsory for all citizens, but is being submitted to deep review that indubitably will have to be resolved by the National Congress. Nevertheless, late jurisprudence by the Supreme court of Justice of the Nation allows to back the hope that, in a concrete case, the issue would be resolved in favour of your position.

6. You can impart on your children the teachings you wish.
7. Under the event of having to declare in front of a tribunal as witnesses, such a declaration will be done under the formalities stated by your beliefs.

After this report, the signatures of the members of the commission follow those of the lawyers, which suggests that they could have thought of it as an agreement. With this immigratory history, it was not unlikely for the government officers to believe that, eventually, a process of integration would happen. Within ten years of their arrival, the provincial Ministry of Education started to pressure the Mennonite colony to make them accept public schooling. Several offers were made regarding the provision of health services, which were refused one after the other by the Mennonites: to build a first aid unit in the colony, to station an ambulance in the colony and to establish a radio or telephone linkage with the hospital. Later, the provincial government tried different ways to impose the national syllabus. First, offering to build provincial public schools, then to send teachers to complement the teaching of the Mennonite schools with partial implementation of the syllabus. In the end, after harsh negotiations they settled on the agreement that children who were born in Argentina (and therefore Argentine through *jus solis*) were to be taught Spanish by their parents, using material provided by the State. This caused several families to migrate to Bolivia, and provided the conditions for a scam artist to approach the Mennonites offering them an interview with the national minister of education in exchange for an important sum of money. The trial in Santa Rosa that took place on my last arrival, together with the demotion of the *eltesta*, were both consequences of this swindle. A new colony was built in the last couple of years in the province of Santiago del Estero, while the colony La Nueva Esperanza is now being portrayed in the media as a touristic attraction (Cañás Bottos 2006).

Excursus: those who stayed behind

It should be stressed that in each one of these schisms and migrations, there was always a group that stayed behind, considering that a future could be forged without migrating yet again. Those who remained in Russia and Canada accepting the impositions of their respective states continued developing and growing, some maintaining the colony way of life and spawning daughter colonies when needed, while others joined the path of rural-urban migration (Loewen 1993; Driedger 2000). Many actively participated in the public political life of their countries, even endorsing the nationalist flag (as for example Urry shows for Mennonites in both Canada and Russia 2006) while others were forced to juggle with the competing loyalties of faith and country during times of war as Perry Bush (1998) and Fred Kniss (1997) show for Mennonites in the US. Yet others were persecuted without even being given the chance to voice their loyalties, as it happened with Mennonites in Stalinist Russia, having to find new havens in Canada, Paraguay, Uruguay, and Brazil.

Paraguay

One of the motivations of the Paraguayan government for encouraging Mennonite settlements in the Chaco was the former's interest in populating it in order to support their pretensions over such a territory before the start of the war with Bolivia. The *Report of the League of Nations Commission on the Chaco Dispute Between Bolivia and Paraguay* (Secretary General to the Council 1934: 152) recognized the Mennonite settlements as supporting evidence of Paraguayan claims of sovereignty over the Chaco. As in the Ukraine, Mennonite colonies were functional to war efforts in terms of the supply of provisions and the stationing of troops. Both Enrique Derksen (1988: 65) and Sandra Siffredi and Susana Santini (1993) mention the good relationships established between the colonists and the Paraguayan army during the war period. Negotiations between Bolivia and Paraguay started at the end of the nineteenth century, and escalated into the Guerra del Chaco (Chaco War) 1932–1935, although first military incidents started in 1927 (Secretary General to the Council 1934: 162). Other motives for the Mennonite acceptance on the Paraguayan Chaco were the development of the region, its integration into the national economy, and a "positive influence" on nomadic indigenous populations, since "settling is a means […] to make them human beings" (Loewen in Hack 1978: 224), and as a former minister of defense said "building up backward people in a country is the best defense against communism" (Graber in Hack 1978: 225).[12] The Mennonites settled on land that traditionally belonged to the indigenous populations. As a consequence they

---

[12] Both quotations are in English in the Spanish edition (which is a translation from the original German).

greatly restricted the movement required to sustain a hunter-gatherer population, and produced friction among them (see Lehner 1989). At the same time, the Mennonites built work camps where indigenous peoples settled, and which provided cheap labour for the colonists (Derksen 1988; Hack 1978, 1979, 1980; Siffredi and Spadafora 1991; Spadafora 1994; Kidd 1995: 55; Renshaw 1987: 337 and ff.; Susnik and Chase-Sardi 1995: 262–263).[13]

The Mennonite colonies in Paraguay are the product of various migrating routes. Some of the privileges given in Paraguay to the Mennonites by the law 514 of 1921 include religious freedom, schooling autonomy allowing them to use German as the language of teaching, and exemption from military service (Derksen 1988: 64; Dyck 1981: 317; Suarez Vilela 1967: 27–28). In the period 1926–27, in the midst of the Paraguayan Chaco (often described as *el infierno verde*—the green hell due to its combination of heat, humidity and forest), Menno colony is found by Bergthaler Mennonites coming from Canada (from the group who decided not to follow Johann Wiebe and the Old Colony but still refused the acceptance of public schooling and of military service). Bergthaler Mennonites later founded Bergthal and Sommerfeld. Mennonites fleeing Stalinist Russia founded several colonies: Fernheim in 1930–32; Neuland in 1947–48 and Volendam, in Eastern Paraguay. In 1937 Friesland was found as a daughter colony of Fernheim (Derksen 1988: 62–67; Dyck 1981: 317–322; Hack 1978: 210; Suarez Vilela 1967: 27,28, 34; Warkentin 1987: 83–85; Smith 1957). These colonies continued to grow and were joined by further waves of immigrants from different Mennonite denominations as well as other Anabaptists such as Amish and Hutterites (although the latter could not secure the same Privilegium from the government and left) Warkentin (1987: 85) reports a total Mennonite population in Paraguay for the year 1986 of 22,570 people.

The colonies in Paraguay have prospered to the point that Trébol (the trademark of a Mennonite dairy cooperative) is today one of the leaders in the Paraguayan market. I have found their products on the shelves of several supermarkets in Santa Cruz (Bolivia).

There are also some Old Colonies in Paraguay formed by immigrants from Belize and Mexico (in order of foundation: Rio Verde, Mexico,

---

[13] These frictions have also been translated into a heated debate in *American Anthropologist* (Basso 1975; Redekop 1975; Basso 1973; Wilson 1975).

Durango and Manitoba), which keep in close contact with their Bolivian counterparts.

Uruguay, Brazil, and Belize

There are three Mennonite colonies in Uruguay, Delta, Gartenthal and El Ombú, but none of them belongs to the Old Colony. El Ombú was formed in 1950 with Mennonites who were forced to leave the delta of the Vistula river in 1945 as a consequence of WWII. Until they could afford to buy land, they lived in urban centres. A few years later Gartenthal was founded and, in 1955, Delta. All were formed with colonists of the same origins, and received economic and logistic support from the Mennonite Central Committee to undertake their migrations (Abramián, Figueiras, and García 1995: 9–12; Dyck 1981: 324–326; Suarez Vilela 1967: 38). Nowadays they seem to have integrated with the rest of the population (they accepted the Uruguayan public schooling system and apparently were not strongly enforcing religious endogamy). A teenager, descendent from a Mennonite family who left the colonies and converted to Catholicism, stated that "only the old ones remain in the colonies."

Colonists from the same group that founded Fernheim in Paraguay, formed Witmarsum and Auhagen in the Brazilian state of Santa Catarina. These colonies did not prosper economically and were soon dissolved. Neue Witmarsum and Colonia Nova were founded from the remnants of the first, while those from Auhagen migrated to the suburbs of Curitiba (Dyck 1981: 323).

Mennonites from different denominations (and some Amish) migrated to Belize after securing a privilegium in 1957. Blue Creek and Shipyard were founded in 1958 by Mennonites from the Old Colony who were coming from Mexico, whereas the Kleine Gemeinde founded Spanish Lookout on the same year (Warkentin 1987: 301–303). There has been quite a lot of movement between colonies as well as denominations (Warkentin 1987: 301–302).

In 1969, families from Shipyard and Spanish Lookout formed Barton Creek, where they ban modern equipment considered necessary by other colonies such as refrigerators, tractors, flashlights, etc. In fact, the motive for moving was to avoid modernizing trends in those colonies. Later, some Amish from the US, Sommerfelders from Mexico, and a few Canadians joined them (Warkentin 1987: 302).

Conclusion: the Mennonites' place in a world of nation-states

This history tells about the ironical place of the Mennonites in the world. Ironical, since one of their tenets is the separation from the world and therefore claim not to belong to this world. This tension has implications beyond the Mennonite case since it lays bare some of the relationships between territoriality, nationality and citizenship while shedding light on the development of the system of nation-states from a marginal perspective.

After an initial contribution to the secularization (and subversion) of the political order in sixteenth-century Europe (and their concomitant persecution and expulsion) we can identify a historical pattern that seems to have characterized the relationships the Mennonites have had with the different empires and nation-states along their migratory history.[14] This pattern consists of a succession of two distinct phases: The first one characterized by the acceptance of the Mennonite colonists. The Mennonites were initially considered as a positive factor for economic development and the consolidation of sovereignty and territory through the settlement and population of marginal areas. Their abilities to striate space with their grids, therefore rendering smooth undifferentiated space into a captured territory, was an object of desire for states, which they could appropriate with little cost, the granting of Privilegia (Deleuze and Guattari 1987: 384–386). Through these Privilegia the Mennonites were transformed into exceptions, benefiting from the differential treatment they received by not being subject to the general conditions that applied to the rest of the population. Although they might have interpreted these negotiations as a way of securing their separation from the world and the state, they actually contributed to the consolidation (materially and symbolically) of the latter as sovereign, since sovereign is he who rules over the exception (Schmitt 2005).

A second stage is entered once the state's initial objectives of consolidating its sovereignty and capturing the territory have been attained. In this change the divinity under whose grace the King was King gave way to 'the people' as the ultimate source of legitimation (Morgan 1988; cf. Kantorowicz 1957). This is a stage where the state sets itself the task

---

[14] See Fix (1987; 1989) for an analysis of the impact of these reformers in the advent of a rational worldview and Urry (2006: 57–62) for the Mennonite's involvement with the Dutch Patriot Movement in the eighteenth century.

of building its own principles of legitimacy: the imposition of 'official nationality' that Anderson argues should be understood as a means of retaining dynastic power through the stretching of the "short, tight skin of the nation over the gigantic body of the empire" (1990: 82). Or in a less phallic way, to inculcate the "fundamental presuppositions of the national self-image" (Bourdieu 1998: 46) into the inhabitants of the territory over which the state claimed sovereignty, achieved mainly through public schooling and military service. Massimo d'Azeglio's phrase clearly summarizes the conduct of the nation-states in these two phases "we have made Italy, now we have to make the Italians" (Hobsbawm 1992: 44). The Mennonites were therefore witnessing, through the change of attitude towards them by the state from recipients of privileges—and therefore being recognized as different—to being subjects to the imposition of 'official nationalisms'—an attempt to homogenize them with the rest of the population, the transformation of empires (and kingdoms) into nations.

Being a Mennonite and being a 'national' are seen by the Mennonites, as well as by the states involved, as being exclusive of each other. As Franz told me (paraphrasing Jesus in Mt. 6:24 and Lk. 16:13) "one heart cannot have two masters." In this way both Jesus and the nation (through the recourse to the naturalization of nationality and its conflation with citizenship) are perceived as competing for the ultimate loyalty. Jesus as God's son and Saviour ought to be witnessed and upheld even in the face of persecution, torture and death. Concomitantly, to defend the Union Jack and the British constitution are concrete expressions of a broader nationalist motto of wide application coined by Horace: *dulce et decorum est pro patria mori* (it is sweet and appropriate to die for one's fatherland), or put more prosaically by a modern anthropologist: "In war, the modern state demands from its citizens not only that they kill and maim others but also that they themselves suffer cruel pain and death" (Asad 2003: 117). These principles and demands are materialized in exemplars to be followed and imitated. Whereas the Mennonites look at martyrs' lives for suitable exemplars to be followed in the keeping of the faith in times of difficulty and persecution—and Thieleman van Braght's (1982) voluminous martyrology can be found in numerous Mennonite houses—nation-states provide their own version in their heroes and monuments to the anonymous unknown soldiers. Therefore, the *Christenvolk* should continue to resist the attempts of the different states in transforming them into nationals. Mennonite and nationalist imaginations of the future are therefore incompatible with each other, each demanding ultimate loyalty, each demanding to be reproduced and inculcated into forthcoming generations.

We can now have a better understanding of the initial vignette: Franz was not speaking about a genealogical succession of nationalities (loyalties and emotional ties), but of citizenships. In recognizing such distinction, Franz had successfully gone beyond "methodological nationalism" (Wimmer and Glick Schiller 2002: 302) and decoded the "double code of nationality" (Habermas 1996: 284) that attempts to make an indissoluble unity out of citizenship and nationality. The Old Colony therefore settles in states, but rejects becoming part of the nation. The succession of citizenships clearly showed that migration was in fact a way of rejecting nationality. If national narratives are based on the building of a common past, that justifies a common present, in order to secure the glorious and eternal future of the fatherland, Old Colony Mennonites can certainly not partake of it. Doing so would imply sharing the same future, belonging to the world, and contributing to the apotheosis of the nation (by accepting a place within the people that replaced the divinity). This rejection was needed because of the conflict between the nation-state requirements and their moral order, and therefore Franz was defining both his and his forefathers' decisions to migrate in moral terms. When later he added: "our fatherland is not of this world, our fatherland is heaven" it became clear which identification he was reclaiming as his own, as well as stating where his ultimate loyalty was and what future community he was imagining and using as guide.

Having initially worked for the state, the Mennonites attempted to remain separate from the nation through migration, searching for a new state that would privilege territorial consolidation over nation-building. The apparent simplicity and state-friendliness of individual Mennonite colonies, displaying a grid, and an arborescent internal hierarchy, was belied by the nomadic potentiality of the combination of the separation from the world, the production of schism and the lines of flight taken thereafter, constructing cross-border rhizomes in an attempt at maintaining their difference from the nation. This, however, is the subject of the next chapter.

CHAPTER THREE

INTER-COLONY DYNAMICS

Introduction

In the previous chapters I have shown the historical process of formation of the internal organization of the colonies, as well as its religious legitimation and transformation. I have highlighted the place of migrations and the founding of new colonies as the Mennonites' answer to the attempts of different nation-states to impose national identities on them. In this chapter, I examine two interlinked processes, the construction of a community that spans across the territories of different states, and the dynamics of colony fission and formation. I argue that these cross border practices and colony fission and formation are the two main strategies the Mennonites deploy in order to cope with the problems of demographic growth, external state impositions, and internal conflict. Furthermore, this change of dynamics from settling in marginal areas and contributing to the territorialization of different nation-states, to the deployment of cross-border strategies to flout their incorporation into the nation seems to be the Mennonite answer to the globalization of the nation-state, which has left no territory beyond its control (except perhaps Antarctica). Having nowhere else to migrate to, it is by keeping as many doors open as possible that they can assure for their coming generations a place where they can continue building and imagining a future separate from that of nations.

The founding of new colonies

We now have the necessary elements to take a closer look at the process of colony schism and formation and to suggest a possible systematization. Initiatives to found new colonies can be classified by following the intersection of two dimensions: the character of the initiative, which can be either schismatic or expansive; and the originators of the initiative, which can range from a single person or small group of individuals, to a *Je'meent* sponsored one that, for the sake of simplicity, I will be referring to as 'individual' and 'collective'.

Expansive initiatives are the response of the Mennonites to predicaments that arise from their own practices, values, and situation. Among the different economic activities, agricultural ones are the most highly valued on their moral scale. They define themselves as farmers, and expect their children to continue tilling the land. Therefore, in order to maintain themselves as farmers over time, without expelling labour outside the colony or deviating it to non-land dependent activities, land acquisition should be matched to demographic growth. This is not an easy task when taking other factors into consideration: First, the Mennonites rejection of contraceptive practices since they are seen to interfere with God's will. Nevertheless, the practice of baptism of adults tends to delay marriage, thus contributing to the reduction of birth-rates. Second, the issue of productivity: as prices for agricultural products fall and the cost of inputs rise, a higher efficiency is required, which is sought after through mechanization. This, in turn, frees more hands to be provided with land if they are to refrain from sinful idleness. Moreover, changes in price structures have made certain activities economically unviable. For example, in Mexico, colonies that required pumping water to irrigate the fields were progressively dismantled after the increasing rise of the price of oil, and moved to Bolivia. In such cases, the relevant colony as a collective undertakes the task to sponsor the founding of a new colony, which would remain part of the same *Je'meent*.

The formation of a new colony is a long process that normally takes a few years to complete. Colony members express the need for more land informally to their authorities until a *broodashoft* (meeting of members) is called to officially formalize the undertaking. Usually the *fäaschta* (elected chief of the colony), accompanied by a small group of members set on finding suitable arable land for sale. They prefer to buy uncleared land, since prices are lower, and then clear it themselves. Qualities they look for are, foremost, closeness to other colonies, price, quality of land, access to water and distance to urban centres and access to means of communication. Of course these qualities cannot be maximized all at once. Prices for land surrounding an established colony are usually extremely inflated when a Mennonite approaches its non-Mennonite owner. Regarding closeness with urban centres and means of communication a balance is strived for; they have to be close enough so as not to make their products unmarketable due to transport costs, but far enough in order to attain a level of isolation that would restrict everyday travel to town, especially for youngsters. After a suitable tract of land is found, and a price agreed upon between the seller and the envoys, a member's meeting is arranged. I attended one of these meetings in La Pampa.

The meeting took place in one of the schools, and it had been announced earlier during the week. Abraham took me there in his *bogge*, but when we arrived, the meeting had already started. All members of the *Leardeenst*, as well as the *fäaschta* and *schulte* were sitting in the front, facing the rest of the male members of the *Je'meent* who sat on the pupil's benches (not a single woman was present since only men are allowed to participate). After the negotiators explained the situation (land quality, price, conditions of payment, etc.), they answered questions and allowed comments. Then, everybody stood up and headed for the door. The *fäaschta*, sitting on a desk next to the door, asked each member on their way out how many hectares he would be willing to buy.

Besides the sum asked for by the seller, plus taxes and other expenses, the price per hectare arrived at includes all the costs incurred by the commission and a variable addition in order to pay for land that will remain colony property and which will either be sold later to newcomers or newlyweds, or kept for the building of churches, schools, and colony-owned buildings such as the cooperative cheese factory or cooperative shop. A number of hectares (variable depending on quality of land) is also set apart as land to provide for landless families on a more or less temporary basis. Then, figures are consolidated and if enough interested buyers are found, the deal is pursued. I later learned the deal was called off due to the lack of sufficient prospective buyers. They also look for possible buyers in other colonies, by either inviting them to the meeting or sponsoring similar meetings in different colonies. Individuals often own land in colonies other than where they reside. This ownership is usually the result of one of two processes. Either land is bought during the initial stages of the formation of a new colony, or (a much lesser occurrence) is land that has been left behind when moving to a new colony. It was explained to me by different colonists that such properties were bought or kept either: a) for their children when they grow up; b) to contribute to the settlement of a new colony (prices in such a stage are much lower since they tend to buy marginal uncleared land) with or without immediate expectations of moving in themselves, and usually including the first reason mentioned; c) in case of a change of government's attitudes towards them; and d) (in the case of land left behind) a combination of the first reason and/or the impossibility of selling it or the unsuitability of the price offered. Cleared land is usually rented to fellow colonists, whereas uncleared land is either left as such or an agreement is made between the owner and an interested candidate whereby the latter clears it in exchange for its usage rights for a number of years.

At this point in the process, the main issue is to find enough buyers for the available surface and location of the land regardless of the internal location of the particular plots (unless internal heterogeneity of soil and condition is readily available). If sufficient interest is raised, then the land is further surveyed, and the plan laid out. If it is a case of a whole colony moving to a different location, they try to retain a similar layout, or at least to keep neighbours together. Then, the streets are cleared, and the land divided among their owners. Although from this moment on it is up to each individual colonist to do the necessary arrangements for clearing their own piece of land and constructing their own buildings, different families nevertheless coordinate their efforts at this stage. A variable number of members of the *Leardeenst* should join the new colony, but this is dependent on the distance to other colonies (of the same denomination). The closer they are, the more possible it is for *prädjasch* from the mother colony to take turns in preaching at the new settlement until a suitable number has been ordained. In addition, until the new colony has their own *eltesta*, the one from the mother colony travels there to perform baptism and the Lord's Supper.

Individuals (or most likely small groups of them) without material support from the community, can also initiate new colonies without losing communion with their colony of origin as long as they obtain consent from the *Leardeenst* and they abide by the same *Ordninj*. Initiatives of this type are not very common not only because of the resources needed, but also because it brings to the surface internal differences and the risk of being labelled a proud individualist, who cannot wait for the collective initiative because he wants to do things his own way. In fact, the land scarcity issue seems to be the publicly offered reason, although disagreements on issues that are not serious enough to cause excommunication are often lurking underneath. In spite of the Old Colonies agreeing on a common *Ordninj*, there are usually some differences in its interpretation and enforcement. The settling in on an already established colony involves the adaptation of the newcomer to the colonies' own peculiarities; the making of a new one gives them the chance to juggle with the rules more freely. For example, one of such differences between the colonies in Bolivia and Argentina dealt with the use of tractors. Whereas in La Pampa a tractor can be used to pull loaded carts, this has to be done by horsepower in certain colonies in Bolivia. Other differences include the type of designs, number and combination of colours that are considered permissible for embellishing women's *düak* (the kerchief they wear on their heads).

Returning to the definition of initiatives, the standing of a member within the community (and the way he handles the whole process) can have important consequences on the labelling of his attempt. Initiatives that start as expansive can easily become considered (by fellow members) as schismatic. Individual expansive attempts can therefore be the result of expansive attempts that failed to gain collective support, and are always on the brink of becoming schismatic.

Schismatic initiatives are those that produce a breaking of communion between the originating colony and the new one to be formed. This implies that one of them loses its standing among the Old Colony and either joins another Mennonite denomination or forms its own. The main cause that gives rise to a collective schismatic initiative is the perception that an important part of the colony has become worldly. This can be the product of two processes: imposition or appropriation of cultural objects, ideas, or practices deemed worldly by the splintering group. Unlike the opinion of Redekop (1969: 25), who claims that the ones who emigrate are those in search for the loosening of discipline and in search of adventure, it is usually those who reject these innovations that emigrate. The main argument is that the separation of the world, the moral cornerstone of the colonies, is no longer possible because the world has invaded it. Therefore, those who wish to remain separate from the world have to vote with their feet, and build a new one to re-establish their separation.

It is important to notice the differences between schisms triggered by processes of imposition from those of appropriation, since the former involve international migration, whereas the latter usually involves the forming of a new colony within the same national borders. This is reflected in Chapter 2, which was concerned mainly with collective schismatic processes triggered by the imposition of schooling and military service, producing migrations from Russia to Canada, and from Canada to Mexico. Longer distances between colonies, the negotiation of the conditions of immigration with different states, and the adaptation to new cultural, social, and ecological environments make these the hardest migrations of all, materially, logistically and emotionally. Another aspect of this difference is the assignment of blame done by the *émigrés*. Whereas impositions are interpreted as acts of persecution done by the world to them, and which tend to strengthen and increase the cohesion of the splintering group (persecution becomes the manifestation of their identity as Christians); appropriations are seen (at least by those who have resisted them) as the indicators of the lack of faith, and of the surrendering to the temptations of the Devil by the Mennonites themselves.

How communion is severed between the two colonies depends on the particular circumstances. It can either be a required renewal of the commitment to the church, a simple *de facto* moving out and the cutting of ties between the colonies, or an escalation of excommunication of individuals, which would render such a punitive measure useless. This is so because excommunication actually involves the prohibition of members in good standing to socially engage with those punished, but nothing prevents those under the ban from continuing life as usual among themselves.

Finally, individual-schismatic attempts can be of two types, depending if excommunication precedes or follows the formation of the colony. In the latter case, it is often the product of a transformation from individual-expansive after 'falling from grace' in the eyes of the other Old Colonists, such as Abraham's attempt in Sachayoj (which can be seen as a continuation of his failed attempt in Córdoba, see Chapter 5). In the former type, where there is a schismatic intention from the outset, we can locate Abraham's current project with the help of Agromac (see Chapter 6).

The following tables summarize this section.[1]

Table 1: Etiology of types of colony formation

	Schismatic	Expansive
Collective	a) Imposition (nation-state influence) b) Adoption (temptations from the world)	Economic and/or demographic
Individual	a) Disagreement (possible transformation from individual-expansive) b) Excommunication	a) Economic (possible failure to become collective-expansive) b) Secular disagreement

---

[1] Subtypes 'a' and 'b' are consistent across tables.

Table 2: Consequences of types of colony formation

	Schismatic	Expansive
Collective	a) Schism + migration to different country b) Schism + formation of new colony (not necessarily in different country)	Formation of new colony, ties and cooperation kept, sharing of *Leardeenst*
Individual	a) Excommunication follows new colony formation (possibility of future repentance and reincorporation) b) Repentance and reincorporation are highly unlikely In both cases, externalization of dissent	a) Can be managed to form a new colony whilst keeping ties (likely to be the result of failure to achieve wide support for a new colony) b) Colony likely to become labelled as schismatic and therefore severing of ties

Table 3: Types of colony formation, cases

	Schismatic	Expansive
Collective	a) Migrations to Canada and Mexico b) Formation of the Old Colony in Canada	Bergthal and Furstenland in Russia; Pinondi and Manitoba in Bolivia; La Nueva Esperanza in Argentina
Individual	a) Abraham's attempt in Sachayoj b) Abraham's Roboré project	a) Abraham's attempt next to Pinondi, Bolivia b) Abraham's attempt in Córdoba, Argentina

Cross-border practices

Different colonies from Bolivia, Argentina, Paraguay, Mexico and Belize belong to the Altkolonier Reinlaender Mennoniten Gemeinde. During my field research, there were a total of forty-one Mennonite colonies in Bolivia, of which fifteen belonged to the Old Colony.[2] In Argentina,

---

[2] These are: Capulín, Casas Grandes, Durango, Fresnillo, Gnadenhoff, Manitoba, Milagrosa, Neuenthal, Oriente, Pinondi, Riva Palacios, San Jose, Santa Rita, Swift

there were two colonies, both belonging to the Old Colony; one in the province of La Pampa, and a smaller one in the province of Santiago del Estero. There is no central authority that joins them, but a mutual genealogy and the agreement on a common *Ordninj*. It is this agreement on a common set of rules and norms that allows individual colonies to be recognized as equals by other colonies. This mutual recognition allows for the building of a community that crosses locales and national boundaries, but at the same time, this translocal community is being constantly constructed and transformed through these practices.

Focusing on these practices is necessary since, for the Mennonites themselves, the definition of 'us' is not a territorially bound one, and therefore references to 'colony', 'us', and 'Mennonites' include those covered by the same *Ordninj*. This is why treating single colonies as basic and total units (or several colonies as simple replicas of one) misses the frame of reference of the Mennonites themselves. For the Mennonites, the simultaneous existence of different colonies, between which relationships are established and a wider community constructed, is what allows for the practice of translocal strategies. Let me illustrate this with a few brief and concrete examples (the last three chapters provide more detailed accounts of some of these strategies).

It is not uncommon for Mennonites to move between colonies, giving reasons that range from no more than the wish to try out a different place; economic situation; or to liberate oneself from a social environment in which they are not happy. Franz was born in Mexico, spent his youth and got married in Riva Palacios (one of the oldest and biggest colonies in Bolivia), where his four children were born. He then moved to Argentina with his wife and children. After a few years, he moved back to Riva Palacios, only to return to Argentina two years later. The last time I saw him in Argentina, he told me he was strongly thinking of returning to Bolivia because of his unhappiness with the new colony authorities. It should be noted that although he did not give me exact dates, the colony in Argentina was found in 1986, and our last meeting took place in the year 2000. A recent letter informed me that he and his children (and their wives) had moved yet again to a new colony in Argentina. That is three changes of country of residence, and at least four colony transfers in 20 years. Jacob was born in the same colony

---

Current, and Tres Cruces in the Department of Santa Cruz; and El Sur and Florida in the Department of Tarija.

as Franz, and he also moved to La Nueva Esperanza, which was where I first met him. The last time I saw him was in Pinondi colony, 300 kilometres south of Santa Cruz de la Sierra. Although he still owned land in Argentina and in another colony in Bolivia, he was living on borrowed land. Jacob was looking for new land in the Charagua area in order to build a new colony where he and other *émigrés* from La Pampa could settle. Like Franz, Jacob was not alone; along with his wife and children were his mother and father, brothers and sisters (all with their respective spouses and children), and all were moving together. Let me mention one last case, that of Abraham on who we will focus on in later chapters. Also born in Mexico, he moved with his parents to Belize and then Bolivia, where he got married. He integrated the mission for arranging the Mennonite entry in Argentina and negotiating the colony land. After much gossip and accusations of not being honest when settling the land deal, he left for Sachayoj, in the province of Santiago del Estero in order to build his own colony. Only his family (including some of his married children) followed him, making his initiative a failure. He was excommunicated, but later repented and returned to Bolivia. He is now in Santa Rita working as a debt collector for a company that sells tractors and agricultural implements to Mennonites, while recruiting settlers for building a colony close to the border with Brazil. These movements are just a small fraction of a wide range of practices that bound the Mennonite community across the territories of different states. Other practices include mutual visiting, be it just for pleasure, to do business, or to attend to ritual occasions (funerals, weddings, baptisms, etc.), private epistolary exchange and the writing of open letters to the *Die Mennonitische Post* (a fortnightly newspaper of wide circulation in the colonies), but more importantly, their mutual recognition of membership. At the same time, these practices manifest the interchangeability of members between colonies. In the eyes of individuals, this interchangeability gives flesh and blood to the abstract, or even imagined, construction of *Christenvolk* that takes place through their acceptance of a common *Ordninj*. Since every so often, when members move between colonies or share their experiences in written form, it provides an opportunity for proving their shared membership and fellowship. It also teaches them that their life strategies need not necessarily be bounded to the colony where they live, but extended to the network of fellow Old Colonies.

In short, although colonies are similar to one another in terms of social organization and expected behaviour of its members, the fact that *other* colonies exist (or can be created) without necessarily requiring a break with the community is the indispensable factor for these strategies to exist. While, at the same time, it is through these practices that the community is maintained materially, and also imagined while being scattered on the territories of different nation states.

Parish records

Although there is no one single authority that centralizes the organization of the Old Colony, there is, however, one very important formal practice in the binding of the colonies at a high institutional level: The keeping and distributing of parish records.

At the end of every year, the *dia'koon* of each colony consolidates the parish records and these are posted to the *eltestasch* of all the other colonies of the *Je'meent*, to be read aloud by a *prädja* in church during the Christmas mass. The *eltesta* of each colony keeps a copy of the reports of every other colony. The report is sent in a short slip of paper, which has been photocopied, with blank spaces to have the appropriate numbers filled in. The blank slip reads as follows:

> During the year ____ there were born within the community ____males and ____females, tallying____. There were a total of ____ dead, of which there were ____males and ____ females, from where a total of ____ were community members,[3] out of which were ____ males and ____ females. Therefore there were ____ more born than dead. There are ____ male community members and ____ females, tallying ____. There were also ____ new members of the community[4] and ____ new marriages. In total, there are ____ souls.

After a long negotiation, I managed to get hold of and copy these records. They cover from 1977 (the year the *eltesta* that gave them to me assumed his position) to the year 2000. One of the problems in this data, which seemed not to be of much concern to the *eltesta*, is that not every colony is represented every year. Either the slips missing were not sent, or got lost on their way. Another problem was that on top of every slip, there was supposed to be the name of the colony to which the figures referred. This was not consistent, sometimes the name of the *eltesta* of the colony was used, sometimes the nearest town.

---

[3] "Community members" (Gemeindeglieder) means baptized members.
[4] Baptisms this year.

Furthermore, since the names given to the colonies are often repeated (a daughter colony in a new country sometimes takes the same name of its originating colony) a process of consolidation was required, taking into account the values given, and cross-referencing these to fieldnotes and other sources regarding the names of the *eltestasch* of different colonies at different periods. In addition, and not in a consistent manner, certain newly built colonies which had not yet had their own *eltesta* ordained, were included in the records of their parent colony. There were also systematic inconsistencies in the records of one of the colonies, the values of fields to be added or subtracted, and the tallying fields did not match. In these cases, I assumed that the fields to be added (or subtracted) were correct and recalculated the 'total' value. One last point to note is that notions of group belonging are superimposed on the making of these records. As soon as a colony ceases to be part of the Old Colony it is no longer included in them. Despite these limitations, they do seem to tell a number of things. This is only a brief descriptive analysis and by no means do I pretend to exhaust this source. The main objective is to present a number of general trends, which provide a rough quantitative picture of the colonies and their population dynamics.

According to what was said earlier regarding their reproductive practices, a steady, regular increase of population would be expected.[5] By calculating, where possible, the population growth for each colony for every single year,[6] showing values between 0.04 and 0.06, which means that a duplication of population should occur between every 12 to 17 years.[7] The records show a total consolidated population for the whole Old Colony (in Mexico, Bolivia, Paraguay, Belize, and Argentina) of 20,489 members for 1977 (the start of the series) and of 34,786 for the year 2000 (the end of the series). The highest value being 42,339 for 1998. This observed consolidated growth does not fit within what could be expected from the natural increase of individual colonies calculated earlier, showing instead a growth rate of 0.03. This

---

[5] It should be noted that regarding reproduction, my research did not go beyond registering their repeated claim of not taking contraceptive measures, although I did not perceive (nor pursue to find) any evidence on the contrary.

[6] $(TB-TD)/TP=NG$. In all the formulas in this chapter, TP = total population at the end of a given year; TB = total births during the given year; TD = total deaths during the given year; TPP = total population for the previous year.

[7] Due to the nature of the data available, all values should be seen more as being well-informed estimations than exact values.

comparison between consolidated natural growth and observed population growth of individual colonies indicates a loss of population through means other than death. This is in fact the result of schisms, and the disaffiliation of colonies from the Old Colony. Whereas the settling of new colonies of the expansive type involve the moving of individuals between different colonies while still belonging to the Old Colony, the disaffiliation of a colony (following a schism) is reflected in no longer submitting their yearly 'slips' and therefore the loss of its population from the records through the ceasing of its representation. For example, the contraction in total Old Colony population which occurred after 1998 (the modal value) can be almost wholly attributed to the fact that the Los Patos colony in Mexico (with 7,579 inhabitants in 1998) left the Old Colony in 1999, being 33,616 the total sum of population for that year.[8] Indeed, during the period 1977–2000 six colonies left the Old Colony (Campeche, Buenos Aires, Durango-Paraguay, La Honda-Mexico, La Honda-Paraguay, Los Patos) and 21 new colonies were founded (Campeche Durango, Capulín, Casas Grandes-Bolivia, Durango-Bolivia, Durango-Paraguay, Fresnillo, Gnadenhoff, Indian Creek, La Batea, La Nueva Esperanza, Little Belize, Manitoba, Milagrosa, Neuenthal, Oriente, Pinondi, Progreso, Sabinal, Santiago, Tres Cruces and Yalnon).

By taking a closer look at individual colonies, it is possible to calculate the migratory balance by applying the same logic of separating the component of population dynamic that is due to natural growth, from the observed total population growth or contraction.[9] This is so since the Old Colony does not incorporate new members that have not been born within one of its member colonies. Colonies show steady positive migratory balances during the first years of creation and, upon reaching a certain value, specific (and almost constant) for each colony, they start to continuously expel members of the population.

One last point that these records show is the participation of colonies within each country towards the total population. Whereas for 1977 the ranking (from higher to lower) was: Mexico, Bolivia, Belize and Paraguay, for the year 2000 Bolivia is by far the country with greatest Old Colony population, followed by Belize, Mexico and Argentina.

---

[8] Missing values from the Casas Grandes (in Bolivia) and Yalnon (in Mexico) seem to account for the rest of the missing population. These colonies showed values of 473 and 1528 for 1998 and of 642 and 1634 respectively; an estimate of those missing values would total just above 2000 people.

[9] TP − TB + TD − TPP.

The year of foundation of the colony in La Pampa in 1986 coincides with a slight loss of population for Mexico (which then continues with a downward trend) and, two years later, Bolivia takes the first place. A final drop in population for Mexico in the year 1999 coincides also with a vertiginous population rise in Bolivia. This is the product of a last wave of migrations to Bolivia before the disaffection of all Mexican colonies from the Old Colony.

Conclusion: externalization of dissent, and cross-border strategies

In this chapter I have shown how the Mennonites apply translocal and cross-border strategies for the maintenance of community, and that these practices are implemented in order to cope with three problems: demographic growth, internal dissent, and state intervention. In this way fission, expulsion and migration, far from being an abnormality, are a constitutive dynamic of their own process of reproduction by, on the one hand, externalizing internal competing imaginations of the future. On the other hand, migration and cross-border practices allow the avoidance of the internalization of competing imaginations from without. More importantly, beyond the economic benefits obtained by agricultural settlements through ecological diversification, the formation of a social body that spans the borders of different states allows the distribution of risk in different polities in order to insure themselves against sudden political changes that might eventually endanger their situation via the restriction of religious freedom, imposition of state schooling, or of military service. Having witnessed and contributed to the rise of the national order of things, they have learned that it is by being simultaneously within various nation states, that they can protect themselves from the attempts at incorporating them into the nation.

CHAPTER FOUR

ARTICULATIONS, CONNECTIONS AND SHORT-CIRCUITS

Introduction

This chapter explores the Mennonite dilemma between their moral value of remaining separate from the world, while maintaining relationships with it. Indeed, one problem the Mennonites encounter when attempting to materialize their imagination of the future is how to apply their guiding principle of separation from the world that lies at the heart of their imagination, while state impositions and material conditions require them to engage with non-Mennonites. In this chapter I show that this dilemma is tackled through the usage and control of the processes of social articulation, (Blok 1988; Hermitte and Herrán 1977; Hermitte and Bartolomé 1977; Hermitte 1979; Bartolomé 1977; Greenfield 1977; Lomnitz 1988), also referred to as structures of mediation (Gould and Fernandez 1989) or interhierarchical and intercalary roles (for an overview of the Manchester-school approach to this problem see Werbner 1984: 164–170) within which specialized agents take in their hands the task of establishing the necessary linkages. Focusing on different activities and contexts, such as doctors and lawyers in Brazil (Greenfield 1977) poncho weavers in North Western Argentina with contacts on the national market (Hermitte 1972, 1979; Hermitte and Herrán 1970) and the Sicilian Mafia (Blok 1988) these authors show how the access to the supra-local level resources are transformed into increased wealth and a loyal political following of the articulator.

A diverse number of labels have been attached to the actors involved in these processes, expressing its wide local variations: brokers, *caciques*, godfathers, patrons, and *coroneis*. What they all share is a structural position between the local community and different levels (regional, national, the state) and spheres (economic, political) that allow them to profit from the channelling and transformation of different types of value between them (Roniger 1987; Michaelson 1976; Greenfield 1977; Hermitte and Herrán 1970, 1977; Rothstein 1979; Eisenstadt and Roniger 1980; Lomnitz-Adler 1992: 169 and ff.). These studies have concentrated on the transformative and accumulative aspects of articulation, and its role in the reproduction of inequality in the differential access to resources. I will propose a different interpretation for the Mennonite case: this differential access should be understood more as an instance for isolation and maintenance of difference rather than inequality.

I argue here that articulators also act as isolators since, in their attempts to establish an oligopoly of inter-group social relationships, the brokers free their fellow Mennonites from establishing them themselves. Furthermore, it is this very aspect of articulation that the Mennonites seem to be most interested in, since it is through them that the separation of the world, and the social interaction across boundaries, are kept under control.

Instances of articulation become simultaneously the loci of conflict and of its resolution. On the one hand, because the process of articulation is the very means that allows communication, exchange, and relationships to occur between different groups. Conflict can therefore arise during this process out of the contrast between aspects of different social entities, each with its values, interests, peculiarities, etc. On the other hand, borders, limits, and their crossing and playing with them has been deemed as both a source of danger as well as power (Turner 1994; Douglas 1985, 1991). In order to avoid, or at least to contain and control those dangers and powers, carefully fenced off domains of interaction and their respective articulation specialists are needed. Another locus of conflict can be found in the definitions of these domains and their respective rules of articulation, which each side attempts to control, define and manage.

In the following pages, I analyse these processes of articulation in concrete situations. I start in a pseudo chronological order, concentrating on my first days in the field, since my introduction to the colony was not only an instance of articulation, but also because almost every single person I was introduced to during those first days were themselves engaging in different domains of articulation. This writing strategy attempts to show these processes in practice while the process of my insertion, and the networks I established, show the level of control they succeeded in establishing over my presence and research. By doing so, I bring to the foreground their border maintenance strategies which were also applied to me. I then move on to analyse a couple of cases where this management has been unsuccessful (from the Mennonite perspective), pointing at the multiplicity of agencies involved in processes of articulation, and the limits of the Mennonite control of brokerage and of their borders.

Whereas in this chapter I focus on the predicaments of border maintenance in the face of inter-group relations, the remaining chapters will focus on how these borders get challenged and crossed. Before delving into the strategies of border maintenance, it is necessary to briefly present how the Mennonites perceive the people that inhabit the world from which they wish to remain separate (for a more detailed analysis that also incorporates how the Mennonites are perceived by others see Cañás Bottos 2005).

Perceptions of others

The Mennonites define themselves as *Christenvolk*, the people of Christ, although alternative terms used are *Dietsch* (German) and *Mennoniten* or *Menonita*. They all have the same referent, but they are used in different situations: *Christenvolk* if they are speaking in religious terms, or want to claim the moral high-ground; *Dietsch* is more neutral, and used in internal conversations whereas *Mennoniten* and *Menonita* are used in communicating with non-Mennonites.

The categories *Weltmensch* (worldly men) and *Ejebuare* (aboriginal, indigenous people) stand in opposition to *Christenvolk* and *Dietsch* respectively. There are different *Weltmensch* and *Ejebuare*, and they are classified according to nationality (or in some instances ethnic categories): such as *Bolivianos* or *Collas* (Bolivians), *Mexa* (Mexicans), *Argentinos* (Argentines). Although they are all part of the world, there is a perceived distinction between the different *Ejebuare* in the way they behave. Despite their differences, what for the Mennonites is certain is that having renounced the world at the time of baptism, they no longer belong to it, and whatever comes from this world is potentially dangerous to them.

For the Mennonites, *Mexas* are more violent than the rest: "on weekends, there is always one that ends up stabbed in their parties because of a fight over a woman." This is also applicable for business making:

> They are very different. In Mexico, they think differently. If you do business, and don't pay your part, then you get killed... If they want to take your money, they come with a revolver. Here [in Argentina], nothing happens. There is a guy named ***, from Guatraché that owes us $15000 in cows and does not pay. In Mexico another Mexa would have killed him. Here you have to be careful because you end up giving the money yourself. They talk to you, and they take more than is due.

Another Mennonite added:

> This is different from Mexico. The Mexa is a *sinvergüenza* [lit. one without shame] because his blood makes him steal, and after stealing, disappears, and if cornered he can be very dangerous. But in Argentina he comes back, and solves it with his mouth. In Bolivia, when they go and ask for a job, they are always keeping an eye on what things they can come back at night to steal.

The first Mennonite summarized: "*Mexas* steal at gunpoint, *Bolivianos* during nighttimes, and *Argentinos* with their mouths in broad daylight." They therefore recommend being very careful in Mexico in order not to trigger violence; to lock everything in Bolivia, and to pay deaf ears to the Argentines' sweet talk.

They are also different in their attitudes towards work. Whereas *Bolivianos* are seen as little more than beasts of burden, who work long hours for very little pay, *Mexas* are perceived as being reluctant to work:

> The Mexas are always drunk, they come to the colonies asking for work, but when the week-end comes, they spend everything on booze. On Mondays they always come with a hangover and can hardly work. You got to wait until Tuesday to get anything done.

Another Mennonite jumped in to the conversation and added: "the government came, and gave land, seed, diesel, fertilizers, and tractors for the Mexas to work, but they sold it to us and then they drank the money."

Although they all seem to pose different physical and economical dangers, *Ejebuare* are all equally dangerous in spiritual ways, since they can also be used by Satan as means to tempt the *Christenvolk* into sin, not only by facilitating their access to modern goods but also by convincing Mennonites into following *false prophets*. From the Mennonite perspective, it becomes clear that contact with the outside is something that should be placed under strict control. How they do it, and what are the problems encountered in the management of their relationships with the *Weltmensch* forms the core of this chapter.

Controlled connections

A chain of anthropologists and missionaries in Buenos Aires, the Argentine Chaco, and in the US, led me to Angel, the pastor of the Evangelical Mennonite Church in Buenos Aires, who facilitated my first entrance to La Nueva Esperanza. I attended several worship meetings at the Church and explained my interests to Angel. He told me that a couple had approached him a year before, in order to be introduced into the colony (whom later turned out to be Sergio and Silvana—Chapters 5 and 6 deal with them more thoroughly). Angel, tried to delay them in order to get to know them better to ascertain their true intentions. However, they never came back to him. Not too long afterwards, on one of his trips to the La Nueva Esperanza, Angel was surprized when he found them wearing the typical Mennonite attire and working in the fields with the colonists, they had managed to get into the colony without his intervention.

A tornado had swept the colony some months before I met Angel. He had to take a donation from both the Mennonite Central Committee and from some Paraguayan colonies in order to contribute with the reconstruction. Angel offered to take me with him and introduce me there. He explicitly told me he made no promises of them accepting me beyond his stay, but that he would help me as much as he could. We took an overnight bus to Santa Rosa, the provincial capital, where Oscar the pastor of the local Mennonite Church and his son Facundo picked us up.

On the way we talked about the colony, the weather, football, and discussed the radio program they were hoping to get on the air to aid their mission efforts. After about four hours, we took a dirt road that led to the colony. The passage of the tornado could still be seen on the bent silos, and strewn metal sheets. Once inside the colony, girls and boys would pretend to ignore us while the car was approaching, but would curiously turn around to look at us as soon as we went pass them. We went straight to Johann's house, the *fäaschta*. Having heard the engine, Johann stepped out. We all shook hands with Johann, and I was introduced as a friend. Immediately, Oscar opened the boot of his car and tried in vain to interest Johann with some locks he had managed to buy at a cheap price. We were then invited into the house. We were led to the bedroom (which, as I later learned, is the place where visits are received), and Johann produced some chairs for us to sit on. Johann's wife who was baking cookies and bread brought us some juice to quench the thirst that the summer heat and the dry dirt road had produced. After a quick chat, Angel started talking about the donation, Facundo stood up immediately, and gestured me to leave with him. We left and had a look at the garden, the barn, and the workshop. When Oscar, Angel and Johann left the house, Angel came to me and said jokingly "you are lucky, we have just been invited to a wedding ceremony. What a reception you had huh? And the chief is going to introduce you, you should become *Mennoniten*." Johann ordered one of his sons to prepare his *bogge*, and when it was ready he told me to go with him while the others followed us with the car. He asked me what I was doing there, and I told him that wanted to write a book about their lifestyle and their religion. He apologized for his Spanish, and told me there was another man, Franz, whom I would be interested in talking to since he "knows more about these things." I learned later he was the father of the groom.

It only took us five minutes to get to the house of the bride's father where the *fe'lafniss* was taking place. Although Mennonites translate this as 'wedding ceremony', a more precise cultural translation would be 'engagement ceremony' since the marriage vows are taken eight days later during a church service. There were groups of people scattered around the *wirtschoft*, divided roughly by gender and age. Children roamed around, members of the *Leardeenst* (wearing their distinctive clothing) and other elderly people were gathered close to the windmill, *junges* (single, adolescent males, but also used as a generic for youngsters) and a few *me'jaleores* (single, adolescent females) were inside the barn, sheltering from the scorching summer sun. Quite a few adults and *me'jaleores* were running around inside the house and kitchen preparing the meals to be served. I saw one young man, wearing blue jeans and a checkered shirt in the middle of the garden. He was wearing a leather hat and a Bible in hand speaking to some youngsters. "Do you believe in salvation by faith or by acts?" He was asking them, opening the Bible to show a verse, while I walked past them. His name was Nicolas, we introduced ourselves, but he refused to be specific about the church he went to or about his interest in the colony. I never saw him again.

Johann introduced me to Franz, the groom's father, to some members of the *Leardeenst*, and to a few other people. Then they told me about the tornado, a draught that had been going on for the last two years and about the new tax legislation and the paperwork it had produced. The father of the bride came towards us and invited us in. I sat on the bench next to a man in his sixties named Jacob, while a young woman placed on the table a plate containing a knife, fork, spoon, and cup. I realized we were only adult men sitting at the table, and while we were eating, another non-Mennonite was invited into the house. He was in his sixties, with a thick but short moustache and a bulbous nose above it. He seemed to be behaving quite proficiently and with knowledge of what was going on, although I did not speak to him on that occasion.

Jacob jokingly dared me to an eating competition to see who was manlier. I interpreted his challenge as an invitation to not be inhibited and eat as much as I liked. As soon as people finished, they would stand up and leave, making place for another guest who would be shown to his place by the bride's father. Considering the stereotypes of isolation surrounding this group, and that this was my very first day in the colony, I was very surprized by the presence of these two Argentines, in addition to Facundo, Oscar, Angel and myself.

After lunch, we went out and, after a few minutes, a man wearing the *Leardeenst*'s attire arrived on his *bogge*. Oscar shook hands with him and asked jokingly "did you have trouble starting the *bogge* that you arrive so late?" To which the man replied in the same tone "my horse ran out of petrol." Oscar introduced the man to me as the *eltesta*, and said to him that I was his friend, wishing to learn and write about their religion and customs. The *eltesta* extended his hand to me and apologized for his Spanish, claiming he had a poor command of the language. He offered his help in whatever I needed, and I asked him to meet him some other day so that we could talk about religion and life in the colony. The *eltesta* agreed with his permanent smile, and Oscar intervened, immediately, starting a negotiation with him for an order of benches for the church in Santa Rosa. In addition to his farm, and the unpaid duty of *eltesta*, he was also a highly skilled carpenter.

After the meal, Facundo, Angel and Oscar, who wanted to buy some cheese, went to the cheese factory. Meanwhile, I was engaging in conversation with Jacob, his son Abraham, and Franz. As soon as they were back, they told me they were leaving. I was surprised, as I thought they might stay the night and assumed that my trip was finished, but they said Johann had told them I could stay at his place until Nicolas vacated Franz's house where I could then move in. All this had been arranged without me knowing.

After lunch everybody was called into the house to do some singing, later on, a mid-afternoon coffee was served, and I left with Johann for his house. We had dinner, and we chatted on the porch in order to get to know each other a little bit more. I was offered a mattress on the floor, beside the dinner table, and the next morning was woken up at around five to milk the cows. Afterwards we had breakfast and we went to church. I followed Johann into the building and a murmur rose as we walked in. The church service lasted slightly more than two hours, and was carried out in German, we then went back to his place, had lunch, and a siesta.

Julius, Johann's brother-in-law who is the colony 'doctor' came with his wife to visit. We sat in the main bedroom, eating sunflower seeds and drinking juice. Most of the conversation was conducted in Plautdietsch. A few times, they resorted to Spanish in order to include me in the conversation. They questioned me on different aspects of life in Buenos Aires, and Julius demonstrated a good knowledge of it. They also mentioned Franz, and his appearance on a TV special on Mennonites. They said that in church they were being constantly admonished not to watch TV when going to town, and that certainly included a ban on appearing on it. Johann continuously stressed the importance of living a humble and poor life, and that agricultural work was more fitting for a true Christian than manufacturing or commerce since it involved fewer opportunities for lying and cheating. Johann thought that engaging in commerce can easily lead a person to a constant struggle between realizing the maximum possible profit, and an honest true price.

The following morning Johann asked me if I would be interested in seeing the cheese factory, I replied positively and he indicated a *bogge* that was coming along the road, which would be going there. He walked me to the road and left. I flagged the *bogge*, and the driver stopped. I introduced myself briefly, but the driver already knew about me. I was invited to climb on the *bogge* and to join them. The driver was called David and he was the owner of one of the cheese factories in the colony. David was accompanied by two of his brothers, who had come from Mexico and Bolivia to visit him. They had not seen each other for twenty years, and were being taken on a tour of the factory.

The production of cheese is a central activity in the colonies. Besides the economic benefits, it is the main synchronizer of activities and through following the path of the milk we can see how the Mennonite domestic unit is at the same time connected with (and isolated from) the national economy through a series of transformations of the product, and the social relationships in which it is embedded.

There are three cheese factories in La Nueva Esperanza: two small privately owned ones and a bigger one, which is run cooperatively by the whole colony. Almost every household in the colony has cows, which are milked twice a day. The milkman collects in the morning and in the evenings (with the exception of Sundays). On Mondays, there is an extra collection trip for Sunday's milk that starts at 1am. The milkman receives a percentage of the value of the milk collected, and milk suppliers are paid on a fortnightly basis. The colonists eagerly await the milk payments as they supply most of their immediate cash needs. Cheese factories produce mainly two types of cheese, mozzarella base paste, and a ready to eat semi-hard cheese. The former is picked up twice a week by a truck, and is taken to mozzarella factories in different cities (Bahia Blanca, Buenos Aires, Santa Rosa), whereas the latter is mostly retailed straight from the factory to tourists, visitors, and fellow Mennonites who sometimes peddle it in town to defray some of the costs of travelling. In its time-synchronizing aspect, the milk industry in the colonies has an effect on the building of community similar to that of newspapers. Paraphrasing Benedict Anderson, every time a Mennonite milks, his actions are being replicated simultaneously by all his fellow coreligionists, "of whose existence he is confident, yet of whose identity he [may or may not have] the slightest notion" (Anderson 1990: 39).

Before setting up the cheese factories, the colonists used to sell the milk to one of the biggest dairy companies in Argentina. A combination of factors then led them to the setting up of these cheese factories, namely: the price paid was based on fat content, which was established unilaterally and measured by the company (therefore beyond the control of the colonists) and, eventually, the company failed to pay them. The benefits they obtained by selling cheese instead of milk include the aggregation of value within the colony (providing jobs) and it also allowed for a rise in the price paid for the milk. Another benefit of this change is that the shelf life of cheese is greater than milk and, therefore, more flexibility is allowed for collection times, and there is therefore less spoilage. David told me that although his cheese factory was not producing much profit, he could at least help other families by buying their milk and providing jobs for his sons or sons-in-law in case they needed them.[1]

The opening of the cheese factories was not without problems. State requirements had to be fulfilled, and David explained, in the following way, his struggle to obtain sanitary permission.

> I had to do an enormous amount of paperwork. Not only registering independently for tax and hiring an accountant, but for opening the factory, an inspector came to check its cleanliness. He came once and he

---

[1] I asked for the price and quantities of the necessary inputs, and after calculating the cost of his production with the income obtained, he was hardly breaking even.

said it was not good. But it was clean. I thought that he wanted a bribe; I asked him if there was another way out, but he got offended. He said he would return the following week to check if everything was sorted. So, the following week, when he came, I invited him for lunch. He saw my house, my family, he saw we were clean people, and then he extended his permission. It was just a matter of getting to know each other. I was wrong when I thought he wanted a bribe. But that was the way to do things in Bolivia and Mexico but in Argentina things are different. You can't just solve everything with a bribe, but when they do ask for it, it is so much higher!

When I returned from the cheese factory, Johann took me to one of the stores. There they were not only Mennonites, but also a few Argentines, including the mobile unit from a local radio station from Bahía Blanca. The wide range of goods for sale impressed me. The shelves behind the counter, and indeed the whole room, was full of cloth, shoes, hats, tools, seeds, foodstuffs (most packed in big-sized containers, such as the five kilogram jars holding the mayonnaise), butane gas, oxygen and acetylene for the welding machines, soft drinks, a wide range of sweets, oil, grease, diesel, petrol, timber, some books (Bibles, Catechisms, hymnals), *Die Mennonitische Post*, medicines for both people and cattle, etc.[2] Most of the goods are bought wholesale in cities such as Bahia Blanca, Santa Rosa, and Buenos Aires, and the printed material is either photocopied and bound by them, or imported from Mexico, Bolivia and Canada. The owners of stores make constant journeys in order to obtain the necessary supplies; nevertheless there are a few things (such as gas, oil, petrol, oxygen, timber, etc.) that are delivered directly by the suppliers. There was also a carton box where correspondence collected from the colony's P.O. Box in town was brought regularly by the storeowner so that colonists could spare their trip to town (and at the same time attract them to the store). Most of the transactions I saw were not paid for, instead, the storekeeper kept a filing desk with cards for each household of the colony. He would note down the items purchased, the date, and the amount due. It took us fifteen minutes by *bogge* to get from Johann's house to the store, he spent half an hour talking and socializing with other Mennonites, and then of course it was another fifteen minutes return trip; this was all just to buy a two litre bottle of concentrated juice and a gas refill for his soda-making siphon.

---

[2] The *Die Mennonitische Post* is a fortnightly newspaper published in Canada and Mexico that circulates among all Mennonite colonies.

The following day I was taken to Franz's house, the groom's father. He was not at his house when I arrived, but Johann told me I could stay there anyway, stressing that it had already been arranged. Peter, the youngest of his sons, was repairing the new Belarus tractor.[3] I joined him and gave him a hand passing him the tools while we did some introductory small talk. When Franz arrived, he asked me if I wanted to have a ride with him. I helped him with the harnessing of the horse and we went to visit a couple of other houses to borrow a plough, which was unfruitful. On the *bogge* I explained to him that I wanted to write about their way of life and religion, and that I needed to be inside the colony as much as I could in order to learn about them. He did not seemed very interested, so in order to show my interest in Mennonites, I gave him a summary of what I had already read about them. Franz was surprized, he then reasserted their belonging to the Altkolonier Reinlaender Mennoniten Gemeinde, characterizing it as the "most conservative of all." Franz then told me that if I could read German, I would not need to stay there, as his personal library would be enough. I emphasized the need to observe actual behaviour, and the learning through participation. He then asked me about my family background and after my reply, he stated: "then it must be something very humiliating for you, coming from the city, with all the comfort and cleanliness, and studying at university, to come to humble yourself and get dirty with us." Once we got back to his house, I asked him to indicate anything I might be doing wrong, or anything that might be a nuisance for them.

> You are not a nuisance, the guys from Channel 2 were.[4] They put pressure on people, forcing them to act as they wanted, and at the end they gave beer and cigarettes to the *junges* in order to be filmed breaking the rules. And now, they are using the video to promote Guatraché for tourism, I have just recovered that copy of the video, I will burn it. They also cut what I said into pieces, and put it together in a way that I was saying things I did not say.

---

[3] These tractors are made in Belorussia, and are indeed branded 'Belarus'. Some jokes were made about their 'common' origin.

[4] The year before, a TV team from Channel 2, a broadcaster from the city of La Plata in the province of Buenos Aires went to the colony to make a documentary about the Mennonites.

I took his words as a warning of what I should not do, if I wanted to continue with my work there. Upon asking him why he participated, he said that they put a lot of pressure on the colony, and then, somebody had to talk to them, and he was instructed to do so because of his command of the Spanish language, in a way similar to how my presence was imposed on him.

He also showed me a pile of receipts that he was in charge of collecting and sorting in order to ease the workload of the chartered accountant they had hired to comply with the new tax regulations:

> Cavallo and this bureaucracy have caused me an ulcer, despite having always been weak on the body and never having digested properly, it is all because of the worries he is producing here.[5]

I helped him sort out the receipts to be filed for the purposes of claiming a tax return. While I read what was being bought, I was surprized by the amount of alcohol and sweets. Abraham was also appointed with the same task, and they spent endless afternoons collecting, sorting, and filing the receipts. Franz was later relieved from these duties because of his zeal to comply with state regulations (to the detriment of the colony's economical interest).

Milking time arrived, and I followed them to the milking parlour. I was puzzled when I saw that the milk from two of the cows was being weighed. I asked Helena while she was doing so, and she told me those were the cows of her brother, who had just got married. The two cows had been given to him as a wedding present from his family. The milk was weighed separately so that he would receive his own money from the milk payment. He would not have a separate account in the cheese factory until he had his own milk jars, which would bear his initials. Upon marriage, the newlyweds usually receive a total of four cows, two from each of the spouses' parents. During the week between the *fe'lafniss* and the consecration of marriage in church, they would receive invitations for meals at friends and kin's houses. There they would receive presents such as crockery, cutlery, furniture, tools, etc.

After being a guest in Franz's house for almost a week, he told me I would have to leave by the time his son got married, since he would be returning home with his wife until they had their own house built. I went to find Abraham and ask him if I could move to his house. He

---

[5] Domingo Felipe Cavallo was at the time the National Minister of Finance.

said that he had already spoken with Franz and that my move had already been arranged. He invited me to go with him on his *bogge* to collect some money from the inhabitants of the *darp* to take to the *fäaschta*. It was part of the payment for the land.

Abraham owned a store together with his brothers and his father, Jacob. They had bought it from Franz, but they had lost all the goods with the tornado. The future looked dim since, in addition, the latest drought had left many colonists without money to pay for the goods they had bought on credit and with slim chances of recovering the money.

It was on a Sunday when I joined the *junges* on their evening *spat'seare*,[6] that I realized the importance of my presence having been legitimized by Johann, the *fäaschta*, when he took me to church the week before. At the end of the evening, I did not know how to return to Abraham's since it was in another *darp* and it would have taken me an hour and a half to walk back. A car was approaching and they told me that it was a taxi. It was pretty late for a taxi to be roaming around the colony (roughly 10pm). I flagged the car down, and just after asking the driver for a ride, I noticed the marks on the door. It was a police car. The driver, a policeman in plain clothes queried me intensely about what I was doing there in the colony. I could have been taken for questioning to the precinct. Fortunately, a Mennonite that was on the passenger seat intervened saying: "he is OK, he is visiting us, I saw him in Church the other day and he is our friend." The officer then told me that I should have reported myself in the precinct before going to the colony (although this was not a legal requirement at all). The car continued, leaving the *junges* laughing at my expense, they knew it was a police car, and had decided to play a joke on me. I asked them what the police were doing there, and they told me they were friends of the manager of the cooperative cheese factory. That he had to go to town to report on some stealing that had been going on. After I returned to Abraham's, I asked him about what the policeman was doing there, and he said that they had to call them in because there had been some stealing (both cheese, and petrol from the store).

---

[6] This term is used generally to refer to 'visiting' or 'going out'. On Sunday evenings, it refers specifically to the courting visits *junges* make to their girlfriends. Those who do not have someone to court, simply get together on the streets to have fun. I joined a group of *junges* in this latter condition.

José, the man with the moustache and the bulbous nose drove Franz and myself on my first trip to Guatraché. José was sceptical about my presence, something he admitted to me on a following visit. "So many people go around the Mennonites trying to take advantage of their naiveté, that one has to be careful with newcomers." He had been working as a driver with his own pick-up truck since the Mennonites arrival, and he has been successful enough to be able to buy a second one, and hire another driver for it. There are many other taxi drivers, including two who even sleep in the colony and have mobile phones, which they let Mennonites use for a fee. There is also a bus service that runs twice a week, picking up the colonists in the morning, and returning in the afternoon. This is a service organized for Mennonites, who can therefore go to town during the day to do their shopping, go to the hospital, etc.

Abraham introduced me to Omar, the owner of a small general goods store in Guatraché who supplies the colony stores. Omar drove to the colony on his pick-up truck almost every single day. Omar had been dealing with the colonists since their arrival, and had gained the trust of many of them. This was reflected in the fact that he not only supplies them with goods but also with 'banking services'. Since only the cheese factories have bank accounts, he is usually given cheques to cash from those who sell products to non-Mennonites. He does not charge for this service, but he benefits from the flow in his account.

I have attempted to show the variety of domains of articulation that exist in the colony, and some successful instances of the construction of borders that keep them separate and, at the same time, deal with the required connections with the outside world. It is now time to focus on the problematic aspects of articulation: in the next section I will explore, through a biographical approach, the dangers, dilemmas and struggles faced by one of these articulators. Afterwards, I focus on the conflicts generated between the colony and the surrounding society.

Franz's balancing act

I will here break the chronological narrative and present a portrait of Franz, taking into consideration my successive fieldwork periods. Franz's career as an articulator is instructive since it shows clearly the dilemmas and dangers of treading the borders of the Old Colony. In this case, it can be considered a successful example in that, unlike Abraham's case (reviewed in Chapter 5), it has not cost him his membership in the church. Franz has always been my main contact in La Nueva Esperanza. Every time I arrived there, his house was the first one I visited, staying there for the first couple of weeks until receiving invitations to stay at other houses, or, more truthfully, to have accommodation sorted out for me. I tried to be invited to stay at other houses but my attempts to break with Franz's circle of friends, and expand my own networks were unsuccessful. I was always referred back to Franz who "will tell you better" about what I wanted to know because "he knows a lot and likes to talk to people from the outside." Even though his only office is as a singer in church, and he has never been *fäaschta*, journalists (and anthropologists) are always sent to him. He has also acted as interpreter during a recent court trial.

In my talks with Franz I discovered that he not only was interested in things from outside the colony, but also that he had a very clear theological position, with great knowledge of things Mennonite and non-Mennonite. He likes to travel and read.

> I wanted to continue studying after finishing school, but my parents did not allow me to do so. Now I realize how right they were in not allowing me to leave the colony. No good can modernity bring us. It is better for us to live a spiritual life, as Jesus told us.

At that time, it appeared to me as a post-factum rationalization, and a way of solving the contradiction between his interest in knowledge and technology and Mennonites' emphasis on separation from the world. It had taken him a few years to understand his parents' position, and it took me a couple of years to receive an explanation of such a change, which came unexpectedly while we were discussing the Godly inspiration of the Bible.

> It is something you feel, you read it and it speaks to your heart. When I got baptized, at the moment when the eltesta was pouring the water on me, I felt this incredible presence, I was overwhelmed, I cannot explain it to you, you have to pray for enlightenment and guidance, and read the Bible, but the Holy Spirit's presence was there. And it was then that I understood that my life had to be led following Christ's teachings.

Franz always asked me not only about my "spiritual development" but also queried me on a diverse range of issues. From technical questions such as how elevators work, or how planes manage to fly, to how life is in other places. Franz mail ordered (without my intervention or suggestion) and read, an ethnography of a Hutterite colony; "he is like you, he lived like them and then wrote about their way of life. It is so nice to read how they can live a Christian life," he commented while showing me the book. Franz also asked me to teach him English, and whenever I taught him, he reciprocated in Plautdietsch, but soon he considered it a waste of time and a dangerous tool for me to acquire since I would then be able to understand what was being said when they switched languages to keep me out of the loop. He also spoke some Portuguese, picked up through his many trips to Porto Alegre (a city in the state of Rio Grande do Sul, Brazil), where he buys the Volkswagen shock-absorbing devices used in Mennonite *Bogges*. He also claims he learned some Quechua and Aymara while in Bolivia.

Franz also has very good business acumen, and his economical success is often looked upon with envy. During my very first fieldwork period in March 1996, he was crunching numbers in order to decide the feasibility of renting land outside the colony. Not only did he invest all his savings, but also he got in debt and borrowed the seeds needed. I accompanied him on that first trip to Guatraché, to meet the veterinarian, from whom he rented 550 ha, which we inspected on our way back to the colony. Heavy rains ruined the crops just weeks before harvest, leaving him, by 1997, with no money and owing the seeds he had borrowed. "A message from God" he said "I would have had too much money and would have felt very proud." That same year (1997), I helped him and his son to build the crane with which he was going to construct two silos in order to pay, in kind, for the seeds he borrowed from a non-Mennonite. In 1998, his silo factory was well established, and on my last fieldtrip to La Nueva Esperanza in the year 2000, he had standing orders for several silos and was also manufacturing an add-on for tractors that transformed them into bulldozers, and an automatic, hydraulic-powered bale shredder. Both implements were of his own design. His son-in-law (Helena's husband), one of his sons and two employees were working full time in the factory. Franz no longer milked cows because he claimed the cheese factory evaded taxes and he did not want to be part of it, "Christ instructed to pay our taxes." Although it is very likely that Franz's time had higher economic returns in his factory than in the milking parlour.

Franz's other source of income, although almost negligible, was his association with Drogueria Suiza. A pharmaceutical company in Buenos Aires that produced a herbal 'panacea' called 'Englischen Wunderbalsam' (English wonder balsam), which was very popular within the colonies. It was used internally as a digestive, but also externally for doing rubs and to sterilize wounds (because of its high alcoholic content). Franz and Abraham were in charge of introducing it to different colonies, making trips to the colonies in Paraguay and Mexico. The colonies in Bolivia were supplied by Martin, Johan's brother and Abraham's brother-in-law, who lives in one of the colonies in Bolivia.

Franz complained that he is often frowned upon because of the close contacts he has established with people from outside of the colony. Nevertheless, he insisted that it was his Christian duty to offer help and housing to anyone in need of them. One of the things to note is that most of the people who stayed as guests in his house visit the colony for *spiritual reasons*, and he repeated that it is that subject which interests him the most. Although he seemed to understand perfectly well my professional standing, he nevertheless interpreted it as an instance of Divine intervention.

> One of the mysterious ways in which the Lord acts for its own purposes, which are often unintelligible to men...You think you came here by yourself, for your writing, but it is God who sent you here, you think you are asking these questions for your book, but I see God asking me those questions, for me to reflect and study the Bible harder.

He always asked me on which bus company I travel, and he always had last minute information on which one offered the most comfortable service. I once contrasted his quest for comfort on bus trips with the avoidance of excessive comfort by ripping cabins from tractors and the prohibition on electricity, to which he replied: "You see, you are pointing out things we ought to change, as we have to always choose the narrow path in order to become Christians."

Besides the envy arising in the colony from his business success, and his sometimes-pretentious attitude of being the one who is always thought of as being the most knowledgeable man in the colony, his relationships with outsiders on religious terms seemed to be what created most of the uneasiness among his fellow colonists. It was nevertheless known, and this adds to the apprehension towards him, that he was theologically well informed, and that there was very little to formally reproach him of his conduct. If this was attempted, he could easily respond, Bible in hand. Therefore, the attacks on him were done on an informal, gossip level, rather than in formal accusations or having the issue raised to the *Leardeenst*. His house was the only one I knew where, after dinner, a couple of hours were dedicated to reading. One hour for individual study, followed by a collective reading of the Bible.

Every day a few chapters of the Holy Scriptures were read in a loud voice by Franz and followed by the rest of the family on their own Bibles. At the end, all the family would comment on what had been read before going to bed.

Over the years, I noted some important changes in Franz's theology, and in his ideas about articulation. During August 2000 he told me

> it would have been a much more Christian thing to do to bring the word of God to town instead of so much business; we are Christians, not businessmen.

Two years before he had told me that missionary work was a command only for the apostles, and nobody else. He replied that Silvana had made him change his position. "True Christians should be the light of the world. They should be an example for the world to follow." He regarded Sergio and Silvana as examples of true Christians who had followed God's call to follow their faith. Franz (as well as Abraham's extended family and a few others) supported Sergio and Silvana to stay in the colony, both socially and economically.

Short-circuits

From the very first days of their arrival to La Pampa, the Mennonites were subject to a series of cheats and tricks. Stories abound about dogs being sold to them, and upon escaping their new owners and returning to town, having their hair cut and being sold on again; to branches in pots sold as trees; crop buyers who would disappear and not pay; the already mentioned event with the dairy company; and many others. Within this context, the police had asked for a contribution to pay for the petrol to patrol the area, as well as to have the colonists pay for the conversion to diesel of the police pick-up truck, which would make patrolling cheaper. Another source of concern among the colonists were the number of poachers that plagued their *monte* (uncleared bush), but since some of these were thought to be police officers, the police were 'unable' to contain them. When in town I headed towards the precinct in order to 'register' my presence, and took the chance to interview the principal, who did not feel very happy to be asked questions and kept his answers and interview short. He claimed that they had good relations with the Mennonites, and that not a single one of them had been accused of any felony or crime. He then proceeded to tell the well-known stories of the Mennonites as victims.

Here I focus on two events that happened in the colony during my fieldwork that arose as a consequence of the Argentine State's attempts to intervene in Mennonite life, in order to show how articulation between the state and the colony occurs and is negotiated. The cases of crisis also show that articulation is a two way process where parties on both sides strategize differently in order to define the scope and sphere of articulation for the pursuit of their own interests. So to say, although Mennonites strive to control the process of articulation in order to maintain isolation while establishing connections is just one side of the coin; state officials, anthropologists, merchants, and swindlers are also agents in search of establishing domains of articulation with the colonies, and for that they deploy their own strategies.

During 1997–98, two conflicts arose between the Mennonites and the provincial and the national State. On the one hand, Julius, who acted as 'doctor' within the colony, was banned from practicing because he did not have the necessary qualifications.[7] Julius had been practicing within the colony since their arrival, and this was a well-known fact in town. Julius was also in close contact with the Guatraché hospital, which turned a blind eye upon his practice. He dealt with accidents, first aid, as well as with deliveries, and used to refer cases that he felt were beyond his abilities to the public hospital in Guatraché. In 1997 two of his patients (children of a very young age) died.

Upon learning of these deaths, the director of the hospital called the police for intervention. Julius' house was searched, and his tools of the trade, together with money and medicaments, were seized. This case was reported in both provincial and national newspapers, which prompted Franz to go to town and call me (for an analysis of the representation of the Mennonites in the Argentine media see Cañás Bottos 2005, 2006). Within 24 hours I was in the colony to advise him; he wanted my opinion on the events and to suggest possible courses of action.

As soon as I arrived at Franz's house, he made me go to his room where he showed me the newspaper articles. He was worried, not only because of the legal implications for Julius, but also because he felt the media had misrepresented life in the colony. Franz told me that the rest of the colonists were "a bunch of ignorants that did not know the possible consequences of the scandal." In Franz's opinion, the schooling

---

[7] The lack of qualifications of Mennonite and Amish 'doctors' is a common source of conflict between these groups and the state (for health-related conflicts with the Amish in the US see Huntington 2003).

issue was the real one behind the current problems: "the government is looking for a back door to impose public schooling, but if they do that, we will leave." He claimed this was a media campaign to deteriorate the image of the Mennonites and make it easier to gain support for the school imposition. Freedom from public schooling was something for which they did not have any signed papers, but was achieved through a verbal agreement between the commission (who went searching for suitable conditions and land to settle) and government officials. Since their arrival, they have been approached several times by the provincial government in order to either impose public schooling, or bring the Mennonite schools in line with national curricula. None of these attempts have been successful, but the fear of it occurring was something that was always lurking in the background.

Franz took me to talk to Julius, who looked very stressed and anxious. He cried as he recalled the events. Julius felt deeply humiliated by the way the police had acted. They had gone straight to his house, with a warrant he could not understand and had proceeded to search his home and professional practice. From his perspective, the police should have first reported to the *fäaschta*, and then, proceed with their search with his company and mediation. Julius regarded the hospital director's (Dr. Gomez) involvement to be a breach in the trust they had. Julius explained to me that Dr. Gomez was up-to-date with his practice. Julius had offered him to stop practicing when he realized he was breaching the law, but was encouraged to continue with his practice (and especially with the referral of patients to the hospital).

I asked them if they had contacted a lawyer, to which they replied negatively, that the colony authorities did not want to, but that their accountant had also suggested contacting one. Franz was also of the opinion of hiring one. Julius was officially banned from continuing with his practice, and after a few months of abiding to it, had to treat a few emergency cases, which gradually brought him to his previous level of activity. In the end, Julius was neither prosecuted nor acquitted, and the case against him was simply forgotten and left to prescribe.

I later knew of a different and unexpected undercurrent regarding these events. Mennonites were becoming increasingly unhappy with the treatment they received from the public hospital, especially regarding the waiting times. Those with means had progressively started to patronize a private clinic in town. Personal differences, previous disagreements, and competition had been going on between the directors of the two institutions in the past years. According to gossip in town, that the doctor who signed the death certificates falsely indicated natural death instead of dehydration caused by mistreated diarrhoea, provided Dr. Gomez with an opportunity to both get rid of competition, and increase his standing within the state health structure as the one who integrated the Mennonites within the national health system (something that previous attempts had been unfruitful at).

As a result of this conflict, Mennonites presence in the Guatraché hospital decreased and, since they were going to the hospital in the neighbouring town of Darregueira, births and deaths that would have otherwise been registered in the Guatraché civil registry, were being done at this other town. The Justice of the Peace was worried since this meant that the records at the Civil Registry were becoming fragmented, making the control of the population increasingly difficult.

After a few years of passivity with the Mennonites, the Provincial Government attempted to enforce the public schooling law in the colony upon a simplistic reading of the 1991 national census (which was the first one to include the Mennonite Colony since it formed in 1986). The census showed an alarming increase of illiteracy in the department of Guatraché, with a total population of slightly more than 5,000 inhabitants where the 1200 Mennonites were classified as illiterate due to their lack of completion (and attendance) at officially recognized schools. One of the arguments set forth by the Provincial authorities during the schooling debate was that, due to *jus solis*, the sons and daughters born to Mennonites in Argentina, were themselves Argentine, and therefore the National and Provincial States had a duty to care for their education as such. A conflict between different principles of belonging was therefore activated in order to define the relevant authority and membership over the new generations; through *jus solis* they were partaking in the Argentine 'people' whereas through *ius sanguinis*, they were claimed as *Christenvolk* by the Old Colony. After a year of negotiations, an agreement was arrived at whereby the public schooling system would not be enforced if parents taught Spanish to their children. Dictionaries and phrase books were distributed.

At the same time as the schooling issue was being debated, the colony was looking for new land to expand or move to another province. The increasing scarcity of land in the colony had already produced the conversion from cash crops into more labour-intensive dairy cattle breeding. In my earlier trips, I noticed that almost every single house had cows for producing milk for the cheese factories. A few years later, the failure to acquire more land had produced a land shortage, which had forced some of them to pursue other endeavours such as carpentry and, more notably, light metalworking. Silo factories had sprung up all around the colony. Between 1996 and 1998, at least fifteen new workshops (mostly carpentries and silo factories) had been created, selling almost all their production to the outside of the colony. Some colonists blamed this change of activity for the attempts of the National and Provincial governments to introduce public schooling and the new taxation laws. They claimed that this change was a breach of their deal for settling in Argentina as agriculturalists. This move towards manufacturing also had the consequence of increasing the number of contacts between Mennonites and non-Mennonites which, in turn, raised the number of swindles and rip-offs. These were explained by both Mennonites and people from Guatraché as due to the colonists' ignorance of how to deal, arising from a combination of being excessively trustful, with blindness towards risk in the eyes of a profit.

Some plots were offered in the province of Santiago del Estero, but the operation was never concluded. I was present in the member's meeting when this deal was explained to the colony members, and each one would voice how much land he would be willing to buy. Malatesta, the agent for the land deal, had been establishing close contacts with some of the members of the community.[8] He was invited to houses and given permission to hunt in the colony's *monte*. After the deal was called off, and in the midst of the uncertainty of the schooling debate, Malatesta offered that for 50,000 US dollars, he could arrange a meeting with the National Minister of Education in order to settle the issue. According to my informants, Malatesta claimed that the Minister herself was requesting the amount. The *eltesta*, without making any consultations with the rest of the colony, signed a document for this amount with the colony's land as collateral. He then went to Santa Rosa (the Provincial capital) to attend the arranged meeting, to find that the Minister was not there but her 'secretary'. The document was later altered, transforming it into 250,000 US dollars and taken to the justice in order to force its payment. Malatesta argued that the amount arose from the services offered regarding the failed acquisition of land in Santiago del Estero.

---

[8] It should be noted I only had access to the Mennonite version of events and never met Malatesta in person.

Consequently, and contrary to the normal practice of lifelong appointment, the *eltesta* was demoted to *prädja*. David (the owner of a cheese factory, and former manager of the cooperative) had already complained to me repeatedly about how the *eltesta* had been trying to interfere with the running of the cheese factories. "We have to obey the *eltesta*, but he should not give his opinion on things he understands nothing about." Indeed, what this shows is the conflict between the *eltesta* as the ultimate authority within the colony, arising from his religious office (and the religious narrative of constitution and legitimation of the Mennonite order) and the specialized knowledge required to perform on different domains. Although strictly speaking the *eltesta* might have not been overstepping his functions when dealing with Malatesta, the proficiency to do so was not a requirement for his election to office. Indeed, from a Mennonite perspective they can even be thought of as the opposite: knowing how to bribe, outmanoeuvring authority, a sense of cunningness to detect a possible swindler and hidden agendas would definitely not appear in the canonical texts as qualities to be looked for in candidates for the spiritual leadership of the church. We can see here conflict between the principle of the submission to the religiously based order, and that specialized knowledge is required to perform with the world.

The Mennonites replied by accusing Malatesta of fraud, and eventually won the case. The trial coincided with my last visit during July–August 2000, and suspicions were raised about me. This was the exact moment when I was requiring permission for a year-long stay in the colony and to do my doctoral fieldwork. A colonist remarked that my presence coincided with other significant events: just after the tornado, the failed negotiations for the land deal, and Julius' problem with the hospital; together with the fact that I did not fit any of the usual types of *Weltmensch* with justifiable reasons to be in the colony such as supplier, buyer, taxi driver, an office holding state agent, journalist, or member of an urban evangelical Mennonite church. With this, he concluded that some of the colonists were convinced I was a spy.

Conclusion: isolation and the management of borders

This chapter showed the ways in which the Mennonites strive to control the management of boundaries as a means to maintain separation while establishing needed contacts with the world beyond their boundaries.

I have suggested that processes of articulation are Janus faced, they act as much as isolators as articulators, and they are dangerous and powerful at the same time. Furthermore, I have also shown that it is always at least two parties who engage in this process, each of them with their own agendas, and deploying different strategies in order to achieve them.

The success in articulation as a Mennonite strategy for maintaining isolation in connection is most evident in cases that channel the flow of material goods, especially the cheese factories and the stores. The case of milk is exemplary in this respect. Cows are given as wedding presents in order to allow the newly-weds to attain economic independence; almost every single domestic unit milks cows twice a day to sell to the cheese factories. The product is then carried from the very core of the community, transformed, and channelled to the outside by a specialist. In this way, producers do not need to interact with Argentine dairy companies under conditions they have little control of, entailing both commercial and moral risk. Members of the community run the cheese factories, and therefore the colony authorities can check their operations while, at the same time, the rest of the milk producers are spared from the potentially damaging contact with the world. The condemnation of commercial and manufacturing activities in contrast with agricultural ones can be seen, in this light, as attempts to avoid the generalization of outward oriented activities.

One of the strategies deployed by all parties involved in order to pursue their agendas has been the multiplexing of relationships. That is, to overlay more than one type of relationship between the partners. The most common one has been imbuing these relationships with an emotional, friendship-like character that raises both parties' stakes in the relationship, contributing to its stabilization and predictability. But, while constructing trust, this can be manipulated by either of the parties in order to carry out their own agenda. The success of this technique can be seen in the cases of David and the sanitary inspector, the cheese factory manager and the police officer, the relationships with the taxi drivers, and with Omar; whereas the case of Malatesta presents an exemplary failure, at least from the Mennonites' perspective.

The contrast between the *eltesta* and David's competence in dealing with outsiders (and in this case in knowing how, when and whom to bribe) and the increase in rip-offs paralleled with an increase in the manufacturing of goods to be sold outside the colony, shows the need for specialized knowledge in order to successfully engage in the processes of articulation. Therefore, if articulation is to be effective in the generation of both isolation and connection, a degree of adequacy is needed between the agent and the domain of articulation within which he or she is attempting to perform. The spectacular cases of mismanagement of the borders point to the disjunction between the requirements to be elected to office and the abilities required to perform the duties assigned. The refusal to distinguish between domains and the consequent "monopolization of the universal" achieved by the *Leardeenst* within the colonies shows its pragmatic limits at the limit of the Old Colony. A short-term solution has been to resort to the establishment of informal, non-official brokers like Franz.

Indeed, although the *fäaschta* is theoretically the one in charge of representing the colony to the outside world, many of his functions have been delegated, albeit unofficially, to Franz. Franz's communicative abilities and knowledge are stressed in the colony and, therefore, journalists, anthropologists, religious seekers, and curious people in general who visit the colony, are all swiftly sent to him. Franz is conscious of this situation and complained to me that at the same time, he is accused of not remaining separate from the world, of appearing on TV, of receiving too many strangers in his house, of travelling too much, therefore calling his loyalty and religiosity into question.

These accusations can be interpreted as signs that indicate that Franz is approaching the limits of what is considered proper Mennonite behaviour. Reminders of what he should do are a way to curb and control the power acquired through the dealings with non-Mennonites, by constantly reminding him of his precarious standing. This serves as a warning that, on his constant border crossings he might get caught betwixt and between. These warnings in conjunction with his role as a cultural broker have led Franz to become an expert in eliciting the Mennonite self-evident world, both to defend himself (and prove his standing) and to communicate with the outside world. In this respect, the presence of Sergio, Silvana, and I, did nothing but encourage this process. By being confronted with questions and discussions that would not have occurred with fellow Mennonites, Franz was led to explore his beliefs, and the relationship between the Old Colony ideals and actual practices, finding tensions and contradictions.[9] The problem is that

---

[9] An exemplary example of this process can be found in David's life story and writings, analysed in Chapters 4 and 5.

this behaviour tends to be schismogenetic (to borrow Bateson's term 1998: 175), since the more he elicits the self-evident world, the more likely he will differ from his fellow Mennonites, who will in turn press him again for further compliance or explanations of his behaviour. The flipside is that from the Old Colony perspective, having Franz to deal with questions from outsiders meant that the rest of the colonists were spared from such a nuisance. Furthermore, as a measure against *Weltmenschen* who would insist on communicating, many colonists would politely apologize either for their poor Spanish speaking skills or lack of knowledge on the issue; followed by an immediate referral to Franz, because "he is the one that knows better."

This chapter has also shown that the state, operating on the ground through its agents (sanitary inspectors, doctors, police officers, Ministry of Education officers), does not always do so according to the principles of rationality, bureaucracy and transparency that theoretically ought to be the hallmark of the administration of the modern state. These cases lift the veil on various aspects of statecraft, and some of the techniques it uses for making itself unreadable and concealing its ultimate ends, while simultaneously claiming a discourse of rational, bureaucratic, transparency. On the one hand, through the processes of certification and assigning practice licenses, the state claims for itself as the functions of the controller of crucial services under the banner of safeguarding the public good. On the other is a way of sustaining its position as the ultimate source of symbolic legitimation. Pierre Bourdieu asks rhetorically:

> Who certifies the validity of the certificate? It is the one who signs the credential giving license to certify. But who then certifies this? We are carried through an infinite regression at the end of which "one has to stop" and where one could, following medieval theologians, choose to give the name of 'state' to the last (or to the first) link in the long chain of official acts of consecration. (1998: 51)

But what happens in cases when those who are licensed to certify, forge certifications? Or when state agents also perform agendas of their own? In this way, the Mennonites are left to speculate about the unifying principles behind the actions of these agents, and producing their own interpretations of their underlying intentions. This creates the conditions for the setting in motion a "semiotics of (the) suspicion" (Faubion 1999: 379) which, when developed (and overlaid on a religious background) provides a ready-made breeding ground for the growth of eschatological and conspiracy theories. The Old Colony has a ready-made script for this situation, that of the persecution of the faithful in the last days. That this script was not fully activated (although intimations of it appeared around the schooling issue) might be due to the perceived scope of the conflict in solely economic terms, and the assignment of blame and guilt to state agents being also private individuals. However, this was a secondary effect of the multiplexing strategy: to insulate the state from the perceived wrongdoing of its agents. In this way the state attempted to prevent the Mennonites from interpreting the conflicts the way Bourdieu suggests (1998: 51), and concealed its attempts to take the place of God as the ultimate source of symbolic legitimation. Although this is yet another veil, behind which lies an invented people (Morgan 1988). How the boundaries and limits of this 'people' are imagined and constructed in relationship with how concrete individuals cross them, is the topic of the following chapter.

CHAPTER FIVE

CAREERS IN THE FAITH

> The destiny of humankind, placed between the Fall and the Judgement, appears to its eyes as a long adventure, of which each life, each individual pilgrimage, is in its turn a reflection. It is in time and, therefore, in history that the great drama of Sin and Redemption, the central axis of all Christian thought, is unfolded. (Bloch 1998: 4)

Introduction

This chapter is based on the life stories of Abraham and Sergio. Both have crossed the Old Colony borders but in opposite directions; Sergio has attempted to become a Mennonite, while Abraham, after a failed attempt at building his own separate settlement in Argentina, was back in Bolivia living in the Santa Rita colony. When I met him there, he was in the process of leaving the Old Colony once again. These sojourns are instructive for two important reasons. The first reason is that the collective imagination of the future requires a concomitant imagination of the individuals that would compose the community. Therefore, this chapter provides an exploration of the notions of Christian self that the Old Colony requires its members to display. Although instead of approaching the problem from the creation of a 'typical' subjectivity, I outline the limits through two cases that have produced both negative and positive reactions. I will have more to say about this approach in the analyses of two dissenters in Chapter 7. The second reason is that through these cases we can see how the Old Colony deals with membership issues. Specifically, I focus on the contrast that arises between the ostensive norms that regulate membership, with those that appear to be acting in practice, through the analysis of concrete processes of (albeit failed) incorporation and expulsion.

In Chapter 4, the individual's membership to a particular group was considered as an unproblematic given. Articulators were crossing borders in order to make goods, services, and information flow between groups, while maintaining the groups as distinct. The issue of membership change, a central one in border building and maintenance, was only tangentially addressed. On the one hand, losing membership of the Old Colony appeared only as a possibility, as an ultimate threat to force Mennonites into compliance. On the other hand, the possibility of incorporation of a *Weltmensch* into the colony was only voiced as a joke. In this chapter, I treat the change in group membership as a central aspect in the analysis of the definition and management of borders, and I do so with a biographical perspective that centres on particular personalities, their agency and their experience.

These narratives are simultaneously life stories (Peacock and Holland 1993: 368) and conversion narratives (which the actors refer to as *witnessing* or *testimonies*). As such, one of their qualities is that they constitute a post-factum re-evaluation of the narrators' own lives; they are subjective documents (see Watson-Franke and Watson 1985). Indeed, as Snow and Machalek argue, conversion involves a biographical reconstruction according to the "new ascendant universe of discourse" (1984: 173) (see also Beckford 1978; Heirich 1977; Saunders 1995). This reconstruction constitutes a "unique vantage point" (Heirich 1977: 677), "from the standpoint of one pervasive schema" (Snow and Machalek 1984: 173), which, because it is not a "perfectly transparent" window (Peacock and Holland 1993: 374) imbues the narratives with the narrator's own perspective and, therefore, becomes a privileged medium for the exploration of his or her own self-transformations and subjectivities (Ochs and Capps 1996). It is not only that the narratives are subjective or positioned, but also that the subjectivity of the narrator and his or her positioning is created in the narrative itself. Therefore the subjective narratives of border crossing individuals such as Sergio and Abraham, become promising standpoints for achieving a decentred view of the Old Colony, the subjectivities required by their imagination of the future, and their boundary definition and maintenance processes. Furthermore, Sergio and Abraham can be seen as examples of what the Old Colony wished to avoid in the processes of articulation; the former as a source of new ideas, the latter, as a broker who went too far in his contacts with the outside world.

The question of why people convert has received different approaches according to the underlying assumptions of the place of religion in the research contexts. According to Richard Werbner, questionable assumptions underlie the modernist paradigm on religious change (his emphasis is on Africa, but his observations are applicable to the rest of the Third World):

In essence changeable and dynamic, sometimes in support of the state and the powers that be, other times in critical even subversive opposition, the Christian religion is assumed to be in time, revelatory of the past, prophetic for the future and devoted to the Crucified God who intervenes in history, ultimately through 'the mysticism of suffering'. All that leaves 'traditional religion' caught in the other half of the dichotomy—the traditional is thus unchanging, static, timeless, out of time and out of history. (Werbner 1997: 312)

This paradigm also assumes that along with modernity goes alienation and commodification, and therefore tradition emerges as resistance to them (Werbner 1997: 312). Studies of conversion have therefore explained the move from 'traditional religion' to Christianity (with the exception of forceful conversion, such as the extirpation of idolatries in colonial Latin America by Christian colonizers), as being simultaneously a means towards modernity, and as resistance to its evils. Religion becomes a proxy for politics, and in itself is only recovered when highlighting the compatibilities, harmony, or points in common with previous religious beliefs and practices (Lewis 1999; Viswanathan 1996; Comaroff and Comaroff 1992; van der Veer 1996; Merrill 1993; Miller 1970, 1979).

By contrast, studies on First World countries (especially of the US) normally invoke factors such as deprivation, strain, (Lofland and Stark 1965) and apply formalist economic theories to explain the choosing of the supernatural explanations and compensators that religions provide (Stark and Bainbridge 1996; Sherkat and Wilson 1995) which lead their followers away from modernity. Therefore, the explanations lie between the two poles of structural external forces and the rational choice of individual actors based on the *homo economicus* model, thereby eliminating any trace of the religious experience itself. In short, while studies which treat the adoption of a world religion as a vehicle away from tradition towards modernity regard this as an unproblematic rational act that in itself needs no further explanation, conversions that apparently lead away from modernity into non-mainstream religious options appear problematic and therefore demand from the analyst the uncovering of deeper layers of rationality.[1] These are expressions of the two sides

---

[1] The emphasis given to the conversion to new religious movements (such as Unification Church—Moonies (Barker 1984), other branches of Pentecostalism (Saunders 1995; Frigerio and Carozzi 1994) Scientology, Hare Krishna (Wright 1991), and those of a more millenaristic stance such as Aum Shinrikyo (Mullins 1997; Castells 1998), People's Temple (Chidester 1991), Branch Dravidians (Anthony and Robbins 1997), and its consideration as problematic (and sometimes even dangerous) from both the

of the same coin, the hegemony of the narrative of modernity and its own implicit imagination of the future. Furthermore, public opinion has tended to consider the followers of alternative movements as "passive, brainwashed victims," as Simon Coleman shows for the followers of Word of Life in Sweden (2000: 208 and ff.; for a compelling critique of the efficacy of brainwashing among the Moonies see Barker 1984). Hence, the question of conversion assumes, from the beginning, a position that empties religion of any particularity and value per se, and negates the fundamental place of religion in the construction of the self (see Asad 1996; Csordas 1994; Hefner 1993a).

I do not want to deny the importance of political, social and economic forces in conversion; indeed, the analysis that follows shows their salience in the personal conversion histories of both men. These external forces, however, are not sufficient to explain religious conversion as a cultural and individual phenomenon. Instead, I favour a multidimensional approach that integrates agency, creativity, self-definition and the meaningful, moral and transcendental experience of religion with broad processes and structures that are simultaneously enabling and constraining (Giddens 1979). As Robert Hefner suggests:

> Self-identification must be at the heart of our efforts to understand individual life-worlds and the creative agency of human beings. Though culture is implicated in the creation of self, its precise effects are mediated by the dispositions of their ongoing efforts—never themselves fully programmed—to assess the meaning and value of all that goes on around them. Little of this interaction can be reduced to the status of sociological fact or considered the passive internalization of cultural symbols, religious or otherwise. (1993b: 26)

Indeed one of the features of these narratives is the creativity displayed by Sergio and Abraham in dealing with the contexts in which they were inserted.

Helpful for understanding the convert's definition of religion in general, and to Christianity in particular, together with the meaningfulness of the conversion experience, are approaches that have focused on the transformation of the self (Saunders 1984; Stromberg 1985, 1993), and on the power of rhetoric and language (Harding 1987, 2000; Stromberg

---

social scientists and the social context attests to this (for comparative, as well as reviews on conversion see also Heirich 1977; Snow and Machalek 1984; Barker 1986). See Richardson and Introvigne (2001) for a critical analysis of the perception of sects as dangerous at the legislative level in Europe.

1990; Coleman 2000: 117 and ff.) as both means and outcomes of religious change.[2] Also, with regard to the structural aspects of the narrative, studies have repeatedly noted the usage of models and scripts (Snow and Machalek 1984; Beckford 1978) that converts use as guidelines for building their own narratives. Each testimony, each witnessing, is simultaneously the product and the means of the reconstruction of the self (Ochs and Capps 1996: 20). The reflection that Marc Bloch refers to in the introductory quote is a reflection in the double sense of pondering and mirroring. It is through the act of reflection upon one's experience of conversion, or, in this case, through witnessing, that the convert produces his or her own (and others') conversion. The experience is reconstituted in accordance with certain models and scripts that are considered to have succeeded through the drama of Sin and Redemption. The reflection on one's life, to produce a narrative that reflects others' lives, which at the same time reconstitutes one's self into that which is being narrated.

Here, I explore Abraham and Sergio's own reflection on their interaction with macro processes and institutions.[3] In this way, I hope to illuminate from a different perspective some of the issues tackled in previous chapters, such as the dilemmas of colony formation and the relationship with the state and processes of globalization (Chapters 1, 2, and 3), articulation and the management of borders (Chapter 4). These narratives will also help frame Abraham and Sergio's writings (Chapter 6) as well as their influence and consequences on other Mennonites (Chapter 7).

First movement: from the inside-out

I first heard of Abraham during my first fieldwork period in a passing reference by Omar: "It seems that Abraham's family are not doing well in Santiago del Estero." People in La Nueva Esperanza, when asked about other colonies in Argentina, had so far only mentioned Pampa de los Guanacos, and that was also the only other colony I knew of. Only later I realized that the existence of Abraham's colony had been

---

[2] The reconstruction of the sense of self is not exclusive to conversion narratives, it can also be seen in procreation stories (Ginsburg 1987), and in memories of trauma (Antze and Lambek 1996).

[3] A good example for the powers of biographical accounts to illuminate macro processes can be found in Werbner (1991).

silenced. In fact, it was Abraham himself who was being banished from any reference by name, a typical consequence of excommunication. On my first visit to Benjamin in Pinondi colony I asked him to help me find people who would be willing to receive me. One of the people he mentioned was Abraham.

> He is the one that tried to make a colony in Santiago del Estero, but he is back in Bolivia. Abraham is also a good friend of Sergio, so he won't have problems receiving you.

After staying in Pinondi for a week, I headed towards Riva Palacios to visit Martin (Franz's brother, and married to a sister of Abraham) for whom I had brought some mail. After some days with him and his family, I returned to Santa Cruz, in a taxi that was already carrying a number of Mennonites. One of them was a *prädja*, to whom I attempted three times to introduce myself in both Spanish and German. The reply was always "I don't understand," in a cold and cutting tone that I had to interpret as his unwillingness to establish any communication with me. We spent the remaining hour and a half in the taxi in silence. Finally, the taxi dropped us at the 6 de Agosto street, where the Mennonites met when in town as a number of shops that cater especially for them were located there.[4] As soon as I had left the taxi I met Pedro (Jacob's younger brother) accompanied by his wife. Having been born in Bolivia, but resident for the past fifteen years in Argentina, they had come to Santa Cruz in order to make an application for a new passport, a procedure which was being dealt with on their behalf by Menno Travel. Hence, their presence was only required to sign the papers and to hand in their photographs. Menno Travel was closed as it was only six o'clock in the morning, and it would not open until eight o'clock. I decided to wait with them and use the opportunity to chat with Pedro, to hear what had happened to him and his family in the three years that we had not seen each other. Some Mennonites that passed by, who were puzzled by the cordiality of our talk, came closer to overhear our conversation, until one of them directly asked Pedro who I was and why we were being so friendly to each other. After a while, a very tall Mennonite, identifiable as such by his dungarees but

---

[4] Among these are Menno Travel (a travel agency owned and run by an 'urban mennonite' who not only deals with air, rail and bus tickets, but also handles governmental paperwork on behalf of the colonists), 'Tractor Menno' (a supplier of agricultural machinery and spare parts), 'Menno Credit Union,' and hosts of other shops.

carrying a plastic attaché, walked by and Pedro said: "have you seen that man, that is Abraham, come with me." We then went to greet him. After Pedro introduced me, Abraham replied:

> Oh yes, I wanted to talk to you, why don't you come to my place one of these days, I invite you. Better still, why don't you come with me today? I will be leaving to the colony on the bus this afternoon. The bus leaves at half past five, but let's meet at the bus stop at five.

I was very surprized at this sudden invitation, especially after the lack of interest in establishing a conversation that my previous travelling partner had showed. I was also puzzled by Abraham's apparent urgency to talk to me.

I had returned to Santa Cruz just to buy a jeep, having found that I needed it to cover the vast distances and for independence of movement, but his invitation meant the car would have to wait. On my acceptance of his invitation, Abraham warned me to be very careful with the paperwork for the car, since there were many fake ones going around, and concluded: "I am going now to Agromac, the company for which I work. I will enquire there for you [about jeeps], but anyway, I will be seeing you again at five." Working for a company? I doubted my ears—old Colony Mennonites were prohibited from working outside their colonies.

At five, I met Abraham where we had arranged. He was sitting on a chair on the sidewalk, and a *prädja* and several Mennonites were around him, one of them holding a cigarette and a tin of beer (and thus setting a bad example, according to Abraham). We then climbed on the bus, and Abraham pointed to a seat. I sat by the window and he sat next to me by the aisle. After a few minutes of small talk, a remark by the *prädja* made Abraham turn to me and say: "we will talk about the important things in my house. There are too many ears in here." His request for secrecy during our trip, after he had already made himself seen publicly with me, only further raised my suspense, expectations and puzzlement. I could sense something was happening, but had no clue what it was. I will deal with the storm that was brewing among the Mennonites in the next chapter; what follows is an analysis of his life story, which he told me later in the privacy of his home.

On that first occasion I stayed three days at Abraham's house. We would spend most of the daytime talking, while his wife did housework, or worked on the sewing machine just a few steps away from us. Listening in on our conversation, she often added her commentaries or helped jog Abraham's memory. Abraham directed most of the conversations, while I listened and often stopped him to elicit further explanations on certain points he was making. He also asked me about my own religious background and my reasons for being around Mennonites. It became clear that Abraham had already heard of me and of my project through Sergio, and eventually asked me for a copy of my undergraduate dissertation.[5] The following small excerpt from my fieldnotes conveys his efforts to control the conversation, to establish a good rapport with me and to whet my interest in what he would have to say.

> Abraham: So, you are writing a book about the Mennonites... How do you do it?
>
> Lorenzo: Well, I will spend all this year collecting stories, and then I will put them together when I return to England.
>
> Abraham: That is interesting, I am also writing a book. I write my ideas as they come up, and then I write them down with a typewriter.
>
> Lorenzo: And what is your book about?
>
> Abraham: It is about how the colonies have changed, how we no longer follow the Christian path...

Inverting the usual anthropologist-informant relation, he took the initiative in building rapport by drawing on our common activity as writers with a common subject, and finally gave me a clue to what was going on. Abraham was claiming the colonies were no longer what they should have been. In his opinion, the colonies had modernized, and therefore had become part of the world. The *Leardeenst* were abusing their power and misapplying holy sacraments, making and enforcing man-made laws, transforming custom into religion, encouraging internal persecution, and not fulfilling their spiritual duties. Because of all this, the *Leardeenst* had become comparable to worldly governments.

The paths to riches, poverty, suffering and enlightenment

Through Abraham's life I wish to bring to the foreground some of the principles and mechanisms of Mennonite membership as applied to someone who, while having been born within the boundaries of the

---

[5] Later, I gave him a copy, and after reading it he said: "Everything is fine, except the land issue, I have already explained to you that we were not ripped off, but I know that that is what you have been told in the colony." The dissertation was only published some years later (Cañás Bottos 2005).

Old Colony, has left it and returned. I will also focus on the processes, resources, and conditions that frame his encounter with his newly awakened faith, and that led him to produce an alternative imagination and project to the Old Colony.

Abraham was born in 1937 in Durango colony, Mexico. As a way of highlighting the poverty in which he was raised, he told me that white bread was only available once a week, and that a piece of fruit was a highly valued reward after good deeds. Since they were late to arrive in Mexico, they could only settle on marginal land, in a *darp* that was separate from the main colony land.

Abraham praised his younger years as an agriculturalist, when he would till the land with a plough pulled by horses, and when he would work in teams with other young people. He remembered the satisfaction of having done a good job and of being appropriately materially rewarded for it, since the prices of crops were better then. He added, "not as nowadays where the crop-buyers calculate how much it cost you to produce it and then pay you only a cent or two on top of it."

It was thanks to such hard work, combined with the favourable prices of crops, that allowed him and his family to progress economically. In 1955 Abraham's father bought his first tractor. It was a second-hand one which some Mennonites had bought in the United States and brought back to sell in the colony. Abraham recalled how on one of their trips to the US these Mennonites also brought the *schlaubbekjse* with them. Before, "we dressed just like you, trousers and shirts, and initially the *schlaubbekjse* was worn only by young people." Only later did dungarees stopped being the mark of rebel Mennonite youths and become the compulsory male attire within the colonies. Abraham had clearly seen through the attempts at naturalization of the relationship between this particular item of clothing and group belonging. Abraham's consciousness of change was indeed contradicting the ideology of immutability that the Old Colony was attempting to impose. Abraham had decoded the operation at place in Old Colony historical consciousness, that of transposing to the past, the idealized features of the present, which would then become the centrepieces of the imagination of the future.

In 1959 Abraham married the sister of his brother's wife, a common marriage pattern among the Mennonites which aims at reducing the extension of kinship networks by concentrating rather than expanding them (for an analysis of this pattern see Cañás Bottos 1999). Being the youngest child in his family, he did not receive any land from his parents since it had already been divided among his elder brothers and sisters. They therefore went to live in his father-in-law's house, in Swift Current colony, because they had available space. Abraham looked further afield for opportunities, which did not take long to arise. A cotton company that was close to the colony had just gone bankrupt, so he went to buy the old machinery, which he put in working condition and sold within the colony. "And with that I made a small fortune." Abraham's first successful enterprise was followed by similar endeavours. In 1963, because of the unlikely prospects of finding suitable arable land in the Swift Current colony and its surrounding area, Abraham went with his family to settle in Blue Creek colony, in Belize, following his parents who had gone there. Being disappointed with the situation, and upon hearing of the new settlements in Bolivia, they moved to Santa Cruz de la Sierra in 1969:

> In Belize I lost all my capital. I was left with 3.500 US dollars to start up in Bolivia. I bought 50 hectares of land at 5 dollars per hectare, I built the house, got a few chickens, and was left without money and had to start searching for a job.

The situation forced him to sell his labour as a bulldozer driver for clearing the bush, and that allowed him to save some money, which he used to buy dairy cows.

> I borrowed a little bit to buy one, but found a whole truckload on sale, so I bought it and sold it inside the colony, and I continued like that, until I bought a lot of 70 heads. After that the colonies were full of cows, so I had to move on.

Then came the tractors he bought in Cochabamba, an important city in south central Bolivia. Thomas Hausmann, a Bolivian who was then on the board of Menoagro later told me the story of those tractors and located it as the beginning of his long lasting business and personal relationship with Abraham:[6]

> During those years, some of the Bolivian exports to Argentina were paid in kind. So there was this lot of 70 small tractors. To give you an idea

---

[6] Menoagro, Agromac, and Theoprax are three companies closely linked to each other; Thomas Hausmann has worked for and/or owned them all at some point. At the time of research, David was working as a debt collector for Theoprax who was providing consultancy, financial, and managerial services to Agromac, which had absorbed Menoagro. The debts David was collecting were the remaining payments for machinery to Menoagro.

of the size of the operation: in Bolivia, as an average, there are sold 150 new tractors per year. So Abraham found them, rusting in the fields, and belonged to the Bolivian Government. So Agromac put part of the money, and Abraham sold them in the colonies.

Abraham then started travelling to Brazil to buy used machinery. He would bring it to the colonies by train, in groups of four or five wagons at a time. Tyrone then heard of a lot Polish tractors (Massey Ferguson clones) abandoned in one of the Brazilian harbours. Thomas and Abraham did the necessary paperwork for them to be considered scrap metal, and brought them into Bolivia, refurbishing and rebranding them 'Menon' before selling them in the colonies. It was all going well until, at some point, a sudden change in the relationship between the Bolivian peso and the US dollar made him lose almost everything once again. Abraham also had grown tired of so much travelling, and decided to try his luck by associating with the brother of his wife. Together they bought a bulldozer to work with.

> It was a brand new Caterpillar, and I drove it for 4.500 hours, but two people owning one machine produces problems. So I sold my part and bought another one for myself. I did 13.000 hours on that one. There were still people—and money—coming from Mexico at the time, so that was good for clearing new fields. That allowed me to buy 150 hectares, and during three years I was the harvest champion of all the Mennonites in Bolivia.

He kept buying as much land as he could. During the dictatorship in the eighties in Bolivia, the Mennonites' Privilegium was suspended. This prompted the colonists to start looking for new horizons in Argentina. Abraham business acumen was required by the *Leardeenst* to take part in the commission to Argentina to search for land and suitable conditions for settling. A young Franz was also a member of the committee, and Abraham angrily recalled the discussion they had in front of one of the officers that interviewed them in order to analyse their request for a Privilegium.

> When we were asked whom we followed, I answered "Jesus Christ," but Franz interrupted and said "Menno Simons," and tried to argue with me there. What an impression we must have given this man, that we could not reach an agreement between ourselves regarding our religion.

This difference in opinion leads to an important distinction made by Abraham: being Mennonite and being Christian are not synonyms and work independently of each other. In this disagreement, Abraham was attempting a reordering of hierarchies; for Abraham, Jesus is the one to be followed, and Menno Simons, a reformer who attempted to correct the course towards Him. Undue emphasis on the reformer meant a shadowing of Jesus; an overrating of the means in relationship to the true end, and of man-made rules over the word of God. For Abraham, a person can be a Christian without being Mennonite and, concomitantly, being born, bred, and living within a Mennonite colony, and abiding to all its regulations, are neither sufficient nor necessary conditions to make one a true Christian. In this way, Abraham is proposing a notion of Christianity that has problematic consequences for the Old Colony, since it breaks with the assumption of coherence between the social sphere and religious membership. In the eyes of most Old Colonists, being a Mennonite is seen as synonymous with being Christian. For them, the limits of the Old Colony are the limits of Christianity. In this way, faith, belief and the possibility of attaining church membership are held by virtue of birth within the Mennonite colonies. Furthermore, it questions the Old Colony as the only way to Jesus, and allows non-Mennonites to become Christians.

They could not get any signed agreements with the government (see Chapter 2). Regarding land, they managed to get two initial arrangements: one with Estancia Remecó, and the other with Estancia La Luna. Abraham was not convinced about the former because of the financial arrangement, which could, and eventually had, negative economical consequences. Since the rest of the commission considered it the best, he decided to go along. Nevertheless, eventually Abraham's colony decided to cancel the plan to move to Argentina, because they saw that the change in legislation in Bolivia had no practical impact. A short time later, a Mexican Mennonite commission was sent to Argentina in search of land and suitable migratory conditions, and Abraham's presence was required in order to continue the negotiations where they had been left. Again, he dissented from the rest of the commission, insisting that La Luna was a better deal, but the others decided to go for Estancia Remecó. There were no major differences regarding the quality of land, the point of difference being the financial agreements for both purchases. Although initially for La Luna the price per hectare was slightly higher, they did not need to buy the whole property. The deal was that they would have to pay in full for the land they settled in, and the rest would be reserved for them for a period of four years to be bought at the same price. The deal with Estancia Remecó involved the paying of an initial amount and the financing of the remainder over a period of ten years, which was dollarized, and with a variable interest rate, but it provided immediate availability of the whole property. The commission decided on Estancia Remecó, and initially it appeared to have been a successful enterprise, but then hyperinflation hit the Argentine economy in 1986, multiplying their debt.[7] Abraham was eventually accused of stealing from his fellow brothers, of having amassed his wealth through the land deal.

Estancia Remecó soon proved to be too small, and the Mennonites started looking for new land. According to Abraham, he had the support of the Bolivian *Leardeenst*, who asked him to look for new land. Abraham decided to go by himself, and out of his own initiative bought an entire property in the province of Córdoba, so as to make the new colony for his Mennonite brethren from Bolivia.

> But those in Argentina did all they could in order to make the Bolivians remove their support. And they succeeded. I had to sell the land, lost a lot of money, and also my trust in the human being. We should not place our trust in men, only in Jesus Christ.

This experience made Abraham leave the colony, and he was excommunicated for doing so. Abraham bought land in Sachayoj, in the Province of Santiago del Estero, and formed a colony with some of his sons, daughters, and their spouses. Three families from the colonies in Paraguay also joined them. "But these families wanted to modernize; they wanted cars. So I gave them their money back and then they went to Canada." Not being able to recruit enough people to join him and make the enterprise viable, after a couple of years he tried to sell the land, but problems with the title deeds arose, which he was still trying to sort out when I spoke with him.

Abraham then returned to Bolivia, where he had to ask for forgiveness for his sin (of having left the colony) in order to be accepted again. His old friend Thomas, through Agromac, gave him not only the initial economic resources needed to start his life anew in Santa Rita colony, but also offered him a job in the company.

Abraham finished his story with a gloomy synthesis of his life, but far from giving up, he was committed to continuing with his new project.

---

[7] See Beckerman (1995) for an analysis of the 1986 Argentine economic crisis.

There is not much else to do in this lifetime. I hope I have a better one in the next one...I realized the world is full of evil; it is difficult for those who want to follow the Lord's path. There is a lot of suffering, it is not easy.

Abraham's narrative revolves around his entrepreneurial activities, which are emphasised in order to highlight two issues of utmost importance for him: the (for him) unjustified accusations on him within the colony, and his spiritual enlightenment. Like Franz, Abraham's articulatory activities have put him in touch with the world beyond the Old Colony, but unlike the former, Abraham went too far when he attempted to create his own settlement. It was during this period, and the suffering he went through, that drove him to an analysis of the scriptures and the *Martyrs' Mirror* in order to find solace and explanations for his predicament. His renewed faith was not the product of a mystical or supernatural experience, but the product of reflection and comparison between his life and those of the martyrs. This new perspective led him to produce a critique of the Old Colony, pointing to contradictions between the publicly held beliefs and those actually in practice. In the light of this position, he consolidated his perception of the distinction between being Mennonite and being Christian, defining his belonging to the latter group. He wrote and then distributed an essay where he argued his position, which will be explored in the next chapter.

Second movement: from the outside-in

In this section, I focus on the case of 'The Sergios'—the affectionate way in which Sergio, Silvana and their children were referred to by their friends in the colonies. They are a family of Argentines who tried to become Mennonites and to be incorporated into the colonies. Their presence and attempt to become part of the Old Colony makes explicit the Mennonite membership principles as they are put in practice. It will also provide the context for the problems and conflicts within the colonies, which will be analysed in Chapter 7.

The material for this section comes mainly from the conversations we had in his home in the mountains of Tarija, although, as the story shows, we have known each other for some years, and Sergio's presences and absences have marked my fieldwork. I visited him and his family three times while they were in Tarija, and stayed with them for roughly a week each time.

The road to Damascus

Sergio was born in 1965 in Quilmes, a district in Greater Buenos Aires. Both of his parents were first generation Argentines from families coming from Spain and Italy. Sergio's father worked in different factories, usually losing his job due to his active participation in the worker's union. Sergio described him as a Marxist-atheist, as someone who, due to his unionism, was always on the brink of being abducted by the military. The 1976 *coup d'etat* established in Argentina a military government of systematic terror, which lasted until 1983. The official report of the Comisión Nacional sobre la Desaparición de Personas [National Commission on the Disappearance of Persons] (1984) which set to investigate what was called in Argentina the acting of the 'Terrorismo de Estado' (state terrorism) documents the kidnapping, torture and murdering of 8,960 *desaparecidos* (the disappeared, or missing ones) although many victims were not represented in the report and estimates put them on the 30,000 mark (see also Pozzi 1988: 114; Feitlowitz 1998; Taylor 1997).

While still in high school, at thirteen years of age, Sergio got his first job at a garage, and, as he told me, he also started shoplifting with some of his friends. Two years later, after a trivial argument with his father (during dinner time, at the family table) that escalated to a mutual rejection of the filial-paternal bond, he left his parent's home and went to live with an aunt, whom he "tortured" with his heavy metal records. Sergio's narrative on his induction to heavy metal music bears strong structural resemblances with religious conversion narratives, and the position of this chapter of his life within his witnessing was in fact used to highlight the importance, power, and meaningfulness of his later conversion to Christ. Let me quote at length his 'conversion' to heavy metal music as he told it to me under the starry sky in the mountains of Tarija:

> So, I am in my fourth year of high school, and the Malvinas [Falklands] war was going on. Imagine how I was, how I started to learn about things. I saw images and things I wish I had never seen, they were blowing me away. I was damning my whole life... my friend Fabián came home one day and made me listen to a record, Iron Maiden's "The Number of the Beast." So I listened to that record, and it made a revolution inside me... I was already listening to heavy rock, but pure, raw, heavy metal, it turned me upside down, my brother, I was possessed by it. From that moment on I started to transform myself into a heavy metaler; in my mentality, in the dressing, and the long hair. But another day Fabian

> brought a record of an Argentine band... The cover was all black, with the v and the 8 of the Ford trucks... "Read the lyrics" he said to me, and after doing so I replied "All that is here is the truth, is what is really going on." So I clung to it, well I felt identified, so to speak.

Sergio also gave his interpretation of the place of the heavy metal movement in Argentina during his younger years, stressing its marginality, mainly lower class composition, and opposition to the dictatorship, although he joined it during the transition years.

> Every one of their lyrics was expressing what I was feeling with every single fibre. For example, that was a time in which part of the Argentine rock scene, which was related to the hippies, were saying, well, they had their slogan, their symbol, that wagon wheel, as we called it. [laughs] And they were saying "peace, dude, peace, everything is OK everything is all right." And it was not. Because we were like burning from the inside (...) we were generally guys from the lower class. We did not see peace and happiness in the world. Nor hoped that things would get better. And we went crazy with that (...) we said [starts reciting a song by V8] "Enough of hippies, enough of begging, an explosion has marked the time of metal. Power embodied in me, roaring it is. No one will stop it. The earth explodes, and in fire remains, these are my feelings, I cannot hide them. Fed up with crisis and with proposals that will not work, I sink in the mud of evil, the end is near. The power of metal escapes time, and peace does not exist. Enough of trickery and of thinking and doing as others want (...) Peace does not exist, peace does not exist, peace does not exist." We did not have peace and we did not see it in other people. So, we could not believe them, and neither could we, in the Christian groups around us.

He recited the song by heart, and claimed that the lyrics were directly reflecting the harsh reality he was living in then. Through heavy metal he found a community who shared with him common predicaments such as discrimination, material poverty, labour insecurity, persecution, indiscriminate state violence, and above all, lack of hope and direction. Regarding his impossibility to believe in any of the Christian groups that surrounded him, it is important to note that the mainstream position of the Catholic Church in Argentina was one of support of the military regime. This was not an isolated phenomenon. Various Christian denominations supported several Latin American military regimes (although with some exceptions such as those of liberation theology who were themselves subject to persecution). For example, in neighbouring Chile, the Chilean Evangelical Church published a declaration in support of Pinochet's 1973 coup, and Luis Palau (an Argentine born, but

US-based mass evangelist) exhorted Bolivians to obey their military governments (Banzer 1971–78, Pereda Asbún, 1978, and García Meza 1980–81) because they were ordained by God (Deiros 1991).

Meanwhile, Sergio got a job in radio as a sports commentator and quit high school in the last year. He then failed in his first attempts at both singing in a heavy metal band, and at racing as a sidecar co-pilot. A series of badly paid jobs (carpenter apprentice, metal workshop worker, sign writer) in the informal economy (with no contract, benefits, security, etc.) followed, until he was drafted. Besides the government of terror, the economic policy of the dictatorship aborted dreams of social mobility. The crushing foreign debt incurred during the military period, the deindustrialization, and the near dismantling of the labour union all took their toll on the working and middle classes (Ranis 1991; Pozzi 1988; Munck 1985; Serulnikov 1994; Beckerman 1995; Taylor 1997).

Strangely, Sergio fondly remembered his conscription year (in 1984, after the fall of the dictatorship), where the worst moment he experienced was "when my hair was cut." Sergio considered himself a 'good soldier' since for him it was easy to follow orders without questioning them. This statement might seem surprising regarding his opposition to the military regime, but its role in Sergio's reconstruction of his life appears to state his willingness to obey, of his accepting an external will to achieve order. In the narrative, it appears as a prelude to his later submission to Divine Will.

Sergio came in touch for the first time with the Scriptures through the almost constant reference to biblical symbology (although in an inverted fashion) in heavy metal, mostly in its 'Black' and 'Death' varieties. Later, when he was experiencing some health problems, Henry, an American Adventist he had met, told him about the Satanism behind what he was listening to, and started explaining the Bible to him. It was not until Daniel, another friend of his, pointed him to the Gospels, and suggested to read the Word of Christ, that the breakthrough occurred:

> So I started reading them and I started feeling something inside me that I could not explain. That surpassed whatever I had felt for a woman, for heavy metal, for sport, for everything else. I started feeling something unexplainable. The words of God started to produce an emotion inside me, and a feeling that I had never experienced before while reading other things... Well, my brother, the evolutionist, Marxist, heavy metal, the whatnot Sergio reaches that moment, and at that very moment, and solely because of the act of reading, believes. I can't explain, here words run out. I don't know how you are going to put it.

For eight months he continued reading the Bible, although still being a heavy metaller, until one day he decided together with Marcelo, another of his friends, to go to an evangelical church in order to further their understanding of the scriptures. For the first time in his life, Sergio prayed to God to ask for forgiveness. Afterwards, following some church members' advice, Sergio burnt all his belongings related to heavy metal (records, posters, t-shirts) with the exception of V8 records. In order to convey as fully as possible the experience of conversion, and the power of words in producing it, I will be quoting at length:

> On Thursday [of the following week] I worked extra hours, and was returning very late. It was raining, and almost dark, and on my way home I met Marcelo who, accompanied by two or three others, was walking in the opposite direction.—"Sergio, we are going to the church in the Capital [...] Come on, come with us [...]" So we went [...] Marcelo was feeling already a member of the community, so in the church he grabbed me by the arm and took me to the front. I was feeling like a fish out of water. Everybody was wearing suit and tie, and short hair [...] So I sat where he told me... So, what happened? The preacher comes in, stands in front, he was fat... He was really fat, and dressed in a suit and tie, and short hair "But this is a moneybag"—I said to myself—"what does he come here to speak about Christ." I imagined Christ as skinny, poor, barefoot, the disciples, you see, all of them. "No, I do not want to have anything to do with evangelicals." That is how I was, stereotyping everybody... But I was stupid, do you understand me? Do you understand? I was stupid. But that is the way I was... So this guy starts preaching—"The ways of God are not as we see them, we are below, God is on top, and we should not try to use our heads to interpret and to pretend understand and judge how God makes things. It is as if there was a rug that divides us. We are below the rug... what can you see from below the rug? You can see that all the threads make no sense, but from the top you can see harmonious designs. Well, all of God's work on earth is harmonious. It has a sense, and He knows why. But we look from below we cannot see it. But in all those threads there, on the other side, there is harmony. Let's accept by faith only, as God tells us." So he said "the path God laid was through faith, and we should recognize him in our condition, and open our hearts, so that the Holy Spirit would give us repentance, and change our life. Only therefore could we live a life that pleased God." At that stage of the meeting there was no longer anybody around me. There was no longer a fat moneybag, and there were no longer people who would notice the way I was dressed. For me, there were only the words that man was saying, the message and myself. Then, suddenly, the preacher—a wise fox—he knew there were many newcomers. Well you did not have to be such a wise fox in order to notice this guy with a lion's mane on his head. So he said "If there is anybody here who has not

received the Holy Spirit in his heart, and has not truly repented, please, come here to the front now, and I will pray for us all." Ah, my brother. There was I, nailed to the chair. Not with nails, but with rivets! And I was saying "God, if you exist, that is what I need." Because I had noticed I had prayed the other day but I hadn't returned to my parents' and that I was an assassin because I hated, even worse, I hated my parents. That my whole life was corruption, that I was full of adultery and fornication, and hatred. And I knew I was lost, and that I would never make it to the Kingdom of God. So I wanted to step forward to pray, and maybe if God could help me with that, because I could not on my own. So I was there, and seconds were ticking away, until suddenly, I was sitting next to the corridor on the first row. And suddenly an old lady stepped forward, and that moved me. "How such an old lady has the guts to do it, and a tough heavy metaller doesn't" I was saying to myself "coward, what a shame, how can I not go forward to pray." So I don't know how, but God broke my chains, I stood up and went forward, closed my eyes and said these words "Lord, God, if you exist, I do not fully understand what this man is saying, but how do you open the doors to the heart? So says your word, please, what I ask you, what shall I do, I open myself up and rip it off, it has been hardened, I cannot open it. All I ask is one thing, touch it please, with the tip of your toes, and I will do the rest." As I was saying these words, my brother, something grabbed me from below, from within, and I start crying. First I am ashamed, tears start rolling down, I am crying. I started gasping for air, and the stomach pulled itself inside. Within a minute I was crying out loud. I was feeling repentance for my sins. I didn't know at the time what it was to repent. Feeling bad about one's sins, feeling bad for having done wrong. I already had a sense of guilt, but I never experienced true repentance. Now I was in pain. Crying in despair, I was no longer ashamed. Shouting, in front of everyone. Soon, I opened my eyes and there were other people shouting and crying, those who had also stepped forward to pray. And I cried and cried, and time passed and it was as if something was coming out from the inside. And it came out, and out and out, and it wasn't just air, and suddenly something strange happened. I am crying and it was an anguish that was killing me, but suddenly I realized that I am crying, with all my will, but of happiness. I also didn't know what it was, it had never happened to me. I am crying of happiness, and I cry, and suddenly I start laughing, and I am laughing, and I started to laugh out really loud, but not the laughter of a joke. I was drowning, my brother... And I start feeling, well, here I can no longer continue, here it is over, I cannot explain it anymore with words. I can only give you a description of my external reactions. My, my, my, my body got straight up. I mean I was broken up to then. I don't stop crying, but I am laughing, of happiness, and then I start feeling peace. I also didn't know what peace was. I also cannot express it with my own mouth. Jesus says "my peace I leave with you, my peace I give you, not as the world gives it, I give it." And Paul says "God gives us a peace that goes over all understanding." I can believe this guy, because I saw it. So I start opening my eyes, because that might have been five minutes, and suddenly I hear the preacher saying over the microphone "This one is inebriated with the Holy Spirit," because I was like drunk. Because the drunken man cries, I also cried and shouted while drunk. Do you understand? And I cried. When Paul says "Do not get drunk with wine, but be full of the Holy Spirit." He makes that parallel, because when the Holy Spirit touches a heart, it gets drunk, my brother. And I was smiling and laughing, and saw the eyes of all the brothers, and the first ones I saw were those of the moneybag [we both laugh]. And when I saw him I loved him, my brother. I loved him with all my heart. I go running and hug him, and was feeling pain for having thought badly of him, and could not stop crying and hugging him. And I hugged him, and hugged him, and he was consoling me, and he didn't know what was going on with me and I didn't tell him because I couldn't speak. Minutes were ticking away, ten, fifteen, twenty.... Lorenzo, I couldn't speak! I was another guy.

Sergio's narrative starts with an initial confrontation that is soon resolved by the preacher and the power of the Word, producing a transformation that prepares him as a listener to the Word that is being delivered. The efficacy (and therefore the authenticity) of the power of the Word is recognized through its effects: "For me, there were only the words that man was saying, the message and myself." Sergio accepts to listen and to go with the flow. The change continues, from a predisposition to listen to the message, Sergio then accepts the framework that was being proposed, and after evaluating his life, adopted, for the first time, in his own speech, the evangelical language, transforming himself into the centurion of Capernaum, negating the believer's agency and worthiness as a means to highlight the divinity's greatness.[8] By dramatizing (Coleman 2000: 125 & ff.) the Centurion, Sergio was not only demonstrating his competence in the newly embodied discourse, he was incorporating himself within the biblical narrative, refashioning himself after an archetype of faithfulness, and simultaneously accepting and demonstrating the authority and authenticity of the Bible. Sergio's belief and faith are simultaneously the requirement, and end product, for such a statement dramatization, as Harding argues for fundamentalist Baptists:

---

[8] "So Jesus went with them. He was not far from the house when the centurion sent friends to tell Jesus, 'Lord, stop troubling yourself. For I am not worthy to have you come under my roof'" (Lk. 7:6). "The centurion replied, 'Lord, I am not worthy to have you come under my roof. But just say the word, and my servant will be healed'" (Mt. 8:8).

Belief also involves an unconscious willingness to join a narrative tradition, a way of knowing and being through Bible-based storytelling and listening. You cannot tell born-again stories, you cannot fashion them, without acknowledging belief, but you can absorb them, and that's how you 'believe' when you are under conviction. (2000: 58)

The appropriation of the biblical language indicates that the conversion was taking place, but he still needed to come to terms with himself and these changes, that are signalled by his feelings of shame, and when these stop, the Holy Spirit takes over to seal the work done. Sergio's inability to explain his experience and his feelings in the church parallels his loss of control over himself at that moment: it has been accomplished, the Word was made flesh in him, and the old Sergio is left speechless, a sign of his transformation into the new Sergio. Finally, Sergio comes to a stage of realizing and accepting the changes that he has gone through: The recital from the Bible becomes simultaneously the privileged mould with which to retrospectively shape his experience (because they were the source of it in the first place) as well as the means for becoming aware of his embodiment of the scripture.

After his conversion, Sergio contacted the members of V8 (the heavy metal band) to tell them his good news, and to his pleasant surprize, they had also converted to Pentecostal Christianity in one of Carlos Anacondia's rallies one of the leading preachers in the Argentine Pentecostal scene (Oro and Semán 2000) which eventually triggered the dissolution of the band. Finally, everything had come full circle to the central aspect of his life, the encounter with Christ: suffering, deprivation, submission, plus the covert entry of the Bible in his life through its inversion in heavy metal, the encounter with V8 and his inability to part with their records. From the perspective of a conversion narrative, it was meant to be that way.

During the following years, Sergio's involvement with the Adventist church increased. In 1988, he entered the Universidad Adventista del Plata (Adventist University of the River Plate) in the Argentine province of Entre Ríos, only to abandon it again a year later. The main reasons he gave me were that, on the one hand, he disagreed with the theology that was being taught, and, on the other, during holidays students were required to go door-to-door selling Bibles in order to pay their student fees. He then returned to Quilmes, where he met Silvana in an Adventist church. Sergio travelled several times within Argentina and Brazil, sharing his view of the Gospel and supporting himself by begging or with minor jobs. Interestingly, he stressed that each one of his travels had lasted exactly 40 days and that he was challenged to avoid a particular sin on each travel. In his narrative, he thus constructed his travels as border experiences as variations of Christ's fasting in the desert and his temptations by the Devil.

After marrying Silvana, in 1992, they settled in Ezpeleta, a working class district on the outskirts of Buenos Aires. During this time, he had several different jobs and actively participated and migrated through different Adventist and Evangelical churches. The constant change in church affiliation was due to theological disagreements with each one of them, which eventually led Sergio and Silvana to the organization of their own Bible study and discussion, worship, and evangelizing group in their house. They also wanted to live outside the city, away from its temptations, and searched some time for protestant agricultural communities, but to no avail.

In 1993, Silvana found an article about the Mennonites in the Province of La Pampa in the old newspaper that wrapped the groceries she had just bought. Upon reading it, and after doing some background theological research on the group, Sergio and Silvana approached the Evangelical Mennonite Church in Buenos Aires, but Angel refused to introduce them to the colony.

But why did they want to join the Mennonites? Their answer comprised several elements. First, they found an initial theological agreement, with the exception of keeping the Sabbath (that is, of Saturday as the holy day of rest). Another point was the Mennonites' living away from a city, away from the temptations of pornography, materialism, and modernity. Another consideration was the education of their daughter. Sergio and Silvana felt that schools that followed the national curricula were at odds with their beliefs (especially regarding the teaching of evolutionism and the encouragement of competition, consumption, and sexuality).

They decided to try by themselves. In November of the same year, they packed up all their belongings and headed towards the colony in La Pampa. They headed towards the *eltesta*, who called for Franz to act as a translator. Both Franz and the *eltesta* were puzzled as that was the first time they were confronted with non-Mennonites that wished to join the colony. After discussing their beliefs, the *eltesta* decided to raise the issue in the *donnadach*, the *Leardeenst*'s fortnightly meeting. They were told that only after the meeting they would be given an answer.

After spending some days in the nearby town of Guatraché, they went back to the colony the following Friday (the *donnadach* takes place on Thursdays). The *Leardeenst* did not reach a final decision that day, but requested further explanations on the motives for joining, and a doctrinal discussion. They lived with different families, working with them in order to contribute to their food and board.

> Time went by, but we could not reach an agreement on certain doctrinal points. We either had to give way to their beliefs or we had to leave...It was basically the Sabbath. It was also that they did not carry out any missionary activities, and we thought that we should preach the gospel. But that was a minor point, because we would not have been prohibited from doing so. We had other minor differences, for example regarding spiritual gifts; their meetings were not what you would call Pentecostal. But they were not so interested in that, and neither were we. I never had a problem in adapting to my brothers, and for me it was enough to sit there and share [the mass] with them. So it [the period of living in the colony] was over, and what I believe, as Paul says "the faith you have, keep it for yourself, and don't be a hindrance to your brother."

Contrasting with his statement on his adaptability (which also contradicts his explanations for his constant pilgrimage between churches), Sergio felt he could not compromise over the Sabbath. He could also keep Sundays, but he refused to work on Saturdays. He was told that keeping the Sabbath, and spreading his ideas in the colony, would generate dissent and conflict. He was therefore asked to remain quiet about them. Under these conditions, Sergio and Silvana decided that they could no longer stay in the colony. Some Mennonites offered to find them a place to live in the surrounding area so that they could be close, but not within the colony. No suitable place was found, and they left the colony to continue their pilgrimage throughout the country in search of a community to join. After a few months of wandering, they went back to Ezpeleta, to take up again with the Bible discussion group they had formed before they had left for the colony.

In 1995, Sergio started writing essays to distribute specifically among heavy metal followers, after he received news that two of his former friends from his "long hair years" had died of AIDS while in jail. Sergio interpreted this as an example of what could have been his future had he not found Christ. Their second daughter was born. The following year, Silvana had health problems during her third pregnancy, which, according to Sergio, were healed through the power of prayer and the Holy Spirit. They had to leave the house in Ezpeleta for economic reasons, and moved to Florencio Varela, a nearby district in Greater Buenos Aires. Meanwhile, Leonardo (one of his friends who converted at the same time as he did) announced that he was to drop the Sabbath and start keeping Sundays. After a discussion, Bible in hand, Sergio decided to fast with his whole family in order to seek enlightenment. He came to the conclusion that as a Gentile, the Sabbath was not the day to be kept, but the Sunday. He communicated his finding to his friends in the Mennonite colony, who, excited, told him to come back since now that their main doctrinal difference had been solved they could entertain the possibility of acceptance by the *Leardeenst*. They said that either Franz or Abraham would eventually go to his place to discuss this with him, and then take them to the colony (it was during this period that I came to his house to visit him, under Franz's recommendation and request). As discussed in Chapter 1, the Old Colony was no longer defined solely in terms of doctrinal agreement. That they would do so indicated how, on the one hand, Sergio and Silvana misread the colony history, and how that history of changes were also kept concealed from their sponsors in the colonies. The symbolic illusion of continuity was casting its spell of opacity, on the gap between openly held values and their actual application in practice in a historical situation.

The times in Florencio Varela were the hardest for him and his family, with a constant lack of jobs, and nothing to feed the family with. Inflation in Argentina had been controlled by the Menem administration with the convertibility plan which pegged the Peso to the US dollar, but the neo-liberal policy of privatization of public companies, and the successive attempts at labour flexibilization contributed to an increase in labour insecurity (Powers 1995; Smith 1991). Eventually this situation led to the 2001 crisis. Franz eventually came to visit and to invite them to the colony. He offered to pay for their bus tickets if they decided to go, and even for the return trip, should they feel after a while that they could not live in the colony.

Sergio decided to take up Franz's offer and to move to the colony. They lived with different families, but a feeling of uneasiness started to overtake him. They were neither formally accepted by the *Leardeenst*, nor told to leave. Not being formally accepted meant that he could not participate in the Lord's Supper, which for Sergio was a major drawback. Nevertheless they stayed, in the hope that eventually, after successfully adapting to the life in the colony, and proving their faith, the *Leardeenst* would accept them. They felt there was strong opposition to their stay by other members of the colony; the issue at stake was Sergio's daughters. Some colonists felt that when they grew up, they would wish to marry Mennonite boys, and they feared the possibility of blood being mixed. Indeed, this had been a recurrent theme in my conversations with Mennonites regarding not only Sergio and Silvana, but *Weltmenschen* in general. From the *Mexas'* blood which makes them steal, to the Mennonite's blood, which makes them the chosen people. We can see here the principle of *jus sanguinis* is, in practice, the one being activated for defining membership against the outside world, in detriment of the ostensive one based on faith. The imagination of the community in terms of a shared blood distinct from the rest can be thought of as the consequence of the historical transformations on the social level, together with the maintenance of the system of symbols of faith mentioned in Chapter 1. The metaphors of a differentiated, chosen people sharing one blood, found a material substratum that confirmed them: Their history of geographic 'separation from the world' and its concomitant closure of marriage possibilities within the group, together with emphasis on the generational transmission of religion (since the practice of evangelization had been pruned).

Not being formally recognized as members meant Sergio and Silvana could not be given a house to live in on their own, even if they could have afforded it (a problem I shared during fieldwork, although I did made it clear from the beginning I was not wishing to gain membership). They felt their parental roles were being undermined, by constantly being guests at other people's homes, and by being under other people's authority.

Furthermore, at the time the Argentine State was attempting to impose public schooling on the colony. The presence of non-Mennonite Argentines would complicate the colony's position vis-à-vis the state, since on the negotiating table, Sergio and Silvana's presence could be brought up to accuse the colonists of attempting to protect law-breaking people.

After three months of living in the colony, Sergio and Silvana were advised to try to go to Bolivia instead, since the Bolivian State seemed less problematic, and because Mennonites had heard of religious agricultural settlements made by Bolivians. They decided to go, and the colony gave them the necessary money for the trip. Also, some of Sergio's friends personally contributed. They also carried a letter of recommendation from one member of the colony, but not from the *Leardeenst* (which would have been more helpful for joining the new colony).

After a long trip, during which their third child was born in Argentina (Sergio and Silvana wanted the birth to occur in Bolivia, therefore making the child Bolivian, which would have contributed to easing their immigratory status), they arrived in Santa Cruz, Bolivia. They were disappointed since there was no colony being made up by Bolivians, but there were members of evangelical churches and Pentecostals, interspersed with the rest of the population. They then went to Swift Current colony where they met Franz's brother, Martin, and Bernard. For a time they travelled between different colonies, always being told that they could not join this one but should try another one. It is clear that the *Leardeenst* of different colonies had reached an agreement on how to deal with Sergio and Silvana: to constantly point them in another direction. In this way, the *Leardeenst* tried to avoid possible internal conflict with the supporters of the Argentines, as well as the open discussion of membership basis.

After three months they returned to La Pampa, and soon left it because of a strong conflict that arose within the colony regarding the position to take towards non-Mennonites, as a consequence of the contrast between the different membership principles: the officially and formally voiced one of faith, versus the racially based one that was occurring in practice. Eventually, most of those who had accepted Sergio, had to leave for other colonies. As I show in Chapter 7, where I analyse the conflicts as a consequence of Sergio's presence, the *Leardeenst* had devised a strategy of putting pressure on Sergio's sympathisers to make the dissenters leave the colonies by themselves, without recourse to excommunication. In this way, they attempted to avoid the open discussions and dissemination of ideas that would have arisen from the excommunication process. This was the situation I found in the colony in La Pampa when I came from England in order to continue my fieldwork.

Sergio and his family then went to visit Abraham in Sachayoj, who was about to go back to Bolivia because his colony had proved to be unviable, and he put Sergio in touch with some Amish in Tarija, Bolivia's southernmost department. In November 1999, they went to Bolivia for the last time, meeting the Lapp family.[9] The Lapps gave them support and found them a place to live, not far from their own

---

[9] The Lapps are an Amish family that was excommunicated from their colony in the United States because the head of the family wanted to wear a moustache and argued that it was not biblically founded that he should shave it. They failed a couple of times in joining other Amish colonies in Paraguay, Belize and Bolivia, deciding to settle on their own.

farm, in the Department of Tarija, where I met them at the time of my last fieldwork.

Mr Hall, a US American, owned the plot of land where Sergio and his family lived after all these travels. Hall bought it from a group of Amish who had failed in their attempt to build a colony. Sergio was given the right to live and use the land, and was granted a small stipend in exchange for taking care of the property. This was in order to avoid the extraction of trees from it and to comply with land ownership regulations in Bolivia that required land to be put to social use (that is by either populating or putting it into production) if title deeds were to remain valid. The property was relatively isolated, the closest neighbour living some forty minutes walk away, and on a busy day one could see only up to five vehicles going along the dirt road that passed by the property.

Sergio established close contacts with several Christian denominations in the area (evangelical, Pentecostal and Adventist), and also with the evangelizing mission the Lapps set up. He also remained in close contact with several Mennonites who still lived in the colonies, such as Abraham, Bernard, Benjamin, Franz, Abraham, and their families.

Sergio seemed satisfied with his new life in Tarija, he considered it a place where he and his family could live a Christian life away from the corruption in the cities, from the impositions of the state, close to nature, and dedicating his life to God. So far, his travels had ended, although not his quest for an ever deepening faith and relationship with God and Jesus Christ. Sergio had also given up his idea of living inside a Mennonite colony, as he had become disenchanted with his experience that had not matched his expectations.

Conclusion: the reconstruction of the Christian self

A number of contrasts can be found by comparing Abraham and Sergio's narratives with regard to the reconstruction of the self that takes place in these narratives: the temporal organization, the model script, the type of divinity and the religious experience. Beyond the narratives, what Sergio and Abraham show through their sojourns, is the interaction between different principles at work in the definition of the Old Colony, and some of the limits of the Christian self required to be a member of it, most notably the insufficiency of doctrinal agreements, and shared descent.

Sergio stressed many times the importance of the Old Testament in terms of the prophesised Messiah. Paraphrasing Sergio's words, the Old Testament is worth nothing without the eventual coming of Christ (because it is the confirmation of the prophecies) and Christ would not *be* without the Old Testament (there would be no way of identifying his divinity). It is this biblical model that Sergio's narrative appears to reflect (upon). Christ is the *telos* of the Old Testament and the centre of the New Testament, as the prophecies are anticipated world history. In the narrative's reflection, Sergio presents his life prior to conversion as predestined, moving under the guidance of the Holy Spirit and leading towards his encounter with Christ; and achieved by his conversion. The purpose of every detail told was to reinforce this, and the very act of telling, was a means to witness His power. After Sergio's conversion, he became an apostle, spreading the faith. Sergio's narrated life story is not only filled with biblical quotations, but is in itself a constant "quotation" of biblical events: his 40 day trips where he was exposed to temptations (Jesus in the desert), his arguments with different religious authorities (Jesus and the sages in the temple), his fleeing from the power of the state over his children (the escape from Herod). All are reflections of/on the biblical script.

Abraham's narrative differs from Sergio's in several aspects. A first difference arises from the sources of exemplars of conversion available to each one of them. On the one hand, Abraham was not as exposed to, nor practiced in the witnessing genre as Sergio was (his pilgrimage through a variety of Adventist, Evangelical and Pentecostal Churches had provided him with the necessary "constitutive language"—the canonical and metaphorical—as Stromberg (1993) calls it, in order to produce such narratives). The model that underlies Abraham's narrative is one constructed from sixteenth-century sources, such as the *Martyrs' Mirror* and especially from Menno Simon's own account of his conversion. Indeed, as Judith Pollmann shows (1996) the Pauline and Augustinian models of conversion were not widespread during the sixteenth century, and conversion was more a matter of discovering the old truths, and of coming out of ignorance than with breaking with and condemning a sinful past. This seems to account for the contrast between the "naturality" of Abraham's religious experience and the "supernaturality" of Sergio's. For Abraham, the existence of God required no proof, it was a known fact, whereas Sergio was in constant need of proving the existence of an omnipresent, omnipotent, and omniscient being as the causal principle behind everything (he was collecting excerpts from the life stories of famous scientists who had converted to Christianity which he showed me on several occasions). This was also due to the main interlocutors each one had, whereas Sergio had experience in addressing non-believers, Abraham did not have to prove the existence of God. Abraham combined these sixteenth-century sources with the success story of the self-made man, probably an influence of his own history of business activities and contacts. Indeed, part of his recent Marxist vocabulary and concerns are most likely the product of his relationship with Thomas. The combination of the two different models produces the narrative of a self-conscious and proactive man, who endures once and again in the face of hardship, and eventually finds in God the comfort, trust and transcendence he cannot find in man. As Menno Simons, Abraham analyses the Holy Scripture, and compares it with the reality he sees around him. Finding differences, he sets out to correct the reality. Abraham is in the centre of his own narrative; it is his own agency that drives the narrative forward, although this agency ought to be tamed by the diligent and humble study of the will of the fearful and righteous God.

Within his own drama of Sin and Redemption, *suffering* has been for Abraham an indication that he was on the narrow path to salvation. According to Abraham, it was through the experience of *suffering* and through a process of empathizing with the martyrs' narratives of persecution and torture, that he had become a member of a small group of true Christians. In this case, suffering is not only a means to join the body of Christ (like in medieval Europe, see Walker-Bynum 1987; Asad 1993) but also of joining of a community of fellow sufferers. Dispersed over time and space, but made available in the present through martyrologies such as the *Martyrs' Mirror* (Braght 1982), the sharing common experiences of persecution, torture and suffering for the keeping of their faith, they all belonged to the same community which would be united at the end of time.[10] The grace of God, made the suffering bearable, and with it, came understanding. Like John in Patmos,[11] it was now his duty to share what he had understood and seen, whatever the consequences for him. From that moment, he saw his life modelled on those of the martyrs. Therefore he assumed the task of writing an essay, and of distributing it, first among a closed circle of like-minded friends and, later, among the colony's authorities.

There is also a contrast regarding the prevalent character from the Trinity, and the relationship established with it. Whereas for Sergio it

---

[10] The place of written texts is one of the cornerstones of Benedict Anderson's argument on the imagination of communities (1990).

[11] John, the author of the Book of Revelation, who was instructed to commit to paper the visions granted to him (see Rev. 1:9–11).

was the power of the Holy Spirit, for Abraham it was the trust in Jesus Christ and the fearfulness of God that characterized this relationship. The ineffability of Sergio's encounter with the divine and the supernatural, contrasts with the rationalized, even "natural" style of Abraham's encounter. This different relationship with the supernatural is coherent with Sergio and Abraham's different attitudes towards the world. Whereas Sergio's main strategy has been one of retreat, Abraham's choice has been to engage actively with the world, in an attempt to produce change in it. Indeed, this contrast is also present in their writings, which provide their religious analysis of the situation in the colonies and the world (see next chapter). True, Abraham and Sergio had different starting points, and therefore the crossing of boundaries was in different directions. What is interesting however, is that the one coming from the apparently 'disenchanted', 'modern' world, was producing the most 'enchanting' narratives, where the supernatural was always present. Meanwhile, the one coming from a group that supposedly held a position that rejected modernity and the disenchantment of the world, produced a narrative so devoid of the supernatural, and where his presence and agency were the driving force.

What impact did events within the wider 'world' have on Sergio's and Abraham's choices and the representation of their narratives? Experiencing the advent of military dictatorships and macroeconomic volatility in Bolivia and Argentina, and the requirements of the different institutions with which they interacted posed concrete challenges they had to confront and master. Their lives, far from being a simple reaction to these challenges, exhibit complex and multidimensional agency and a creativity that cannot be contained by the application of a single model to their narratives.

Finally, what these two cases bring to the foreground, is the layering of two principles that define the Old Colony: One *de jure*, that of shared faith, and the other *de facto* of shared descent. Abraham was part of the Mennonite social order by virtue of his birth. Upon this, the faith based principle was applied to grant and remove his church affiliation (his faith or lack of it was evidenced by his behaviour). On the contrary, what made it impossible for Sergio and his family to become members was the lack of common descent. What the *Leardeenst* avoided stating clearly in words, (because it would have contradicted their own *de jure* principle of membership), was that common faith and doctrinal agreements became irrelevant when the individual lacked common descent with the group. In this way, for the *Leardeenst*, only certain kind of people, of certain descent and of certain blood can become Christians.

CHAPTER SIX

SCRIPTURAL PRACTICES

Introduction

In this chapter I analyse Abraham and Sergio's critique of the Old Colony, as well as their projects for the building of a community of believers; which, with the exception of Abraham's project in Roboré, have been disseminated in written form. Through them, I explore in this chapter the process of creation and dissemination of alternative imaginations of the future. These texts contain an interpretation of the world within which the colonies and the authors' ideas of how to make a Christian community are embedded. They have challenged the basic ideological tenets of the Old Colony, in this case, the definition of Christianity and the basis of group membership, proposing a self centred, internal, and processual definition as opposed to the communitarian, inherited and externalized one of the Old Colony. The *Leardeenst* responded to this challenge not only by attempting to restrict the circulation of Sergio's writings, but also by taking concrete actions against those who shared the views expressed in them (analysed in Chapter 7). Abraham acknowledged to me that it was under Sergio's inspiration that he decided to put his views in writing, and was expecting a similar reaction to his own, although he had not widely distributed it at the time of fieldwork.

The writings of Abraham and Sergio present an opportunity not only to gain a perspective on the contents—an analysis of the Old Colony from its margins, but also on situated uses of literacy (Kulick and Stroud 1990; Collins 1995). Jack Goody's work on literacy (Goody and Watt 1963; Goody 1968b, 1986) has sparked an ongoing debate in anthropology regarding the consequences of technologies of writing in the development of logic and knowledge. A recurrent critique has been Goody's treatment of systems of writing as neutral technologies, shadowing the actual, culturally bound practices of literacy (Niezen 1991; Kulick and Stroud 1990; Collins 1995). Here I focus on the use of writing as a tool for both challenging the established order and for bringing forth social change. Within the domain of Mennonite religious practices, reading is privileged over writing in a situation similar to Thai Buddhist monks:

> Novices and monks were primarily trained to read the scripts and only secondarily to write. Writing was not so much creative composition as copying. The literature read and copied was composed of religious texts or traditional tales which could not in theory be changed, only transmitted. (Tambiah 1968: 121)

Indeed, the sermons *prädjasch* read in the mass were written in the past and handed down over generations. Only a minority of *prädjasch* contribute to the growth of this corpus, and many do not write a single sermon in their whole career. The same is the case for the Hutterites, who, according to Karl Peter (1983: 229), resorted to the fixation in writing of the sermons in order to avoid different biblical interpretations (see also Goody 1986: 17). Abraham and Sergio's challenge is therefore a particular case of the encounter of two potentialities of literacy, the one that codifies and maintains orthodoxy through the emphasis in reading (and where writing is left to copying), with the one that through reflection and creativity, attempts to subvert it with an emphasis on writing.

The ostensive position of the Mennonites regarding texts and knowledge is that everything worth knowing comes from the Bible. The Bible as the revealed word of God is inerrant, what it says is eternal truth, and its prophecies will become reality. Biblical inerrancy, in this context, has two consequences: first, that it not only becomes a Procrustean bed where world events are to be accommodated, but also becomes also the benchmark for establishing what reality is, therefore simultaneously constituting it (see Goody 1986: 20). Second, the textual authority of the biblical text is transferred to other texts, by their virtue of being written, although this is especially the case if they appear to fit the biblical narrative. It is therefore not only as a technological means of aiding the dissemination of ideas that writing is used in this context, but because the mere act of having the words in print provides them with a higher degree of authority. The phrase "it is written in the Bible" as a means of claiming authority is transformed into a simple "it is written" (which also echoes the way Jesus is quoted as referring to the prophecies in the Old Testament). Whereas Maurice Bloch (1968) identifies a rather similar power of the written word in Madagascar attributing it mainly to the scarcity and difficulty of obtaining books as objects. I suggest here that such power arises in the case of the Old Colony, from a combination of the mystification of authorship (reinforced by restrictive writing), and from a synecdochical relation between the Bible and the rest of the books. The authority of the text needs then to be complemented by rhetorical strategies that attempt to convince the reader of its biblical inspiration and adequacy. The rhetorical success of the interpretation lies in establishing its biblicality on the eyes of the readers, rather than in its "(ostensibly) rational" authority as Stephen O'Leary argues (1994: 13), together with the establishment of linkages with the world *as perceived* by the potential readers, therefore providing an "uncanny contemporaneity" to the prophecies (Boyer 1992: 296).

Here I show that the strategies used by Abraham and Sergio in order to convince their readers of their point of view, and to induce change are based on the identification of the Old Colony with its purported nemesis, the Devil, the state, and the modern world. These texts go beyond a mere critique, they also constitute foundational texts for the creation of new social orders where the author's interpretation of Christianity can be achieved in this world: veritable blueprints of alternative imaginations of the future.

Writing dissent

Becoming worldly, becoming Christian

After Abraham gave me an oral overview of the content of his essay, I told him that I suspected that it might cause him trouble within the colonies if the *prädjasch* found about it. He replied that that was exactly what he wanted, to force the *Leardeenst* to summon him to give explanations, and at the same time force them to show him "with the Bible" that he was wrong. Abraham was acting as if he had read and followed Kai Erikson's (1966) thesis that deviance forces the elicitation of the limits of acceptable conduct, although he was most likely emulating the written disputational style common during the Reformation, which he had learned from reading the works of Menno Simons. If they showed him to be wrong, he said, he would be ready to repent but if they could not do so, the *Leardeenst* would then be forced to accept his ideas and enforce the appropriate changes in the colonies. His attempt was bold and had serious consequences. Printing and distributing his essay meant his views would become part of the public domain and, therefore, could not be ignored as mere gossip. Furthermore, they would attain a degree of authority by being written. Abraham was therefore very likely to be called to give explanations. If he could not produce the changes he wanted, he would strike back, transforming the *Leardeenst* from judges and jury into defendants. Hence, if the *Leardeenst* failed in conducting the disciplinary process in a way consistent with the Bible, and unjustly punished him, it would confirm that they had left the narrow path, and he would no longer abide by them. If such a situation should arise, Abraham was well prepared to leave, he would build a new colony with the help of a private company, within which a community of true believers could follow their Christian path (which I focus on in the next section).

Throughout his essay, Abraham highlights several aspects of life in the Mennonite colonies which he considers as deviations from what they ought to be if they were to remain true to their commitment of forming a true Christian community. Abraham explains how to become a Christian through a set of counterpoints with his interpretation of the situation of the colonies and how they have deviated from the path to Salvation by becoming worldly and accepting modernity. The main points that Abraham directs his attention to are: the decay of faith, several instances in which the colonies have acquired different traces that erase the separation from the world, while at the same time providing a brief interpretation of the New World Order and how it relates to the colonies.

Abraham starts indicating some aspects of the New World Order that makes it fit within the apocalyptic chronology in the Book of Revelation. A far from novel reading indeed, since the identification of the current state of the world (from the interpreters perspective) in relation to the biblical prophecies is a common exercise undertaken by reformers urging for immediate change.[1]

The unification of countries and currencies through supra-national entities such as the NAFTA and European Union are considered the concrete materializations set forth in the prophecies (although at this point he does not indicate to which verses they correspond). He characterizes the world as "living under governments of injustice, full of

---

[1] From medieval and early modern Europe (Cohn 1957; Hobsbawm 1971; Klaassen 1992; Lerner 1981) to Melanesia (Worsley 1970; Lattas 1998), eighteenth to twentieth-century America, (Anthony and Robbins 1997; Bloch 1985; Davidson 1977; Introvigne 1997; O'Leary 1994), Japan (Castells 1998; Mullins 1997), indigenous south America (Clastres 1995; Cordeu and Siffredi 1971; Pereira de Queiroz 1965; Regher 1981; Siffredi and Spadafora 1991) etc.

cunningness, fraud and lies."[2] These governments will eventually enforce embodied devices: "a tiny microchip, the size of a dot in a typewriter or through the incorporation of barcodes in either the right hand or the forehead" which would not only work as a means of identification, but would also allow the tracking of the location of each bearer, as well as acting as a means of payment (this is a common interpretation, see Boyer 1992: 287). For Abraham, this device is the Mark of the Beast referred to in the Book of Revelation, "without which no one would be able to buy or sell." Being the Mark of the Beast, Christians should therefore abstain from such devices. Within this context, the underdeveloped and poor economic situation of Bolivia is considered an asset, since it would take longer for its State to implement such measures due to their lack of resources.

But Abraham had not developed these ideas on his own. He was actively collecting and reading a wide variety of books, pamphlets and treatises (beyond the canonical ones such as the Bible, and Menno Simon's works). Indeed, the topics and interpretations are identical with those of post World War II US American apocalypticism (Boyer 1992: 254 and ff.). Some of Abraham sources included *En Route to Global Occupation* (Kah 1978), which is a blend of US American Christian fundamentalism with conspiracy theory and is what some Mennonites use as a confirmation of some of the ideas of worldwide political and economic centralization. A few articles dealing with debit cards, the place of bankers in the world economy, and supporting a theory that the central computer that administered the EU was nicknamed 'The Beast' from a journal published by a Canadian Catholic group named 'The Pilgrims of St. Michael'. The one that surprised me most was a photocopy of a pamphlet "Project 666" authored under a pseudonym. The author, a Dominican living in Sweden also claims to be 'The 666' who "aspires to the presidency of the European Union," and who wishes to implement "the 666 identification code," "the 666 business model," for "the making of a paradise on earth" and transforming the European Union into the New Holy Roman Empire. It is not hard to

---

[2] Note the contrast between Abraham's characterization of worldly governments with the functions assigned to them by the Amish, which, according to Yoder (2003: 25) are: "vengeance," "punishment," and "restraint." Whereas David negatively evaluates the worldly governments in order to later transfer those characteristics to the colonies; Yoder attempts to harmonize these qualifications in order to justify the Amish belief of divinely instituted worldly governments.

see that for a prophecy interpreter the aspiration to be elected president of the European Union which seeks to apply a program that bears not only the dreaded figure (the triple six), but that resembles the one prophesised for the government of the last days, can easily be read as the actual project of the European Union. It is through the reading of these works, and by establishing links between them and the Book of Revelation, that Abraham attempts to put forward the idea that the world is reaching to its end, giving a sense of urgency to his message in his call for reformation.

Having characterized the situation of the world, he sets out on the task of framing the Old Colony's position within the narrative of the Book of Revelation. Inside the colonies, he identifies a situation of total apostasy, which is considered as another sign of the end of time, and the product of the work of the Devil. The imminence of Judgement Day drives the necessity of identifying who will be saved and who will not, which can only be done after a thorough search of the signs that place a group or individual on either side of the saved/damned, Christian/worldly divide. Only after a proper identification is made, can a call for the reformation of the latter be done.

According to Abraham, the Devil, through the lure of modernity, has driven even those who consider themselves as Christians to pursue a happy city life, where they freely indulge in stealing, killing and fornication. At the same time, God is denied, and replaced by the TV, which is worshiped in a manner similar to the Beast (Rev. 13:15; Dan. 7:24).

> And also in Revelation 12:4 we see how the scarlet Dragon dragged the stars from the sky and threw them upon the world. What else can we say about satellites, car-bombs, air travel, computers, internet, television and whatnot, whatever has created the world in the last century. To this should be added big machinery, vehicles such as cars and pick-up trucks, motorcycles [...] Modernity counts on things like these, and all of these are signs of the end of time.

According to Abraham all this has made the world lose faith in God, a situation that is also occurring within the colonies, with "materialism and individualism" on the rise, and which has made "fraternal love" disappear. "We have made our own Gods out of our property [...] this should be enough of a sign to tell us where we build up our treasures." This is a paraphrasing of Mt. 6:19–21, which indicates that the place where treasures are built, is where affections are directed. Therefore, through a double metaphorical layer, Abraham indicates that the hearts of humans are focused on material gain, the world, and therefore, away from God.

For Abraham the adoption of individualism and materialism (for him the two driving values of modernism) has created wealth differences within the colonies, generating not only a group of haves and of have-nots, but also connivance between the former and the *Leardeenst*. He condemns the situation in the colonies that economic success has been transformed into moral authority and influence on spiritual matters. In a Marxian tone Abraham asks rhetorically:

> Who sells his labour, and who rents land? Is this done by those who have plenty or by the poor man that needs it? And then, who is the one who judges the poor? The poor or the rich? Why shouldn't he dare work outside the colony?

The poor, stripped from their means of production and with no other opportunities inside the colony, are being forced to search for jobs outside the borders of the colony. They are then punished for doing so, because working outside the colony boundaries is forbidden. The argument that in the opinion of Abraham is brandished by the authorities to justify such prohibition is "because they do not keep themselves in order" when beyond the controlling gaze of fellow Mennonites.

> I think that a Christian community is one where solutions are searched for, where mutual help exists, and lives in communion. That is why it is called a "community." But nowadays it is like this: one has material abundance, much land and tools, but not for others, therefore we are no longer in communion as in the time of the apostles "one heart, and one soul" according to Acts 4:32.

In short, the acceptance of modernism, individualism, and private property, all of it product of the Devil, are the causes that make it impossible to form a true community, hence making the colonies a part of the world, and the damned. Although Abraham attributes these ills to the conflation of modernity as ideological justification with the work of the devil and the spiritual weakness of the Old Colony, this is a means of attempting to come to terms with the actual processes of social change occurring within the colonies, especially on the economic level.

Together with modernity, and with the loss of faith in God go the rise of *idolatry* and the adoration of the Antichrist, which has materialized in the figure of Nicolas. According to Abraham, the figure of Nicolas, who was accepted by the parents and would leave presents for the children, displaced the adoration of Jesus Christ on the evening of the 24th of December:

> All this was done on the 24th, and on the 25th, when the children would wake up, their parents would say to them "all this has been brought to you by Nicolas," and with this, all forms of lies were taught to the children, and such horrible idolatry was forced into them.

Not only Father Christmas was appropriated within the colonies but also Halloween. Abraham states that this was a "game of the enemy," in a clear reference to the Devil. Nevertheless, and much to his liking and opinion, these practices had been eradicated, although not completely as I witnessed some figures of Father Christmas in some houses.

Abraham claims that it is his worry and fear for the spiritual destiny of "our sons and grandsons" that he felt compelled to write his essay. His worry can be sensed all along the essay, and he repeatedly shows concern about their behaviour. He interprets the separation that occurred between the liturgical and written language (Hüagdietsch-High German) and the everyday Plautdietsch (during the Mennonite's stay in Prussia) as a trick of the Devil to confuse the souls of the youngsters, and impede the assimilation of the word of God. He also interprets the different attempts on the part of different states to impose public schooling and/or conscription as punishments from God for not having kept their faith. Therefore reversing the causality identified in the historical narrative. In a multiple pronged attack, the youngsters "have been lost to the world." He also interprets that throughout the history of the colonies, the youngsters have presented a problem for the community. This is evidenced by the fact that Abraham recognizes that the 'youth' are not literally "sons and grandsons" of a particular generation what attract his attention, but of youngsters in general, including those of past, present, and future generations, and that nowadays the degree of their apostasy is such that they seem to behave worse than those from outside the colonies. For Abraham, the youngsters generate trouble through their indulgence in forbidden practices such as alcohol drinking, smoking, rowdiness, pre-marital sex, and by either adopting new styles of clothes, or wearing them in a different way; all this, under the influence of the Devil. Nevertheless, he does not blame it on them, but on their parents, and on the authorities of the colonies who, "during those tender years when it is most easy and necessary to implant in them the Fear of God, they are left to their own devices, to roam around with no controls over them." Instead of instilling them the true

Christian doctrine, they are taught "customs and traditions, which is something forbidden by God." In order to solve this problem, Abraham advocates the creation of Sunday Bible school, and other activities to structure and orient their youth, but his attempts have been ignored by the Old Colony. In other words, the problem is double sided. On the one hand, the contents of the current imagination of the future are flawed, and this imagination is inappropriately transmitted to the forthcoming generation. A new guiding project and a programme for its construction are needed and Abraham will supply them both in his call for reformation and re-reading the Scripture. Despite Abraham's acumen for producing a very modern, materialist, and historical critique of the Old Colony, he then proceeds to produce a project that is completely ahistorical, a veritable utopia: it is one based on the eternal word of God, and therefore of universal application. As many utopias, it is an order imagined once and for all, where change is eliminated by design, as are history and agency.

Furthermore, Abraham counter argues against those who claim that the incorporation of machinery and the usage of modern tools is only an accommodation to time. The defense of accommodation, as interpreted by Abraham, is based on the claim that "it would be impossible to live without it in this time." Abraham argues that those who accommodate have become (quoting Menno Simons) "servants of time," and therefore "temporal," hence "worldly." In opposition to change and temporality, Abraham poses God's eternity, and the immutability of His word and His commandments to men. Indeed an imagined future inspired in the eternal word of God, would therefore by immutable, and today's imagination of the future ought to be the future's future too. Abraham's imagination of the future is therefore one that externalizes both history and time. Ironically, in this sense, Abraham's project approaches the romanticized and idealized image that prevails in representations of Amish and Mennonites analysed at the beginning of this book.

For Abraham, it is not only modernism, individualism, and the practice of idolatry that takes part in the colonies becoming the world; the *Leardeenst* are concomitantly becoming like worldly governments, and faith is 'becoming custom'. In the last part of his essay Abraham argues with plenty of biblical quotations that not only Mennonites are no longer following the Christian path, but that the *Leardeenst* is deviating in its practices from its biblically prescribed duties and forms.

Abraham claims that faith as the foundation of belief has been replaced by custom and rule following. For Abraham, this is not a direct process: faith as a gift of God, which arises from the intervention of the Holy Spirit in reading the Bible, has been replaced in the following of the rules set forth in the Scripture. From there, the control of behaviour has shifted from the enlightened reading of the Scripture towards a *man made* set of rules, in this case made by the *Leardeenst*. In short, Abraham identifies a process of secularization of the moral order of the colonies.

The aforementioned shift has been accompanied by a change in the object of faith. The Mennonites have transferred their "faith in God," to "faith in humans," and more particularly, faith in the *Leardeenst*. According to Abraham, the *Leardeenst* itself has reinforced this shift by claiming that since persecution from the outside has eased, they will be the ones to warn them in case of potential spiritual dangers. This transference of faith in God to faith in humans makes man "a miserable creature" since without God comes "disgrace." He then goes on to quote several biblical passages to sustain justification by faith, as opposed to justification by deeds and rule following and continues with Menno Simons highlighting the fear of God as the cornerstone and source of faith.[3] Abraham's interest here is to contribute to his argument about faith having been replaced by custom, and trying to sort out the proper hierarchies. If even the law in the Bible has to be subsumed to faith, then man made rules and customs should not only be subsumed to those in the Bible, but also to faith, and therefore to fearfulness of God. It is the diminishing, or even non-existent fear of God that for him, is the central cause of all the problems, including the breaching of the proper hierarchy between texts. In short, and following the *Martyrs' Mirror*, Abraham states:

> It is when human laws dominate when the poor hearts are being seduced. Where Jesus Christ is not the sole Lord, who constructs and takes care, no building can last. Everything crumbles down in ruins, and even if the world elevates them and holds them in high esteem, they are worthless in front of God. Custom has grown stronger in us than the word of God.

Abraham's earlier mention of the origins of the *schlaubbekjse* can be seen as a concrete example of this situation: "Many Mennonites believe that

---

[3] Rom. 2:15, 3:20–22, 4:5–7, 4:15, 6:16, 7:6, 10:2–4; Gal. 2:16, 3:2–3, 2:21, 5:4.

because they wear *schlaubbekjse*, they are saved." The process of sacralization of external symbols (in this case clothing) within the colonies, is here identified by Abraham as a process of traditionalization that goes hand in hand with that of the autonomization of behaviours from their religious basis, in short, secularization. This traditionalization is also the abuse of the *Leardeenst's* power, who have succumbed to being "proud in themselves" and therefore claim for them law-making attributes reserved for God and Jesus. The *Leardeenst* have not only failed to preach with their own example, but have also become "proud" and "arrogant," and have taken an active part in this shift: "setting down laws, commandments, and agreements which neither Jesus Christ nor the apostles have used." This point is of the utmost importance, since it shows that Abraham is clear in his position regarding authority. He is not attempting to go against the *Leardeenst* legitimacy in itself, but against the concrete behaviours and occupiers of office, Abraham is therefore not a revolutionary, but a reformer. As such, he is replicating the exemplary model of Menno Simons and many others that followed him in the Mennonite history of schisms over how to define and build the Church of Christ on earth.

> We were forbidden to add or take anything out of the Bible (Rev. 22:18–19). My position is that agreements within the community remain as agreements, and is not our faith, because through this, the word of God is diminished, and many souls are then confused in the faith.

At the same time, this shift on the basis of normativity has been accompanied by a change in the activities of the *Leardeenst*, who spend much energy enforcing the *Ordninj* but (Abraham notices) not enough on deviations that are indeed strictly forbidden by the Bible. To this should be added the *Leardeenst's* discouragement of the reading of the Scriptures: "they say that what they teach us in church is enough and we shouldn't go into reading." Also, "opening the Bible with *Ejebuare*," that is, discussing biblical arguments with non-Mennonites was also being forbidden. In such a way attempting to unjustifiably claim for themselves the monopoly on the interpretation of the sacred texts, and closing up opportunities for different interpretations to gain ground within the community. Indeed, according to Jack Goody, strategies to implement the restriction of literacy "tend to arise wherever people have an interest in maintaining a monopoly of the sources of their power" (1968a: 12). In Abraham's opinion, the worst consequence is that through these prohibitions, the *Leardeenst* is going against the relationship that a believer can establish with God through the reading of His word.

In addition, the *Leardeenst* is no longer using "their true sword, which is brotherly love, with which the heart of the sinner is softened and induced to repentance." Instead, they resort to undue use of the *Kjoakjebaun*, to calumny, and refuse to both forgive and ask for forgiveness when they are wrong. According to Abraham, excommunication is used to punish the breaking of man made laws, but not applied when failing to follow God's commandments. This makes him question the application of excommunication as it is practiced by the *Leardeenst*.

> What do the Holy Scriptures teach us regarding the correct use of excommunication? Is true evangelical excommunication to be used for keeping the agreements of the communities? It is useful to keep the agreements, and to support them, but not to place God's commandments behind them. Those should be the first and most important ones. Nowadays spiritual sins have become custom to us, but people believe that it is enough just keeping the community agreements. So they believe that they are already true Christians, and they fall into a spiritual sleep, and this is why everything has cooled down so much.

In Abraham's opinion, this shift not only "makes injustice" on the word of God, by replacing it with a set of human rules, but also reinforces the loss of faith in God with the concomitant rise of faith in humans. A phrase he constantly repeated during our conversations was indeed stressing this same point: "I only trust God, I do not put my faith in any human being anymore." The discovery of where to place his faith is, indeed, a direct product of his own path of suffering. Here Abraham approaches Franz's understanding of the epistemic qualities of suffering, providing a means towards spiritual, and therefore the highest type of knowledge, also bringing grace and spiritual happiness. Abraham attempts to demonstrate this by pointing to the symmetric opposite of the happiness pursued through individualism and material gain that he considers is on the rise within the colonies, and that that was exemplary pursued in the time of Menno Simons:

> Although they were under a heavy cross, the community flowered like a rose amidst thorny bushes, and through this, it grew constantly because many people saw the light shining from the darkness.

Upon comparing his interpretation of the colonies with the time of Menno Simons, he makes two important points. On the one hand how persecution, poverty and suffering has led them to not only be "stronger in the faith," but also in making the communities grow. On the other, how the community in those times, was truly acting as the "light of the world," showing with their exemplary lives how true Christians should act. Something that, according to Abraham, is no longer the case with the Mennonites. Abraham rhetorically asks how to be the light of the world, and he answers:

> With our fidelity, justice, truth, love and meekness towards the world. Our "yes" should be "yes" and our "no" always "no." But we have it all changed, we believe that if we have a different dress from the world, and the machinery, that is all that is needed, but some are too proud of their attires, as well as being proud of their machinery.

Therefore, he is identifying a process at work within the Old Colony of transformation from spiritual internal faith, into external identity and group markers.

According to Abraham, the Mennonites are no longer persecuted by the outside world: "Mennonites now enjoy peace and security." If the world no longer persecutes them, Abraham reasons, then it means that they have become part of it, since persecution and tribulation are some of the signs that mark the community of believers during the last days. Abraham then identifies repeatedly the "losing of the faith" and the increasing disorder of the colonies with moments where persecution on the part of the state had eased, and the concomitant rise of economic welfare and pride within the communities. In doing so, he praises the work of a few *eltestasch* who attempted to both "put everything back in order" and to reject further state impositions such as conscription and public schooling. Nevertheless, he claims the different schisms and migrations through which those *eltestasch* tried to re-found and re-order the communities failed because "they carried the old yeast with them...and also brought disorder with them."

In Abraham's eyes, now that the persecution from without had eased, a persecution from within was being put in practice:

> Dear reader, our time is terribly dangerous, many preachers have cooled down spiritually, and apparently calumny has become custom among the Leardeenst. That is something I have personally and abundantly experienced. They also lie and are treacherous (with the exception of a few ones that watch the sad state of our communities and lament themselves with tears).

In Abraham's opinion, the *Leardeenst*'s behavioural deviation from their biblically prescribed duties and procedures have transformed them into the new persecutors. "Mennonites are no longer persecuted by the world but by themselves." Being persecuted is one of the signs of the true Christian during the end of time, and being a persecutor, is equalled with the world, using state-like powers. The qualities of the governments of the modern world (deceitful and treacherous) are also applied to the *Leardeenst*. In such a manner, then, the colonies have become a microcosm of the world, where those in power, acting in a manner worthy of worldly governments persecute the just ones. In addition, Abraham mentions the case of the son of a member of the *Leardeenst*, who, upon being elected as a *prädja*, embarrassed himself publicly in Church when he could not read the sermon, nor the Bible. Bringing into question both the carelessness of the education of the youth, as well as accusing the *Leardeenst* of attempting to establish hereditary principles in the succession of office.

Abraham recognizes and does not contest, in principle, the *Leardeenst*'s legitimacy to the monopoly of power within the colony as he interprets their power to punish and control the population as biblically founded attributes. Instead, he undermines their discretionary use in practice of those powers. Because for Abraham there is only one Religion (with a capital *R*), his accusations of their failure to behave as Christians ministers (biblical selectiveness, their making of man made norms to be retained in the same level as the word of God, their discouragement on independent reading of the Bible and their claim to the monopoly of its interpretation) means that they have lost its religious legitimacy, and become worldly. As a worldly institution, they have become the new persecutors of the few Mennonites who still attempt to walk the *narrow path* towards salvation.

For Abraham, being a true Christian is a process rather than a state of being. It is during this worldly life that this process takes place, reaching its confirmation on Judgement Day, after which, being Christian and being Saved become not only synonyms but definitive eternal states. Therefore, it is faith in Jesus Christ as Saviour that allows the following of His teachings, and through the examples set forth by those who followed Him that one strives to become a Christian although never being sure of attaining it. This situation causes anxiety for those embarked on the path to become Christian, and signs are searched to check one's progress towards the desired end. It should be noted these signs are not signs of being predestined to Salvation (as in Calvinism as studied by Weber [1991; cf. Peter 1983: 228]) but signs that show that their physical, mental, emotional and spiritual behaviour are in accordance with the teachings of Christ, or modelled after those who are believed to have followed Him. It is here that the *Martyrs' Mirror* becomes of the utmost importance, since it provides a corpus of concrete experiences to which to relate one's own predicaments, especially during hard times. Unlike Franz, who found his faith in a direct, mystical experience with the sacred at the time of his baptism, and Sergio for whom the power of the word opened the path to the inebriating Holy Spirit, Abraham's path is one arising from attempting to understand his own suffering. Whereas for Franz and Sergio, the Bible speaks to their hearts, for Abraham, it is a concrete model both of, and for, life.

Abraham also regrets the treatment that certain non-Mennonite Christians have received within the colonies. This is a clear reference to Sergio and his family but without naming them. He claimed that not only should they have been accepted on the basis of their faith and proper Christian behaviour but, he added orally in an interview, that Sergio should not have left the colonies. He should have remained to continue "enlightening the hearts and spirits" of his fellow colonists. The refusal to accept Sergio, together with the long abandoned mission work (since their time in Prussia) meant that they were no longer behaving as true Christians whose duty was to spread the word of God, to form a community of "brothers in faith" regardless of race and cultural background, which would become the "light of the world" setting an example of Christian living. Through this, he was indicating a failure on the part of the *Leardeenst* not only to comply with the commandments set forth to the apostles (to establish a church whose membership was based on faith and not on blood) but also of their selectiveness in their reading of the Scriptures, "taking what suits them, and leaving out what does not."

In short, Abraham is claiming that the current state of the world and the colonies are indications of the end of time. Also, that the colonies have had the wrong type of connection with the world: to accept their ideas and practices, and renouncing both, to spread the Gospel and to become exemplary Christians who would bring light to the world. At the same time, faith has been replaced by normativism and custom. In such a 'becoming,' the Mennonites have stopped 'becoming Christian,' to tread on the path of 'becoming the world,' under the *Leardeenst's* guidance who, in turn, are 'becoming a worldly government' through their secularization, and unbiblical use of power, thereby losing their religious legitimacy. These claims are far from novel they bear not only a strong resemblance to Menno Simons' differences with Catholics and

Lutherans, but are typical of the church-sect cycle where the principle of individual interpretation of the Bible collides with the institutionalization of belief. For Abraham these are the processes he wishes to revert in order to come back to the 'narrow path' towards salvation. If he fails in producing the changes from within, he is ready to attempt his own project in Roboré.

The Roboré project

As indicated earlier, Abraham had a plan to leave the Old Colony to found a new community. This new community would abide by what he thought were the principles of the true Church of Christ, getting rid of the *old yeast* that was still within the Mennonite colonies, remaining separate from the world and avoiding materialism, modernity and individuality through the establishment of commonality of goods.[4] At least these were Abraham's ideals, and all he would say about it. The community would be built in association with Thomas Hausmann, the director of Theoprax; a company that had sprung from Agromac, and Menoagro. Thomas had a more practical approach to the project.

Thomas had been very active within university politics during his younger years, his participation in a left-wing party, which cost him being abducted and tortured during the García Meza dictatorship.[5] He also did consultancy for foreign aid agencies, organized peasant cooperatives, and then moved to the private sector. Upon asking him about the meaning of the title of his last company Theoprax, Thomas went on to an explanation about Marx's Theses on Feuerbach, and the emphasis on a theoretically and scientifically driven approach to practice, therefore becoming praxis which was to be the spirit and orientation of the company. More specifically, regarding the Roboré project, he had a double motivation for embarking on it. On the one hand, it was a way to put in practice his own little social experiment, the making of his own utopia. On the other, the more practical motivation

---

[4] During our talk, Abraham repeatedly used this biblical metaphor to refer to the winnowing process that ought to take place within the church. "So let us keep celebrating the festival, not with the old yeast or with the yeast of vice and wickedness, but with the bread of purity and truth that has no yeast" (1 Cor. 5:8).

[5] The wave of simultaneous military dictatorships in Latin America was a product of the US' security doctrine at the time, many of its officers were graduates from the "School of the Americas" where torture was part of the curricula (see Munck 1985; Feitlowitz 1998: 9 and ff.).

that he owned land that according to current legislation, had to be put into social use in order for his title deeds to remain valid.

The initial arrangement was that of the 15,000 ha Thomas owned in Roboré, 5,000 would be immediately put into production by the settlers. This would be done with capital provided mainly by Thomas; Abraham would be the one in charge of recruiting colonists within the Mennonite colonies. Theoprax would economically support them during the first couple of years. Of those 5,000 ha Abraham and his group would receive the property deeds of 4,000 ha and, in exchange, they would put into production the remainder 1,000 ha that would be kept as Thomas' own property. Abraham's idea was that within the new settlement, and with the exception of Thomas' land, all goods were to be held in common, and settlers would be there to pursue a Christian lifestyle, separate from the world, abiding to the New Testament, and living as "one heart and one soul." The abolition of private property, together with the geographical isolation, were the two main points for Abraham to make a Christian community viable since, with the former, modernism, consumerism and pride would be eliminated and, with the latter, negative influences from the world could be kept at bay. During my last week of fieldwork, Abraham was dedicated to the task of finding like-minded people (mainly Mennonites, but he was also open to others) that would join him in his endeavour.

At the end of our interview, Thomas asked for my professional opinion and advice on the project. I was surprised at the request, but could not refuse. I pointed out three issues that I thought should be taken into account: first regarding the stages of the domestic cycle of the families to be settled, which would have a direct effect on the possibilities and limits of the economic success; second, that the long term sustainability of the project depended to a great extent on the matching of the demographic growth (which considering the Christian rejection of family planning would inevitably be high) with either constant land acquisition, by increasing productivity, or by being prepared to eventually expel people. Third, I pointed out that the issue of the prevalence of man made rules (something which Abraham was criticizing in the colonies), would eventually crop up. He agreed on the diagnosis and his immediate thoughts were the negative aspects of large demographic growth, and that the demographic composition was something that had not yet been discussed. He started getting worried that selection of candidates had apparently been so far based solely on ideological agreement with the project. Regarding my last commentary regarding the establishments of rules in the new settlement, he pointed out it was the "eternal problem in the transmutation from critique, to the making of concrete projects." I left Bolivia the following week, and was unable to track down the progress of the project.

Interpreting the world and the Word

Sergio wrote several treatises, but two of them are of special importance here. On the one hand, conflict arose within the colonies when they were translated into German and distributed among the Mennonites. On the other hand, because they contain Sergio's interpretation of what a true Christian church should be, and how he sees the world through his interpretation of the symbols in the Book of Revelation. They therefore form alternative imaginations of the future which some Mennonites adopted as their own (and that the Old Colony authorities tried to suppress).

The Church of God

Sergio's essay "The Church of God: How and for what purpose the Lord wishes me to live in this world" is divided in two parts. The first one, entitled "The Church of God and Ecology" where he puts forward a theologically derived green argument, and "The simple and crucified life of the church" where he gives general guidelines on the principles that should be followed by the true Christian church.

The first part starts with an exemplification of the things that some Amish, Baptist, and other Christian groups *do not do* that harm the natural environment.

> They do not use tractors, engines and similar machinery and therefore they do not toil large extensions of land, neither do they uncontrollably deforest the bush, therefore avoiding the destruction of forest on a large scale with the consequential and irreparable desertification and disappearance of fauna and flora...By not using engines, aerosols, refrigerators and gas, they avoid the pollution of the air and the destruction of the ozone layer...By not using hydroelectric energy, they avoid the construction of dams with their terrible consequences for the flora and fauna...through the breakage of their delicate biological cycles and equilibriums...

Because the exemplification is done in a negative way, Sergio puts into practice a process of construction of the "other," and implicitly inviting the reader to think from whom is he separating them from. By taking into the account the contents of mentioned practices, it becomes clear that the reference groups from which they are being distinguished are the modern world, and the Mennonites (while at the same time collapsing the latter with the former in their simultaneous opposition to the praised 'not doers'). The more direct references to the Mennonites come at the end of the second part, where the first person in the plural is used: "We say we live separate from the world, from its craziness and inventions," and followed by a reference to "colonies with 2000 to 5000 inhabitants." Therefore suggesting both, that he considers himself a Mennonite, and that the Mennonites are his intended readership.

Sergio's next step is to establish the biblical foundations for the avoidance of the destruction of the earth. He shows that the process has been prophesised (Isa. 24:4–6; Hos. 4:1–3; Rev. 11:18). In the case of the first two biblical quotations, the destruction of the environment seems to be a God-sent punishment for the breaking of the covenant. In the quotation from the book of Rev. (11:18) the causality is reversed; punishment is due when men proceed to the destruction of the earth, but Sergio does not identify this contrast, which would have led him to recognize the existence of contradictory principles for the causation of natural disasters within the Bible. Having stated the prophecies (and shown that they were indeed being fulfilled in the present) Sergio proceeds to justify the conservation of nature in Neotestamentarian terms, that is, that the true Christian church should follow the example of Christ, and part of that example relates to the not harming of the earth nor any part of God's creation.

> Jesus Christ still lives on earth (Mt. 28:20, Jn. 14:18). He has resurrected, and standing on the right hand side of the Father, inhabits the hearts of men through the Holy Spirit that He has given (to those who believe in Him and in the Word of His Father. Jn. 14:16–23). He lives in his church, which is His body (Eph. 1:22,23; Col. 1:18), and He works through it (Phil. 2:13; Gal. 2:20; Heb. 13:20,21), and He cannot do anything bad (Job 34:10,12) neither to men, to animals, to any part of the creation.

It follows that those who do harm God's creation cannot be considered Christian. Sergio does not explicitly link this consequence with the definition of groups made earlier, but it does come through very clearly: the Mennonite colonies can no longer be considered Christian because they harm the environment. There is a widespread concern in Santa Cruz, and to a much lesser extent in La Pampa, about the ecological soundness of the Mennonite's agricultural practices. In Santa Cruz, it is their apparently indiscriminate clearing of the forest and its transformation into arable land, in La Pampa, it is because of their use of a type of plough that facilitates desertification.

The second part, "The simple and crucified life of the church" starts with the biblical foundation of Jesus Christ as an exemplar to be followed if a church claims to be Christian. Jesus and the apostles' words are to be abided by, and their deeds to be emulated, which include the conversion of the unfaithful, the spreading of the gospel, poverty, suffering, and the washing of feet.[6] He quotes several biblical passages that support each one of these positions. It is important to note that with the exception of suffering and poverty, which are difficult to measure conclusively and are subject to interpretation, the Mennonites do not conform to the rest of the commanded practices.

That Sergio's expected readership consists of Mennonites is also suggested in his choosing of Menno Simons as guidance in the identification of the Church of Christ. Especially his focus on the "Reply to Gellius Faber" (Simons 1983b: 77) (already explored in Chapter 2), where the signs for the identification of the true church from that of the anti-Christ are given. Sergio claims that some (without mentioning the colonies, but some Mennonites have made this point to me) understand that the spreading of the gospel was a task given only to the apostles, together with the washing of the feet, and the charismatic gifts. In contrast, Sergio argues that this has the same degree of biblical backing as baptism, excommunication and the Lord's Supper, which the Mennonites do in fact practice. In this way, he agrees with Abraham on the biblical selectivity within the Old Colony. After calling for a revision and change of these issues, Sergio foresees some possible objections Mennonites would give him, and attempts to defuse them in advance. The first one is a fusion of the genealogical argument that claims spiritual descent from David (the King of Israel), and that of race and custom.

> The son of a son of God is not God's son automatically (despite wearing the same clothes, speaking the same language, and keeping the same books in the house). He must also be born again, and do Godly deeds. In this matter, the usage of names is useless. The sons of God are not born of flesh, blood, or tradition, but of God (Jn. 1:12,13;1 Pet. 1:22–25) and by the power of His Word...The flesh, the blood, the colour, the language, customs, for Him, in His very presence, they are nothing.

---

[6] 1 Jn. 2:6; Eph. 5:1,2; 1 Cor. 1:11; Phil. 3:17; Acts 10:38.

Here Sergio is implicitly accusing the Old Colony for racializing and traditionalizing the notion of Christianity. In short, neither nature nor culture can provide salvation, only individual conversion and faith.[7]

In one of the latest paragraphs, Sergio addresses the issue of the separation of the world, claiming that the colonies are no longer separate, despite them believing so.

> How can we live separate from the world when we are dependent on its fuels, on its repair parts, on its batteries, on its gas, on its electrical machinery, on its tractors, on its fertilizers.

In a nutshell, that the separation of the world is impossible with economical interdependency. Since the mark of the Beast will be implemented shortly, and without it, buying and selling would be impossible, absolute self-sufficiency is necessary for resisting its imposition, and continuing to be Christians.

The Beasts of the Book of Revelation

It is now time to explore another of Sergio's treatises "The Beasts of the Book of Revelation, Chapter 13: Their Identification." Here, in a manner similar to Abraham, Sergio attempts to situate both world history and the current state of the world within the prophetic biblical narrative. Sergio's starting point is that the key to interpreting the Book of Revelation and its symbols lie in the rest of the Bible. He makes a list of the different symbols appearing in chapter thirteen of the Book of Revelation, and searches for their meaning in the rest of the Bible (see Table 4).

After establishing his main exegetic key, he proceeds to decoding the text, while also taking into account historical events. His first task is the identification of the "Beast that came from the sea." He claims that there has been only one power in world history that satisfies the characteristics set forth in chapter thirteen: a) raising its power after the Greek Empire, b) with its capital city edified over seven hills, c) boasting world-wide power, d) its city would dominate in time of John, d) it would persecute and kill Christians, e) it would temporarily lose its power (in 1798) and would recover it afterwards (1929 with the treatise of Letran), f) and would join, at the end of time with the most

---

[7] A similar passage is used by Charismatics in the US, but for arguing that children must establish their own unmediated connection with God (Csordas 1997: 184).

Table 4: Sergio's exegetical key

Symbol	Meaning	Source of meaning
Beast	Kingdom, Empire, World Power	Dan. 7:23
Sea	Peoples, masses, nations, languages	Rev. 17:15
Horns	Powers, kings	Lk. 1: 68; Rev. 17:12
Heads	Mounts, kingdoms	Rev. 17:9
Crowns	Royal attributes	2 Kings 11:12; Heb. 2:7–9
Leopard, Bear and Lion	Characteristics of the three kingdoms prophesised by Daniel (Greek, Medo-Persian, Babylonian)	Dan. 7
Dragon	Satan	Rev. 12:9
Deadly wound	The defeat of a kingdom or the losing of its power	Dan. 8:7, 19–21; Isa. 1:6, 14:5, 14:6, 24:12
Healed wound	A kingdom being re-established	Isa. 30:26; Jer. 10:17–19, 30:10–18; Hos. 5:13
Sacrificed lamb	The Son of God, Jesus Christ	Jn. 1:29; Rev. 5:5–9
To rise from the earth	As opposed to a kingdom that rises from the waters, this is one that is brought to being on a space not previously occupied by other peoples and kingdoms and that does not resort to them for its organization	Rev. 13:11; 12:6,14,16; 17:15
Horns like those of a lamb	Exterior appearance of righteousness, of love of justice and fearfulness of God	Mt. 7:15; Acts 20:29
To speak like a serpent	Despite righteous appearance, to show its true evil personality	Prov. 10:32; Mt. 12:34
Image	Copy, representation	Ex. 20:4; Deut. 4:15–18; Ps. 106:19,20; Ez. 8:10; 23:14; Mk. 12:16; Rom. 1:23
To infuse breath	To give life and movement	Gen. 2:7; Ez. 37:1–10; Rev. 11:11,12
The number of a name	The total of the sum of the numeric values of each of the letters that compose a name	

powerful empire. "That power is the Roman-Papal Empire." Since from Medieval times, it has been a recurrent topic for Christian dissenters and reformists to identify the Pope as the Beast (Boyer 1992: 274). In addition to this historical interpretation, Sergio reproduces several systems that, when counting the values of the letters of the different appellatives of the Pope, add up to 666.

The other Beast, the one that came from the earth is for Sergio, the US. The characteristics of this Beast (or empire) are: a) It would not be built over the remains of a previous, conquered empire (indigenous populations are dismissed on the basis that there was no *traslatio imperii* between the indigenous populations and the pilgrims of the thirteen colonies, and that its organization was not based on the previous one); b) would not fall until the end of time; c) will have a relatively short period of existence; d) would exert world power in the presence of the first Beast; e) would help re-establish the power of the first Beast and would join it; f) together, would have enough power to establish a new politico, economic, religious order that would reach all corners of the earth.

Sergio claims that the alliance between the US and the Vatican was established during Pope John Paul II's visit to America in the 1990s and was received by its president, Bill Clinton.

> This alliance was not with king or president of a nation, but a pact with the bishop of a religion. Therefore, since the 90s the most powerful country in the world has an official religion: Roman Catholicism. From then onwards an empire in which state and church are united is dominating the world.

Sergio's writings confirm Faubion's suggestion that:

> [T]he affinities between millenarianism and the theorization of conspiracy are intimate and enduring. Millennialism may regularly offer a theodicy for which the most cynical theory of conspiracy fails to provide even a functional equivalent [...] Millennialism may proffer a philosophy of the historical process while the theory of conspiracy merely proffers piecemeal empirical speculation (1999: 379).

This new unification of Church and State forms the basis for it being an *image* of the first Beast, and paves the way for the repetition of persecution on the basis of consciousness and religion. The history of the Mennonites, which parallels the constitution of the national order of things, ends with the consolidation of a single world power, with a single religion which persecutes the true Christians.

Conclusion: alternative imaginations

In this chapter, I have set out to approach Abraham and Sergio's writings as vehicles for the promotion of social change. Throughout, I have shown their strategies for identifying the situation in the Old Colonies as identical with what they were supposed to be shunning: evil, modernity and the state. The most important one being the use of sources such as the Bible, *Martyrs' Mirror,* and Menno Simons' work, which the Old Colony accepts as both sources of authority and as foundational texts, which provide the legitimation of the existent order. By bringing to the foreground discrepancies between these texts and the reality they see in the Old Colony, Abraham and Sergio accuse them of having left the Christian path. These discrepancies include the definition of Christianity, the use of authority, and the relationship towards the world. In this way, Abraham and Sergio's writings become the foundational texts for a new imagination of the future, based on their interpretations of how the Christian community was in the time of the apostles as described in the New Testament.

One of the lessons from the diverse range of original times and places for millenarist groups is that almost any situation can be made to fit with prophecies for the end of time, and especially biblical ones (although periods of sudden change, crisis, and of suffering seem especially propitious). This versatility of the Book of Revelation, is therefore exploited as a strategy for giving urgency to the call for change, by bringing judgement day closer to the present. This sense of urgency for the needed change contributes to strengthen the appeal of the alternative and transcendental projects to construct a new social order, posing them as attempts towards restoring the principles laid out in the Bible, and the way to Christianity and Salvation. What these apocalyptic interpretations show, at least in the fact that they have been accepted by some colonists, is that the limits of the Old Colony are not the limits of their world. Furthermore, they can be read as a continuation or even mimesis of the historical relationship between Mennonites, states and modernity. Through the unification of church and state into one single government and economy, with hearts bound to material possessions, with economic dependence, and unable to trade without the Mark of the Beast, the Devil has launched a multiple pronged attack on humanity. It is in this way that nationality, microchips and barcodes are different aspects through which the body of the Mennonites becomes subject of the state and technology. Modernity and the state share the same telos: the unification into a single apparatus of capture that, through the control and appropriation of bodies, minds and affections of the Mennonites (and the rest of humanity), would lead them away from Christ into eternal death, all this with the connivance of the *Leardeenst*.

Sergio's challenges to the Old Order orthodoxy sparked a number of conflicts when his texts were disseminated (at the time of research, Abraham was distributing his work very selectively, and had not been read by any member of the *Leardeenst*). In the next chapter, I will show how the main strategy of the *Leardeenst* has been to silence these views, and altering their purported rules for dealing with dissent, which would have aided the dissenters in spreading their critique.

CHAPTER SEVEN

THE HANDLING OF DISSENTERS

> Beliefs are most clearly and systematically articulated when they are formed *via negativa*. The boundaries of what is true and acceptable are marked out through a systematic identification of what is false and unacceptable. What people do not believe is often more clearly defined than what they do believe, and it is through battles with heresies and heretics that orthodoxy is most sharply delineated. (Kurtz 1983: 1085)
>
> The existence of an orthodoxy is an invitation to seek alternatives. (Goody 1986: 22)

Introduction

In this chapter, I focus on the 'battle with heresies' that was sparked by the spread of Sergio's ideas within the colonies. Through the biographic perspective of two individuals (Bernard and Benjamin) who supported and disseminated Sergio's ideas, this chapter examines the process by which the *Leardeenst* attempted to maintain control over dissent and heresy. I show that the *Leardeenst* avoided the Old Colony's excommunication process, which through the open exposition of the allegedly reproachable conducts, would have contributed to the spread of the dissenters' ideas; instead, they attempted to silence the dissenters by either ostracizing them, or by forcing them to leave the colony. Thus, this situation points to two separate, but related issues. On the one hand, the emergence of dissent and heresy in opposition to the established order, orthodoxy and orthopraxis. On the other, the avoidance, redefinition, and modification of the excommunication process in order to maintain orthodoxy.

Michael Angrosino argues that it is the typicality of the life story in relation to its social context that allows its usage in anthropology; even if the individual is an extraordinary one, whose remarkability lies in the "fulfilment of a culture's highest expectations, it can be seen as a sort of 'typical personality' writ large" (1976: 134–5). Here I consider the opposite approach, focusing instead on individuals who are not only atypical, but considered deviant, an approach based on Emile Durkheim (1962) and Kai Erikson's (1966) work. In Erikson's words, deviance is:

> conduct which the people of a group consider so dangerous, or embarrassing or irritating that they bring special sanctions to bear against the persons who exhibit it. Deviance is not a property *inherent in* any particular kind of behaviour; it is a property *conferred upon* that behaviour by the people who come into direct or indirect contact with it. The only way an observer can tell whether or not a given style of behaviour is deviant, then, is to learn something about the standards of the audience which responds to it. (1966: 6, emphasis in original)

The position I take here is not the classical functionalist argument that deviance provides an opportunity for the system to reinforce itself, but one that considers it as a methodological standpoint for the elicitation of the norms. If (reverting Erikson's argument) we start with the 'native' labelling of certain beliefs and conducts as deviant, then we can learn about the norms that have been broken, even if they have not yet found an explicit discursive formulation. The benefit (and also, limitation) of this approach is that it is only able to shed light on the norms that are actually active (irrespective of having been previously revealed), and which have been perceived as broken or transgressed. Furthermore, and as Erikson demonstrates, it was through this very process that the New England colonists found a way of eliciting their own beliefs (1966). In this way, it is possible to grasp the process of contestation and enforcement of competing imaginations of the future by focusing on how different configurations of beliefs and practices are either promoted as challengers of the established order, or concomitantly, being excluded from it by its deviant labelling and attempts at their exclusion. Bernard and Benjamin's deviant status arises from the Mennonite's negative evaluation of their behaviours, evidenced by the existence of reproach or punishment, which simultaneously serves as an indicator to the researcher of the existence of a norm that has been perceived to have been breached. Therefore, it is precisely in their *atypicality* and in their deviant status that through their own ideas and practices, Benjamin and Bernard provide a perspective that shows some of the limits of allowed behaviour and belief of the Old Colony, or, in other words, the limits of the dominant imagination of the future as applied to the present.

The second issue that this chapter deals with is the use, or rather the avoidance of the excommunication process within the Old Colony.

This avoidance of the excommunication process, I suggest here, has its roots in the recognition by the *Leardeenst* of the dangers and limits of excommunication as a tool for social control. On the one hand, the procedure of excommunication would have contributed to the dissemination of the dissenters' ideas. Indeed, a recurrent topic during my conversations with Mennonites regarding their history has been the way in which the martyrdom of heretics during the sixteenth century aided in the diffusion of Anabaptists beliefs. On the other hand, as Kniss points out, a crucial feature of religious conflict is the relative lack of commensurability and fungibility of the ideas and symbols at stake, which makes compromise an almost impossible task (1997: 134 and ff.). In this situation, openly acknowledging the existence of dissent would have forced the *Leardeenst* to only two courses of action: excommunicating the dissenters, or the acceptance of the new ideas. I argue that in an attempt to avoid social change within the colonies, those in charge of administering the excommunication process have circumvented it, redefining the rules of the game as it was being played. They were forced to do so by the contradiction between two principles that are common to protestant groups: on the one hand, the establishment and continuity of the Body of Christ on earth, the church, which requires the institutionalization and consolidation of a body of ideas and beliefs, the building of an orthodoxy and an appropriate orthopraxis. On the other hand, the principles of free examination and *sola scriptura*, comprising the individual reading and interpretation of the Bible that open the floodgates of heterodoxy and the biblical legitimation of new practices.[1] In other words, how to maintain and continue reproducing an established and consolidated moral order and imagination of the future where one of its principles allows the generation of alternative imaginations and orders. While the *Leardeenst* had to choose between these two principles, Bernard and Benjamin had to bear the burden of the decision. In this chapter I trace, through a biographical perspective, the way in which religious ideas were disseminated and appropriated by Bernard and Benjamin, and their experience of treading on the margins of Old Colony orthodoxy and orthopraxis.

---

[1] This is the classic sociological argument of the church-sect cycle (Weber 1946; Wilson 1967, 1981).

Translations and transgressions

Benjamin was born in 1970 in Colonia Norte, and one year later moved with his parents to Capulín colony (both in Mexico) following the *eltesta* and a group of *prädjasch* that decided to leave because of the modernization process that was taking place in the colony. His father died of a brain tumour in 1978, and the following year his mother remarried. They left Capulín in 1986 in order to join La Nueva Esperanza, in Argentina, where he got baptised and, after two years of courting, married one of the *eltesta's* daughters.[2] Benjamin did not consider his baptism as producing much of a change in his life as he claimed he kept on smoking, drinking, and was only thinking about making money. The "great change," as Benjamin himself called it, was a product of his meeting with Sergio, in 1998. They had already met briefly during Sergio's previous visit, but this time, Benjamin had invited him to his house. According to Benjamin, he picked Sergio and his daughters up from Abraham's house and, while on the *bogge*, Sergio indicated to one of his daughters that the wheat was ripe for harvesting, and to separate the wheat that should be saved from the chaff that should be burned. It was an analogy taken from the Bible, one that has been repeatedly used by postmillennialists since it urges believers to prepare the ground for Christ's second coming (see Robbins and Palmer 1997). Retrospectively, those words were not aimed at her, but at Benjamin. Afterwards, when they arrived at Benjamin's place, Sergio started:

> So, here it is, you have your house, you have your cows, your bales, your tractor, but we are going to talk about something more important, we are going to talk about our lives, of what is going to happen to us after this life.

Sergio then started to hammer the missionary message of the Bible, Menno Simons' active position in the spreading of the Gospel, and reflecting on stories from the *Martyrs' Mirror*. Afterwards, Sergio gave his testimony. Benjamin remembered his emotions at the moment, evidencing the power of the Word, and of witnessing in producing change in those who listen to it (Harding 1987):

---

[2] The *eltesta* who was removed from his position after the Malatesta incident; see Chapter 4.

> My heart was burning, because he spoke of the love of Jesus, and of accepting him inside each one's heart. Not in traditions or customs, but personally, within one's heart. The majority of us wrongly believe that we are God's people, the elected people, the Christians, they carry their clothes and think that with that is enough to become the light of the world.

From that day onwards, Benjamin considers Sergio as a "brother in Christ." Benjamin then started reading the Bible, Menno Simons' works, and the *Martyrs' Mirror*. He claimed that he discovered, during this process of reading and discussing with Sergio, that he had previously believed in things that were either wrong or of no importance: that the Mennonites were Israelites, and that the only way of being a Christian was to live in a colony. These changes show not only the adoption of a definition of Christianity that differs from the one held by the Old Colony (spiritual kinship instead of descent and custom based one), but of a differing interpretation of the role of Mennonites in the world, from one of separation towards one of example and leadership towards Christ.

The adoption of this new definition of Christianity also triggered a process of self-examination: Benjamin started doubting about the truthfulness and validity of his own baptism since it was not done out of a desire to follow God's will.

> Going to church every Sunday, getting baptised, attending the Lord's Supper, and then going back home, and living a tranquil life, without much further reflection. Outside ceremonies have no value for God if they are not simultaneously carried within your heart. You have to have a clean heart, follow his will. You have to follow everything that Jesus taught, not just a few things.

The seeds of doubt had been planted, and the trip towards heresy was initiated. The process of internal self-examination was followed by a revision of the Old Colony in the light of his new findings. As a result of his revision of Old Colony beliefs and practices, he discovered "certain things" (as Benjamin called them) that had been left out in the colonies. One of these was the washing of each other's feet. This practice was revived each time they met with Sergio and Bernard. "Until the next foot washing" was the salutatory formula with which they ended each communication in their heavy epistolary exchange, and wholeheartedly accepted my joking label of them as the 'feet-washers' after my refusals to their repeated attempts at handling my feet. Another important issue was the spreading of the Gospel, and becoming a witness of Christ. After reading my undergraduate thesis, and referring to my first meeting with members of the *Leardeenst*, Benjamin told me it was a sad fact that, taking into account my interest in their beliefs, none of the members of the *Leardeenst* offered me a New Testament, nor attempted to teach me their faith. Instead, they had focused on the weather, taxation, the schooling issue, and business matters, thus demonstrating their preference for worldly instead of spiritual matters.

During an interview with Benjamin, we started talking about the *Martyrs' Mirror*, of how he used it in times of hardship to console himself, and during good times in order not to forget where his path was. As with Abraham, the topic of persecution arose:

> We are not being persecuted anymore. Maybe in some countries they want to impose the school and language on us, but not everywhere. So from the outside, there is no more persecution towards the Mennonites.

Benjamin left this sentence hanging, with a deep silence. His words were carefully phrased, in order to suggest he knew what I was interested in, that I already knew, but I had to make it explicit. "So, the Mennonites are no longer persecuted, but persecution exists..." I replied. We were luring each other, to see who would be the first to tread on the topic that both wanted to talk about, but none dared to start. I made a first attempt by asking him his opinion on the internal situation in the colonies. Benjamin told me that spiritual life had cooled down. After querying him further, he referred to the refusal to accept Sergio for not being "one of us, German. And those who were with him, are seen as if they had changed as if they were looking for something new." We were getting closer. First emphasizing the absence of persecution from the outside, without denying the existence of persecution, then the suggestion that the victims were the ones who had been in contact with Sergio, there was one more step to be taken. I had heard the story: both Sergio and Bernard had already told me, but I wanted a first hand version. Suddenly I remembered that on previous occasions he had refused to speak about himself: "I don't want to become proud, and make myself bigger." Therefore, I asked him in the third person, if he could tell me about the Mennonite who had to leave the colony in Argentina. We both knew the other person was Benjamin himself, and following my prompt, he started to tell it in the third person, as if it had indeed happened to somebody else.

Letters to the Mennonites

After he had gone to Bolivia, Sergio wrote letters to several of his friends in the colonies sending "The Church of God" to Benjamin, and later, "The Beasts of the Book of Revelation" to Bernard.

> In these letters he was showing the errors that Mennonites were making, and there was not a single word in those letters that was not backed up by a verse in the New Testament, or by resorting to other books such as Menno Simons' works or the *Martyrs' Mirror*.

That is, Sergio had written to them using only the books recognized as canonical by the Mennonites themselves, and succeeded in establishing its biblicality. To the power of the text in itself, it successfully incorporated canonical authority. Furthermore, his essays were referred to as 'letters'. When Benjamin told me that the life story of Sergio I was writing should be entitled "Acts 29" (as a new chapter of the neotestamentarian book of Acts which consists of twenty eight chapters) it became clear that by referring to the essays as 'letters' they were being considered in a manner similar to those written by the Apostle Paul.

Benjamin, without asking for consent from the author, translated "The Church of God," photocopied and distributed the copies within the colony, thinking that it was a good idea in order to awaken the faith in Christ. He even gave it to a *prädja* who had been a close friend of Sergio, and supportive of him. This *prädja* gave the letter to the newly appointed *eltesta*, who summoned Benjamin immediately and said to him:

> A *Weltmensch* wrote you a letter and you translated it and then spread it in the colonies. You have to retrieve all the copies, and not give it to anybody else, otherwise, it will cause trouble in the colonies. There is no way out other than retrieving them so that nobody else can read them.

Benjamin refused to collect the letters, until it was proven to him that the letter was wrong, and (as I heard from another source) even suggested leaving the colony without retrieving them. The *eltesta* then threatened him with not giving the required letter of transference in order to be accepted in another Mennonite colony. Benjamin had to return five times to the *eltesta*'s house, because another Mennonite would refuse to return the letters, on the basis that it was a constructive and Christian piece of writing, and also wanted the *eltesta* to explain what was wrong with it. Upon hearing about the possibility of Benjamin's punishment, he returned the letter to Benjamin, but only after making photocopies for himself and his sons. They were expecting a biblical refutation by the *eltesta*, or if there was no conflict between the letter and the Scriptures and the other canonical books, they wished to retain it as any other type of literature. The *eltesta's* reply was harsh and disappointing for them: "There is nothing wrong with the letter, but we do not need a *Weltmensch* to teach us on these topics. We already have those books in our houses, that is enough." For the *eltesta*, there was obviously something wrong with the letter, but by denying it, he silenced the discussion and at the same time made the case stronger that his objection was its authorship. It is important to remember here the derogatoriness of the term *Weltmensch*. Literally meaning 'worldly man' but, in this context, laden with heavy undertones of sinfulness, evil, cunning, etc. In short, it stands in opposition to all that is Godly, Christian, and virtuous. The term is also used to refer to anybody that is not a Mennonite, such as *Mexa* (Mexican) and *Ejebuare* (indigenous people). Whether or not the *eltesta* had intended to insult Sergio, using the term in its 'non-mennonite' definition, is something I do not know. Nevertheless, Benjamin interpreted it in its religious meaning in order, not only to make his point regarding Sergio's standing, but because it was in accordance with the notions of Christianity within the letter that he had adopted. As such, in an attempt to defend his friend, and to debunk the *eltesta's* ad-hominem statement, Benjamin asked what was worldly about Sergio, because, according to Benjamin: "Sergio lived a Christian life, with his faith, his deeds, even more separate and backwards than the Mennonites." Benjamin also compared Sergio with the Apostle Paul, who was even a persecutor of Christians before his conversion. If Paul changed from one extreme to the other, why could Sergio not? It was not only a matter of where Sergio belonged, but that of the definition of the most basic categories, 'us' and 'them'; in short, of what made a person a Christian and a Mennonite, if by birth and blood or by faith and practice. Although at this point this distinction is no longer religious, but political (Schmitt 1996). Furthermore, as shown in the previous chapter, this issue was part of the content of the letter itself. The discussion of the exclusion/inclusion of Sergio was therefore one that attempted to redefine the political constitution of the Old Colony (albeit through the use of religious idiom). This redefinition might have led to the questioning or even subversion of the *Leardeenst's* legitimacy. The *eltesta's* answer, which attempted to safeguard and reinforce his position of authority, remained on the same tone: "we do not need to discuss this." Benjamin had not been summoned for a discussion of either Sergio's religiosity, or biblical hermeneutics; he had been summoned to obey. Furthermore, Benjamin was explicitly forbidden to "open the Bible with non-Mennonites." In such a way, the *eltesta* was using his office-based authority for closing down avenues for the emergence of dissenting biblical interpretations that were threatening to undermine his own position.

It should be added that during the period of this incident, several Mennonite families had decided to go to Bolivia, anticipating an unhappy ending on the schooling issue. The *eltesta* had obtained his position after his predecessor's involvement in the Malatesta case, which had cost him his office. A minor group, which was formed by Jacob and his extended family, including a *prädja* (married to one of Jacob's daughters) had additional reasons besides the schooling issue.[3] Besides a general disagreement over the way the colony was being managed, they disagreed on the demise of the previous *eltesta*, and they wanted to accept Sergio within the colony. Unlike most of the other émigrés to Bolivia, they did not want to join an existing colony, but rather to form their own—although maintaining official association with the Old Colony. They already had a *prädja* to lead them, and the old *eltesta*, who would be reinstated as such in the new settlement. During my fieldwork, they were living in Pinondi colony, from where they were prospecting for suitable land for their project.

It was also mentioned that after the Malatesta incident the members of the family of the former *eltesta* were being heavily scrutinized and were the major target of gossip (as well as those that had befriended Sergio). Benjamin fell into both categories and, within this context, in addition to his own differences with the new *eltesta* he also decided to leave for Pinondi colony, where not only his mother and stepfather had moved there some time before, but also where Jacob and his family had just gone.

When moving between colonies, it is necessary to obtain two letters. One, from the *fäaschta*, who certifies the debt situation of the individual; the other, from the *eltesta*, is an evaluation of the individual in religious terms which proves that the person involved is a member in good standing, and their acceptance in another colony recommended.

---

[3] It is unusual for a *Prädja* to leave the colony where he had been elected without being a formal schismatic separation, or following his constituency.

When Benjamin left La Nueva Esperanza towards Pinondi, he had only secured the first letter. Benjamin explained his situation to the *eltesta* in Pinondi, and was temporarily accepted, although he was required to produce the letter of transference within a certain period. This put him in a liminal (Turner 1995) situation since he was neither excommunicated, nor recommended for acceptance in another colony. Without proof of his good standing or his having been excommunicated, he was neither in or out, but betwixt and between. When Benjamin went back to Argentina to secure his letter of transference, the *eltesta* initially refused claiming that Benjamin had treated him with disrespect and lack of love. Apparently, the discussion had been on stronger terms than those conveyed to me by Benjamin himself. Furthermore, he had committed an act of insubordination in asking the *eltesta* for the copy of Sergio's essay that the *prädja* gave him. Apparently, Benjamin, in a pedantic tone, said to the *eltesta*: "I have come to collect the copy of the letter, as you ordered me to do," obtaining as an answer that that copy would not be returned but kept, and later analysed with the *Leardeenst* of different colonies. Benjamin was told to repent, and returned empty handed to Pinondi, with a promise to receive his letter shortly. He was still waiting for it the last time I saw him.

The *eltesta* in La Nueva Esperanza had to move carefully due to his contested legitimacy, which combined with the unrest within the colony after the schooling issue, the Malatesta case, Sergio, and the contingents that slowly but steadily were leaving towards Bolivia (and some others who eventually made a new colony in the Argentine province of Santiago del Estero). This made the situation a delicate one. His dealing with Benjamin was an act towards the consolidation of authority, sending a signal to any other possible dissenters to refrain from voicing their views. The effect went further, since those who shared Benjamin's ideas perceived the *eltesta's* manipulation of the excommunication process. This, in turn, gave them further reasons to vote with their feet, leaving for Bolivia. No formal schism occurred, dissent was silenced and externalized, and the problem was transferred to Pinondi colony, in Bolivia. In Pinondi, Benjamin's chances of success were reduced by a combination of factors. On the one hand, because he would not have a ready made network of support, and would have to build it from scratch. This would in turn be made more difficult by the widespread knowledge of his previous conflict. On the other hand, not only was the *eltesta* of Pinondi in an uncontested position, but Benjamin's lack of letter of transfer meant that he could be stripped of his temporary membership at any moment. In refusing Benjamin his letter, the *eltesta* of La Nueva Esperanza not only avoided the process of excommunication himself, but also freed his peers too, by providing them with a ready-made reason for non-acceptance in the slightest event of non-compliance.

Blessing as disguise

One day Benjamin told me that he had just been appointed as teacher in one of the schools in the Pinondi colony. They needed a teacher and Benjamin's stepfather recommended him for the post. This news surprised me because I thought his unsolved membership position within the colony seemed to clash with the responsibilities involved. I speculated that it could have been his scriptural abilities and his degree of literacy, which were indeed much higher than the Mennonite average, which were the reasons behind his appointment. It was later that I discovered how wrong I was. For a couple of months we had been trying to organize a joint trip to visit Sergio, but the agricultural calendar was on the way, and we had to wait.[4] One day, while I was visiting Martin (Franz's brother) who lives in Swift Current, he told me that Benjamin wanted to get back in touch with me as soon as possible. Martin had already arranged to telephone Jacob in Pinondi the following day (who would be waiting for the call in the call shop in town), so I asked him if he would pass a message to Benjamin to call me as soon as he could. When we talked on the telephone, Benjamin said he was ready to go, and that that weekend was his last chance to visit Sergio because the school period was starting. I would take the next train from Santa Cruz towards Yacuiba, and he would join me in Charagua station. When I met him at the station, he told me he could not come with me, since his stepfather did not want him to go. "Mennonites can go wherever they want, but for me, there is a small plot of land in Tarija that has been forbidden." This, together with the telephone conversation we had had a few days before, and with the knowledge I had on Bernard's situation (see below) made me realize what was really going on.

---

[4] Not only did we enjoy each other's company, which would have made the three-day long trip to Sergio's more bearable, but I had found that many Mennonites found it easier to speak freely when outside the colony and there were no other fellow colonists around.

As a teacher, Benjamin received land, housing, a salary, and free water.[5] The teaching schedule, with classes both in the morning and in the afternoon, meant that there was little spare time to receive and make visits. Because he was living in a house that was not his, but colony property, he was not as free to receive visitors as if he would have had his own; especially for receiving those from the outside of the colony who would have required overnight stays. He was also having his movements restricted. Since he had to teach six days a week, he was virtually confined to the colony, as the only day left was Sunday, when he had to attend church, and being the Lord's day, no kind of work is permissible. Since the only valid reasons for leaving the colony are either visiting other colonies, going to Hospital, doing necessary paperwork, or conducting business, he had no way to leave the colony on a Sunday, except in case of a medical emergency. Furthermore, having to teach from the scriptures meant that other members could check any deviations from the established interpretations by asking the children what they were being taught. What I had originally thought was a sign of trust and responsibility, was in fact something akin to house arrest. The control was both physical and ideological, with the twist that it was presented as a generous opportunity, and the controllers as benefactors. In this way, a sort of internal ostracism and intensification of social control was added to his precarious membership status. Furthermore, being employed by the colony meant, as Bernard was to suffer later, that his means of subsistence would provide the colony authorities with another means of forcing him to comply. In the years after his appointment, his epistolary contact with Sergio, and the other dissenters has been significantly reduced.

The uninvited host

When I met Bernard for the first time, he was still living in Swift Current colony. I arrived at his house in a taxi. Upon hearing the engine, a short and skinny man came out from the co-operative store, just a few metres from the house, and came to the car. With a soft and gentle voice he approached me, and as soon as I mentioned my name he told

---

[5] Due to the depth of the aquifers in Pinondi, water has to be pumped out with combustion engines. There is usually one well per *darp*, to which each household contributes to its running costs based on the basis of the amount of cattle owned.

me he was the person I was looking for, and enthusiastically asked me to unload the taxi and stay. Sergio had already spoken to him about me, but since he was still on duty at the store, he asked me to wait for him at the house until he finished. I unloaded the car and sent the taxi away. Seating on a plastic chair, I waited under his porch, making and reading my notes.

About an hour later, Bernard reappeared and I gave him the letters that Sergio had entrusted me with. Bernard brought some more chairs from inside the house, and we sat in the porch—his wife and children included. Bernard read the letters aloud to his family, simultaneously translating them from Spanish into Plautdietsch. As soon as he finished with one, he would pass it for me to read, while he would continue with his translation. One was a letter of presentation, where Sergio explained who I was and what I was doing, and urged him to receive me "as his very own brother" and to "bear witness of the faith." After reading the letters and talking for a while, I accompanied him to prepare his small stable to milk the cows. When we were done, we went back to the house. It was the smallest house I have ever seen in a colony. It comprised of a main room with a kitchen, table and benches, and a curtain to keep the shower water from spreading around. At the back there was the storage room and, on the side facing the street, another room which was divided by a curtain. The space in the room was crammed with two double beds and several cots. I was to discover later that Bernard and his wife used one of the beds, and Bernard's brother and his own wife, the other. The cots were for the children of both couples.

Since Bernard had been one of the latecomers to Bolivia (and his brother one of the last to make the move) it was almost impossible for him to buy land in the established colonies since due to its scarcity, prices had skyrocketed. Bernard had no land of his own, and his brother was in no better situation. His brother had just arrived from Mexico, with all his travelling expenses being taken care of by the colony, and was "without a single dollar in his pocket." The house where they were living was part of the benefits of Bernard's job as a store attendant, as was the small plot of land he cultivated. Bernard owned no tractors, nor any other agricultural machinery I had grown accustomed to seeing in the colonies.

After dinner I accompanied Bernard to his neighbours to borrow a bench, which he put side by side with his own, on top of this he placed a few folded blankets as makeshift mattress, and my sleeping arrangements were ready. I had the whole kitchen to myself, while the two families crammed into the other room. The next morning Bernard woke up early and asked his neighbour to cover him at the store for the day, as he had a visitor to take care of. After milking, breakfast was served, and we then proceeded to sit in the *bogge*, under the shade of a tree and with a jug of water to calm the intensive heat throughout our long conversation. As with Benjamin, the encounter with Sergio proved to be a turning point in Bernard's life. Furthermore, it carried similar consequences and conflicts to which I now turn.

Encounter with Sergio

One of the interesting aspects of Bernard's narrative is that the meeting with Sergio was a focal point. Events that otherwise could have been forgotten, were retold as early signs of what was going to happen in the future. The two most notable ones are those related to issues of faith, and the interpretation of the modern world. The first incident happened while a teenager, as he was preparing himself for baptism. Bernard was given a "Confession of Faith" in the Centro Menno, in Casas Grandes (Mexico).[6] There were two particular points that attracted his attention at the time: the washing of feet, and the search for the lost souls. Although later in the interview, when speaking about Sergio's ideas, he added two points that are central in Pentecostal groups: the anointment with oil, and the praying of the elders for the healing of the sick. Bernard went to his father to clear his doubt, and showed him what he had been reading.

> He read it, and when we met again afterwards told me "some points yes, some points we no longer practice, and there are others that we have never practiced. But why are you looking for writings from the outside? We should read the New Testament, the Gesangbuch, and that is enough." But the New Testament itself was saying these things to us.

As soon as Bernard arrived in Bolivia, Abraham gave him a book (a German summary of Kah 1978). According to Bernard, the analysis of the processes of globalization portrayed in that book, which was done

---

[6] "Centro Menno" is the preferred name for the local mission headquarters of the Mennonite Central Committee, a US-Canadian organization made of an array of different types of Mennonites but which does not include the Old Colony. In the words of one missionary of the Centro Menno in Santa Cruz, their objective (in addition to evangelize the native populations) is to "accompany" the Old Colony Mennonites in "discovering their true religion."

from a biblical perspective, acted as an invitation for him to study the Bible and reflect on the current world situation. The conclusion was that biblical prophecies were being fulfilled, and that he was living in the period prophesised in the Book of Revelation.

> So I decided to read the Bible, and I saw what was going on. The prophecies were being fulfilled, and that moved something in my heart. Then I read another book by a Sabbath keeper, a man named Jan Marcussen.[7] That one broke my heart, because he argued with the scripture that the Sabbath should be kept, and not Sunday. The seventh day, and not the first. So I got scared, we were going the wrong way by keeping Sundays. I thought of taking the book to the *eltesta*, to get his opinion, but I never did.

Bernard's memory of his father's reaction towards his previous doubt was decisive in making him keep his new doubts to himself, since he had the inkling that involving the *eltesta* would have created problems for him.

The seeds of doubt had been planted, and were awaiting, like those of grass, a storm to brew. The storm did not take long to start, Sergio appeared in the colony during December 1998, between Christmas and New Year's Eve, when Mennonites refrain from working, and have plenty of time for *spat´seare*. Bernard had heard about him, and upon seeing Sergio for the first time, invited him to his house to talk.

> We found out they were staying at Whilhelm's... We picked them up and brought them here, and after talking to Sergio for a while I realized that he was a person of faith, of a very strong faith in Jesus Christ; he was very religious. He told me about the *Martyrs' Mirror*, of things I knew and of things I was about to know. I realized that he had a good understanding of these things so I liked it... When I took him back, we continued our talk with Whilhelm, and this made me make contact with Whilhelm, and we were two. There we were, realizing that we had become brothers in the Spirit, and Sergio was the one bringing us together.

After positively evaluating Sergio's religious position, Bernard became a listener to Sergio's testimony. Unlike for the rest of the Old Colony, for whom Sergio's influence was considered divisive, for Bernard he was not only a uniting force, but also provided a different basis for the establishment of social relationships: spiritual kinship. Furthermore, the final remarks "we were two" followed by the statement on the spiritual

---

[7] Jan Marcussen, an Adventist pastor from Illinois, Bernard is probably referring to his popular *National Sunday Law* (1983).

kin bond, rings like the words of Jesus in Mt. 18:20 "For where two or three have come together in my name, I am there among them." A new sociality was in the making.

Bernard spent the rest of those holidays visiting and being visited by Sergio, speaking about the Bible, *Martyrs' Mirror*, and Menno Simons' works.

> And I started believing in all this, and since Sergio wanted to become a member of the colonies, I offered him and said to him "if you want to go and speak to the *eltesta*, I can go with you" and he accepted. So we went to the *eltesta's* house, and the *eltesta* started asking him questions, and at some point he told Sergio to look for a religion in his own language, and continued. It seemed that the *eltesta* did not want him. So that is when I jumped in. I did not want to talk there, but reaching that point, I felt I had to; Sergio had told me about his life, I knew Sergio's life, and I did not think that he was getting the answer he deserved. I knew Sergio had suffered a lot. Since the beginning of our lives, we have always slept in our own beds. So I spoke to the *eltesta* about Sergio's life. And I did it, there, in front of him. Sergio kept his mouth shut and I spoke. After this, the *eltesta* changed his opinion, and suggested we go to the other colony [Riva Palacios] and speak to the *eltesta* there too.

On this occasion the *eltesta* of Swift Current did say what the one in La Nueva Esperanza tried to avoid (see Chapter 5), although through the proxy of language, he was referring to the community of descent as a basis for membership. Bernard thought he had succeeded in convincing the *eltesta* to change his mind, but a second opinion was required, although with the caveat that it was going to be a difficult process. Bernard then asked the *eltesta* for permission for a house to be occupied by Sergio and his family. There was a vacant house in the cheese factory, and another one next to one of the churches (the house given to landless people in exchange for the keeping of the church building). The *eltesta's* initial acceptance of this idea set out the never-ending process of inconclusive answers, and the constant avoidance by each one of those consulted of making any decision. Although the *eltesta* posed no further objections, he did not accept Sergio formally, and indicated to Bernard the need for further consultation with the *schult* as to where the cheese factory would be located.

> So we came and spoke to the *schult* of the *darp* where the cheese factory was. The *eltesta* had told us that permission from the *schult* was enough. But the *schult* had a different view... He said that since the house belongs to the cooperative, permission was needed from the schulte of every *darp*

> that has a share in the factory... I realized it was going to be difficult, but the *eltesta* also suggested the church's house. We thought, we will ask the members of the *darp*, and it will be enough, everything will come out alright. We went and spoke to the schulte of the two *darpa*. One of them received us with love, treated us very nicely, and even offered a few cows if the deal was struck. But he needed to speak to another *schult* and the members of the *darp* before any decision could be made. At some point he asked us: "Have you spoken with the dia´koon?" He told us he thought it was a good idea for us to speak with the *dia´koon* first. So we came back home, hoping to speak to the *dia´koon* the following day... The following day, just before setting off to the *dia´koon's* someone came to my house and said "the members of the *darp* will not allow it." I was surprized at how they were disregarding the words of the *eltesta*. However, they said it was not going to happen. Well, I never told Sergio, he still wanted to go and speak to the *dia´koon*, so we went, but after the meeting Sergio said "I have to leave the colony."

The merry-go-round in search for the impossible brass ring of permission was finally broken. The responsibility for deciding the denial of Bernard and Sergio's request was finally diluted in the "people of the *darp*" and carried by an "anonymous" messenger. In this way, the *eltesta*, *dia´koon*, and *schulte* were spared of both, the responsibility for the decision, and the task of confronting Bernard with the bad news.

> This produced a great pain in my heart... This relationship with Sergio, we were studying together the Holy Scriptures, and I was discovering things that I could not understand before. And we heard that people were angry with those receiving him... They were seen with very bad eyes, eyes that saw badly, and tongues that spoke badly. So Sergio saw this, and decided to pull out, but we were embarked on a job. Sergio and I were writing something together, and we managed to finish it before they left. But here the members of the cooperative that own the shop once said to us "this couple, Sergio and his family they have to leave the colony, and if we cannot drive them out on their own, we will do it with the workers." They were speaking about us. They wanted to kick us out, but I decided that I would stay here for as long as possible, inviting Sergio to my house, and staying until they kicked out all of us together.

Although not everything that was going on was reported to Sergio at the time, he nevertheless understood that he was generating trouble, and left the colony. Although his absence was felt physically, his presence was to remain through an intense epistolary exchange, which would lead to the writing of a few treatises in co-authorship, and some other translations. Some of the letters from Sergio to Bernard were intercepted and read by the colony authorities before being handed over to him.

Simultaneously with Sergio's presence in the colony was also that of a group of Jehovah's Witnesses who started to proselytize, and succeeded in converting a few families. Gossip was that Jehovah's Witnesses were going around naked, and engaged in incestuous practices as well as in other kinds of 'non-human' activities.

It did not take a long time for Mennonites to build a new category, that of *Jehovah's Witness*, to include either non-Mennonites who were interested in speaking about the Bible, and fellow colonists who engaged in such discussions. In this way, by applying the libel of non-humanity, a *Jehovah's Witness* was the Old Colony idiom of referring to witchcraft (see Douglas 1991). Apparently, Jehovah's Witnesses were still actively proselytizing in the colonies during my fieldwork. From the Mennonite perspective, I was already a classificatory dilemma. The presence of Jehovah's Witnesses and Sergio did not help in my positioning as a researcher. I was soon on the edge of being considered a missionary for the Watchtower. In such a situation, I could neither visit nor check their existence and gossip about them, since it would have consolidated the suspicions of my religious affiliation, as well as endangering the standing of colony members with whom I had close relationships. Needless to say, being a *Jehovah's Witness* was considered to be engaged in a false doctrine, and therefore being an apostate to be duly excommunicated. Despite this, however, they remained physically living within the colony's boundaries. This case supports my interpretation of the transformation of the definition of Mennonite from doctrinal agreement, to the sharing of blood. Although excommunicated and converted to a different branch of christianism, they remained within the colonies, their presence accepted because of their genealogical ties.

The visitors

When Sergio went to live in Tarija, he spoke about Bernard to the Lapps, his Amish neighbours. One day, the Lapps decided to go and pay Bernard a visit on one of their trips to Santa Cruz. In addition to the Amish, a couple of Russian Christian colonists (Old Believers) coming from Brazil also befriended Sergio, and duly visited Bernard.

> I received a visit from these brothers, with whom we spoke a lot about the Scriptures and religion. I was feeling stronger in the faith, I was very happy with these new brothers. But after a few days, two *prädjasch* came here to tell me that on the Thursday meeting [*donnadach*] they had reached the agreement that I should stop receiving visits from those

people. I should stop because continuing to receive them was bound to create problems within the colony. They said that the rest of the brothers simply do not want me to do it, full-stop. I should stop receiving these people with beards and moustaches. So I told them "According to the Holy Scriptures I am obliged to accept any visits" I don't know how to say this to you exactly, but by accepting visitors, some have received angels in their homes, without knowing they were angels. But they did not want to hear. I told them "treat me with love, and convince me, with the Holy Scripture, that I am going on the wrong path and I will immediately stop doing it, but otherwise, I cannot tell my brothers not to come." But where I cannot be convinced with the Holy Scriptures, and with love, I think I should follow God instead of men. Well, they refused to refer to the Bible. They did not even mention a single word. They just said "We have come to warn you not to do it anymore." That was it, they were gone.

The matter was getting out of hand, Bernard was continuing to incorporate people into his spiritual kinship network, and the *Leardeenst* had decided to stop from the very beginning what they interpreted as the repetition of the spread of the *Jehovah's Witnesses*. The expansion of further interpretations had to be stopped as soon as possible. They did so in exactly the same fashion as with Benjamin in La Nueva Esperanza, no defense, discussion or negotiation was allowed. The party was sent to relay orders, not to discuss them.

> That same day I went to see the *eltesta*...And I explained my position on receiving visits, and he understood it all. He even agreed with me because the Holy Scriptures say it, and he told me "It is not that we had agreed that you should not receive anybody, I also receive visits. Even today, I have received visits from Europe. Religious people, and I have received them. They even left some books." The *eltesta* understood me in everything...He told me he did not see why I should completely stop receiving visits.

Despite these contradictory messages, it was clear that Bernard's persistence in receiving visits would cause him trouble, even if the *eltesta* had taken a more conciliatory approach.

In December, Bernard received the notice that from the beginning of the new year his services would no longer be needed in the store, and that he had an extra month to find himself a place to live and to vacate the house by the end of January. The matter was settled as a simple laying-off of an employee. The reasons were known to everybody, it had little to do with his performance in the store, but his receiving of people from the outside and their incorporation into his group of brothers—although no religious argumentation was given. The consequences were that Bernard, unable to pay the inflated land prices in Riva Palacios, had to move to a newly established colony (Capulín, in the southern department of Tarija), where he managed to buy 20 hectares of uncleared land, of which he lost more than half giving it away in exchange for the clearing of the remainder. Bernard's problems were not solved by his move; gossip travelled faster than he did, and he found, on his arrival, that his new neighbours were convinced that he was a *Jehovah's Witness*. The process was indeed the same as that described by Douglas (1991: 728) for the Lele of Kasai, where those accused of sorcery and banished from their settlement, carried their infamy with them wherever they went. Bernard was kept under control, and his visits had first to report to one of the *prädjasch* to ask for permission to stay at Bernard's house. When I was going through this process, the *prädja*, while granting me permission, told me to let Bernard know that if he wanted to change the lifestyle of the colony, he should leave it for good.

Meanwhile, Bernard kept in close contact with Sergio, Benjamin, and Abraham. The possibility of moving to Tarija with Sergio, always remained present. Bernard was also offered a place in Abraham and Thomas' project in Roboré. At the end of my fieldwork, he was still in the colony, growing and packing chilli peppers, and milking cows to eke out a living. A letter sent to me by Sergio, while I was writing this book, stated that Bernard, together with a couple of other Mennonite families and one from the Russian Old Believers, had settled with him in Tarija.

Conclusion: patterns in dealing with dissent

In this chapter, I have shown how, through focusing on the lives and experiences of deviants and heretics, it was possible to gain a perspective on the norms and beliefs actually at play within the Old Colony. On the one hand, Benjamin and Bernard had recognized the distance existing between the concrete actual community, and its guiding fiction. With the help of the 'letters', Benjamin and Bernard identified a series of discrepancies between the ostensive religious beliefs and practices stated in their own canonical literature that were not being followed in the Old Colony: the washing of the feet, the anointment with oil, and the spreading of the Gospel. It was an accusation that the *Leardeenst* had failed in building the future imagined by their ancestors (or, more precisely what Bernard and Benjamin thought their ancestors imagined). In addition, they were also proposing an internal, affective relationship with Jesus Christ, qualified as 'hot' in opposition to the cold, emptied, ritualized, externalized and custom-based one of the Old Colony, as well as faith as the basis of religious membership, against that of common descent.

On the other hand, it became clear that the main norm that was broken was the establishment of relationships with non-Mennonites in overt religious terms. Challenging the established (and also, imagined) way in which these relations ought to be established as well as the basic distinction between Mennonites and the others. This has been expressed by the authorities of the colonies in various forms, from direct admonishing against receiving people, to prohibitions of both reading the Bible with them, and the dissemination of literature originating from the outside. The *Leardeenst* had attempted to focus more on the origin of the texts and ideas, so as not to have to discuss the actual contents. Indeed, by framing the problem as one arising from the worldly origin of the authors of the ideas, they subsumed the conflict to a relationship between *Christenvolk* and *Weltmensch*. In this way the conflict became thoroughly political due to the resort to the friendly-enemy distinction (Schmitt 1996) although compounded by the fact that said distinction was one of the issues at stake. These cases are exemplary in showing the extent to which the *Leardeenst* had simultaneously absorbed and concealed the political under the veil of religion, controlling the main sources of reality construction, and the exercise of legitimate violence.

It is still unclear whether and how the *Leardeenst* allowed Jehovah's Witnesses to gain a foothold in the Swift Current colony (and if so why) or if it was unable to do so. In any case, they seemed to have learned from the experience and decided not to allow the story to be repeated with Bernard and his spiritual brothers. In the handling of dissent on the part of the different colony authorities, the control of the spread of ideas seems to have been the prime directive. This was achieved in a threefold way: first, by attempting to sever the links between the dissenters and their sources of ideas through the prohibitions of receiving visitors, reading the Bible with non-Mennonites, and by attempting to reduce opportunities for contact with non-Mennonites. This was a clear measure of damage control and attempt at avoiding both the consolidation of the accusations and of the alternative imagination of the future.

Second, the *Leardeenst* avoided the process of excommunication. What Bernard and Benjamin misread, was that the process of excommunication was not a disputation Bible in hand in order to arrive at the proper interpretation of the bible. Although this expectation was based on the previous reformers' examples, it was based on the assumption that truth could be arrived at by rational argument over the biblical text, and that all parties involved would be susceptible of being convinced by the arguments sustained, a very modern attitude to religion. The process of excommunication was instead a performance of a public transcript, a performance designed to reinforce the status quo (Scott 1990: Chapter 3). In such a performance, their assigned role would have been to ask for forgiveness, recognizing their mistakes in their different interpretations and behaviour. However, Benjamin and Bernard's eagerness to enter into a public discussion Bible in hand in order to defend their ideas meant they were not going to play their assigned script in the ritual of obedience. They would have transformed it into a forum for the dissenters to voice their ideas, and this the *Leardeenst* could not afford. Avoiding the process was preferable to having it appropriated as a means to disseminate the dissenters' ideas, especially since the *Leardeenst* had other means of obtaining compliance, which leads us to the third point. A process of externalization of dissenters was set in place. Dissenters were progressively pushed towards the margins of the Old Colony, leaving it up to them to either comply, or leave at their own initiative. This process of externalization was first set in movement through gossip and the tarnishing of reputations, then through the threats to Bernard of losing his means of survival, and to Benjamin of permanent structural liminality. Whereas Benjamin entered into economic dependency on the *Leardeenst* (after arguing—following Sergio—for the total economic disengagement of the colonies from their surrounding economies in order to avoid being forced by stealth to accept the mark of the beast) and seems to have submitted to accepting the higher degree of isolation and ideological control his position requires, Bernard has left the Old Colony. The alternative imaginations of the future were either silenced and asphyxiated through internal ostracism, or externalized. What consequences will the consolidation of the manipulation of due process as a strategy to avoid change have on the constitution of the Old Colony? Will Bernard attempt to spread his ideas in the colonies from without? Will Benjamin abandon his silence? What will happen with the next wave of dissenters? I do not have answers to these questions. What is certain is that although things have changed, the illusion of immutability has been maintained, although illusively.

CONCLUSIONS

One of the aims of this book was to apply the concept of the imagination of the future for analysing processes of social and cultural change. Through the concept of the imagination of the future, I have shown how the Old Colony Mennonites construct the moral projects that guide its reproduction along time. Unlike previous studies, where the ideologies of immutability and equality espoused by Mennonites and related groups had been taken as empirical qualities of the social systems, and where the former were assumed to be 'silently' practiced instead of argued, I focused on the problematic relationships between systems of ideas and religious practices, and between dominant and alternative interpretations. I presented an analysis of the guiding ideas that form the imagination of the future in constant relationship with both, changes in the social conditions of existence, as well as changes in their interpretation and practice. In this process, the imagination of the future emerged as a structure, simultaneously enabling and constraining, and the means and outcome of action and history. In these last pages, I summarize the results of this study and to point some further thoughts as they pertain to three related domains: the making of nation-states, modernity and religion, and the internal politico-religious aspects of the Old Colony.

I have shown how the Mennonite's relationship with different nation-states have transformed their social order from a fragmented and heterogeneous religious movement based on a system of beliefs of voluntary adhesion into geographically bounded agricultural settlements where these beliefs have been transformed into concrete and compulsory identity markers. This change in social conditions required a new imagination of the future to provide a suitable legitimation. Therefore, the separation from the world was transformed from its spiritual meaning into a literal geographical concept, and an orthopraxis established, enforcing internal homogeneity, and where farming becoming the preferred occupation for the leading of a Christian life. Concomitantly, internal institutions were created (and in some instances such as with the *fäaschta* and *schult*, an appropriation following an imposition) in order to deal with states and to establish the necessary linkages with the world beyond the colonies. A trend that started on their 'second generation' in sixteenth-century Europe, whereby externally oriented proselytism gave way towards the transmission of the faith to their own descendents, was then consolidated by both, the prohibition to evangelize in Ukraine as a condition of settlement, and the construction of the 'closed' settlements themselves. In this way, baptism was routinized, becoming a combination of a coming of age ritual and a 'social contract' (renewed periodically in the Lord's Supper), while excommunication became a tool for worldly social control. In this transformation, where the social unit became coterminous with the religious, the *Leardeenst* absorbed the political, and concealed it within the religious. The *Leardeenst* assumed both, the task of definition of *Christenvolk* and *Weltmensch* on the friend/enemy dichotomy, as well as holding the keys to both entry and exit of the *Christenvolk*.

The repeated migrations and schisms that went with them can be interpreted as the concrete ways in which different imaginations of the future were being accepted and rejected, what conditions were deemed suitable for the appropriate reproduction of the Old Colony moral order, and which were not. Furthermore, the use of excommunication became a prime source for the externalization of competing projects. In addition, when the process itself would have contributed to the dissemination of those projects, strategies of isolation and progressive expulsion were undertaken. That these measures were taken against the spreading of these alternative imaginations of the future evidences that the transformations indicated had indeed become dominant.

This new imagination of the future presented new requirements to individuals to qualify for membership in the community. Interspersed in various chapters I have shown evidence of the changes in the basis of membership, which shifted from individual faith, into the sharing of descent and racialized group belonging. Examples that indicate this change include the acceptance of Abraham back into the community, the permanence in the colonies of those who became *Jehovah's Witnesses*, the idioms of kinship for defining community, the lack of incorporation of people not born to Mennonite parents, the perception of Sergio's daughters as a danger to the purity of their blood, and reinforced in such rituals as the Lord's Supper and Baptism. In addition, through the *Ordninj* it promoted the construction of a Christian self based on a series of oppositions: body/soul, individual/community, and worldly/Christian. This orthodoxy on the level of principles was translated into a codified orthopraxis (the *Ordninj*), consisting of an inventory of proscribed and prescribed practices and elements that ranged from prohibitions to own cars and musical instruments, to a prescribed dress code to the limits in the usage of tractors and electricity. Through them, Old Colony Mennonites were therefore required to control their bodies in order to save their souls, quench their individuality for the sake of community, and refrain from engaging with the world (or doing so in a regulated context).

With the advent of modernity, and the speeding up of change in the world that surrounded them, the Old Colony found in the control of technological acquisition a means of marking their separation from the world. If the Mennonites were 'early moderns' as suggested in Chapters 1 and 2 due to their initial distinction between the political and the religious (a first step in the structural differentiation of domains), the privatization of faith and the fostering of individual responsibility for ones' acts (as expressed in adult baptism), they then defined themselves against modernity. The diacritics used were assumed to be the consequences of the following of biblical principles, therefore becoming sacralized, and their upholding not only compulsory, but indicators of faith and membership. In attempting to separate themselves from modernity (as a proxy for understanding, practicing, and conceiving their separation from the world), the Old Colony incorporated its exclusion as a mark of belonging and difference from the world.

This rejection of modernity and the nation points to an important question for understanding the religious experience and the imaginations of the future of Mennonites like Abraham, with that of Sergio's. Narratives of modernity posit the disenchantment of the world and the decline of religion as the outcome of processes of structural and functional differentiation. Secularisation theorists argue this is due to the advance of rationalization and science (Bruce 1996; Berger 1969; cf. Asad 2003). The expansion of rationalization and science is necessarily accompanied by the expansion of the natural over the supernatural; the latter becoming a residual category (this movement was already suggested by Emile Durkheim when dismissing the possibilities of defining religion through recourse to the supernatural [2001]). This process led to what Bruno Latour calls the crossing out of God as one of the guarantees of the constitution of the modern (1993: 32). God receives within this narrative of modernity, the same treatment as modernity receives from the Mennonites, the inclusion through exclusion. Religion, once captured by modernity as one among other domains in the process of differentiation is subject to a process of constant encroachment by the expansion of the natural, leaving for it the sphere of the supernatural or as a traditional source of ethics and morality. This is what was at the bottom of the romanticization of groups like the Amish and Mennonites, a transposition of the meaning of religion in the two contexts without realizing the different grammars at work.

Meanwhile, within the Old Colony, the existence of Jesus Christ and God is not a belief but considered a fact, and their powers 'natural'. The world is disenchanted not because of the powers of reason to uncover the hidden natural causalities, but because, by definition there *is no* supernatural. To the avoidance of this distinction is superimposed the sacralisation of the social order and the exclusion of the profane. It is wholly within this sphere (a sacred order devoid of the supernatural) that Abraham's alternative project is imagined. What worried Abraham was the process of absorption and concealment of the political by religion, threatening the Old Colony's sacred order with the incorporation of the secular. As such he was promoting a reformation of the Old Colony imagined future back into the exclusion (or rather promoting a new process of concealment) of the secular from the sacred order. In other words, his was an attempt to bring back the Old Colony from the new secular time proposed by modernity (which in German means precisely that, *Neuzeit*) into which the Old Colony was slipping into, back into sacred time. In other words, his imagination of the future continued with the dominant Mennonite imagination of it being a non-enchanted sacred order. The former aspect allowed its construction of earth through the promise of factibility, whereas the latter provided its moral imperative, but also locating it outside history. Being sacred and revealed, with origins in an omniscient and all-powerful God, it would be immutable. Its realization would effectively eliminate time, just as the Old Colony was attempting to do by basing their imagination of the future on their past. Abraham unveiled and discovered the effects of history in the Old Colony; his project was to exclude it. In this light, and despite Abraham, the differences between the Old Colony and his own imaginations of the future were built with the same building blocks, and obeying the same logic. What Abraham pointed to, was the failure of the Old Colony of maintaining the illusion of immutability (the fact that he could make a historical analysis was its proof), of the *Leardeenst* unwittingly allowing to slip out of the sacred order, becoming worldly and historical.

What are the meanings of the sacred, the profane, the natural and supernatural when the total social system is sacralized and the profane externalized? What is the meaning of religion when it becomes naturalized? I would suggest that the sacred becomes secularised, as the limits between the supernatural and natural are not allowed to be built. Unlike Abraham, Sergio, Benjamin and Bernard were promoting a very different imagination of the future based on a different understanding of religion. What Sergio brought into the colonies was a version of religion that, within the modern world's fragmentation and specialization of domains, had specialized in the field of the supernatural. Against secularising discourses, he had gone to great lengths to prove the existence of God and its powers. Indeed, the perception of Sergio as a prophet, evidences his follower's understanding of him as in touch with the supernatural (unlike Abraham, who remained wholly within the sphere of 'rational' interpretation of scriptures and social conditions). What Sergio showed them, was the existence of said supernatural—constructed and transmitted through his witnessing, which was reproduced later on by his followers. This version, contrasted with the disenchanted, and generalized one within the colonies, erecting distinctions between the natural and supernatural, the sacred and the secular. This is what their followers discovered, and towards which were oriented their efforts to 'heat up' the 'cold' spirituality within the colonies. Even if Sergio's call to the avoidance of modernity in terms of technology and practices, the religious experience and definition remained wholly within the grammar of "modern" religion.

In the same way as the analysis of conflict and deviants has shown the process of transformation of the Mennonite imagination of the future, focusing on the Mennonites has, in turn, provided insights in the process of the transformation of the political world into the national order of things (Malkki 1995b). First by showing the transformation of the legitimation of political authority: from divine right, to nationalist coherence. In their attempts to build a community of believers, the Mennonites contributed to the territorial consolidation of states, as well as to their economic development. They nevertheless rejected, through negotiations and migrations, the processes through which the inhabitants of those territories were being transformed into nationals, showing that the nation is a product of the state. Distinguishing nationality from citizenship, and in order to avoid the former, they constructed a cross-border network of colonies, joined by relations of common origins, a putative acceptance of a common moral and legal code, and a self-identification as *Christenvolk*. This self-identification, although originally a religious metaphor was, in practice, constructed in opposition to national identifications while at the same time accepting citizenship. The simultaneous existence of colonies in different countries allowed them not only to diversify their political stakes, but also provided their members and the *Leardeenst* with new possibilities for avoiding nationality, controlling internal dissent, and enforcing the dominant imagination of the future.

States and the *Leardeenst* were involved in similar but complementary processes in their relationship with the religious and the political. Whereas through the process of modernization and the changing of the basis of legitimation of states proceeded by excluding the religious from the political followed by the reincorporation of its dynamics through the building and apotheosizing of 'the people' and 'the nation', the *Leardeenst* went through an inverse process: attempting to exclude and conceal the political by denouncing the sword, but internalizing the monopoly on legitimate violence and biblical interpretation that provides its legitimation. They strove to externalize the political, but with the building of the colonies they reabsorbed and concealed it. The legitimacy of the *Leardeenst's* internal use of force, taxation, and enumeration practices; its control of membership; its struggle for territoriality, and intimations of a semi autonomous legal order; its establishment and collective negotiations of exception status with states; its control of the processes of imagination and reproduction of its members as a people different from the rest, based on common descent, through the construction of an appropriate self (via their own schooling system), and the exclusive loyalty demanded from their members points to an ironical transformation: The Old Colony have transformed itself into something very similar to a nation, while the *Leardeenst* into something that, in many ways resembles a state. An ironical situation for a group whose one of its main symbols of origin lie in the separation of church and state and voluntary adhesion to the symbols of faith regardless of origin. I doubt this was the future sixteenth-century Mennonites imagined. Likewise, their future presents are likely to be different from their present imagined future, as will be their future futures.

GLOSSARY

brauntschult: Lit. 'fire chief', fire insurance officer.
broodashoft: General meeting of members.
bogge, pl -s: Four-wheeled cart usually pulled by a single horse. Main means of transportation within the colonies.
Christenvolk: People of Christ.
darp, pl -a: Main geographical and political division of a colony, it consists of a linear village and its adjacent cultivated land.
dia'koon: Deacon, one of the members of the *Leardeenst*. He is in charge of help and charity issues.
Dietsch: German.
donnadach: Thursday, day of thunder, or of reckoning.
düak: Embroidered women's kerchief. White for singles, and black for married and widows.
Ejebuare: Natives, aboriginals.
eltesta, pl -sch: Lit. 'the eldest', main authority within the colonies. Translated into Spanish by Mennonites themselves as 'obispo' [bishop].
fäaschta: Main administrative authority of the colony and officially in charge of managing relations with outside officers and institutions.
fe'lafniss: Party organized by the bride's father where the newlyweds announce their intentions of marrying (usually the Sunday the following week).
Gesangbuch: Hymnal.
Hüagdietsch: High-German.
Je'meent: Community, church.
jung, pl -es: Young men.
Kjoakjebaun: Lit. 'Church ban', excommunication.
Leardeenst: Collective formed by the *eltesta*, *prädjasch*, and *dia'koon* of a colony.
me'jal, pl -eores: Young women.
Ordninj: Rulebook, constitution.
prädja, pl -sch: Preacher.
schlaubbekjse: Dungarees, main male attire.
schult, pl -e: Administrative chief of a *darp*. Report to the *fäaschta*.
senja: Church singers.
spat'seare: To visit, date or go out.

wirtschofte: An individual farm, consisting of buildings such as the main house, barn, workshop, etc.

weisenaumt: Person in charge of managing the assets of underage orphans, loaning it to other Mennonites who pay a fixed interest rate on the funds.

Weltmensch, pl -e: Men of the world, worldly people.

REFERENCES

Abramián, Beatriz, Mónica Figueiras, and Josefina García. 1995. "El cooperativismo en las colonias menonitas alemanas en el Uruguay." Paper read at V Jornadas Sobre Alternativas Religiosas en Latinoamérica: Sociedad y Diversidad Religiosa, 26–29 April 1995, at Santiago de Chile.

Agamben, Giorgio. 2005. *State of exception*. Translated by K. Attell. Chicago.

Anderson, Benedict. 1990. *Imagined communities: Reflections on the origin and spread of nationalism*. London.

Anderson, Perry. 1974. *Lineages of the absolutist state*. London.

Angrosino, Michael V. 1976. "The use of autobiography as 'Life history': The case of albert gomes." *Ethos* 4 (2):133–154.

Anthony, Dick, and Thomas Robbins. 1997. "Religious totalism, exemplary dualism, and the Waco tragedy." Pp. 261–284 in *Millennium, messiahs, and mayhem: Contemporary apocalyptic movements*, edited by T. Robbins and S. J. Palmer. London.

Antze, Paul, and Michael Lambek. 1996. *Tense past: Cultural essays in trauma and memory*. London.

Archetti, Eduardo P., and Kristi Anne Stølen. 1975. *Explotación familiar y acumulación de capital en el campo Argentino*. Buenos Aires.

Asad, Talal. 1983. "Anthropological conceptions of religion—reflections on Geertz." *Man* 18 (2):237–259.

———. 1993. *Genealogies of religion: Discipline and reasons of power in Christianity and Islam*. Baltimore, MD.

———. 1996. "Comments on conversion." Pp. 263–274 in *Conversion to modernities: The globalization of Christianity*, edited by P. van der Veer. New York.

———. 2003. *Formations of the secular: Christianity, Islam, modernity*. Stanford, CA.

Bargman, Daniel. 1992. "Un ámbito para las relaciones interétnicas: Las colonias agrícolas judías en argentina." *Revista de Antropología* 7 (11):50–58.

Bargman, Daniel, Guadalupe Barúa, Mirta Bialogorski, Estela Biondi Assali, and Isabel Lemounier. 1992. "Los grupos étnicos de origen extranjero como objeto de estudio de la antropología en la Argentina." Pp. 189–198 in *Etnicidad e identidad*, edited by C. Hidalgo and L. Tamagno. Buenos Aires.

Barker, Eileen. 1984. *The making of a moonie: Choice or brainwashing?* Oxford.

———. 1986. Religious movements—cult and anticult since Jonestown. *Annual Review of Sociology* 12:329–346.

Bartolomé, Leopoldo J. 1977. "Sistemas de actividad y estrategias adaptativas en la articulación regional y nacional de colonias agrícolas étnicas: El caso de apóstoles (misiones)." Pp. 257–281 in *Procesos de articulación social*. Buenos Aires.

———. 1990. *The colonos of Apóstoles. Adaptive strategy and ethnicity in a Polish-Ukrainian settlement in northeast Argentina*. New York.

Basso, Ellen B. 1973. Book review: "The situation of the Indian in South America: Contributions to the study of inter-ethnic conflict in the non-Andean regions of South America" by W. Dostal. *American Anthropologist* 75 (6):1865–1868.

———. 1975. "Reply to Calvin Redekop." *American Anthropologist* 77 (1):83–84.

Bateson, Gregory. 1998. *Naven. A survey of the problems suggested by a composite picture of the culture of a New Guinea tribe drawn from three points of view*. Stanford, CA. Original edition, 1958.

Beckerman, Paul. 1995. "Central-bank 'distress' and hyperinflation in Argentina, 1989–90." *Journal of Latin American Studies* 27 (3):663–682.

Beckford, James A. 1978. Accounting for conversion. *British Journal of Sociology* 29 (2):249–262.
Bender, Harold S. 1950. *Conrad grebel 1498–1526. The founder of the swiss brethren.* Goshen, IN.
———. 1957. "Migrations of mennonites." Pp. 684–687 in *The Mennonite Encyclopedia. A comprehensive reference work on the Anabaptist-Mennonite movement*, edited by H. S. Bender and C. H. Smith. V vols. Vol. III. Scottdale, PA.
Bennett, John W. 1967. *Hutterian brethren: The agricultural economy and social organization of a communal people.* Stanford, CA.
Berger, Peter L. 1969. *The social reality of religion.* London.
Bloch, Marc. 1998. *The historian's craft.* Translated by P. Putnam. Manchester. Original edition, 1954.
Bloch, Maurice. 1968. "Astrology and writing in Madagascar." Pp. 277–297 in *Literacy in traditional societies*, edited by J. Goody. Cambridge.
Bloch, Ruth H. 1985. *Visionary republic: Millenial themes in American thought, 1756–1800.* Cambridge.
Blok, Anton. 1988. *The mafia of a Sicilian village, 1860–1960: A study of violent peasant entrepreneurs.* Long Grove, IL. Original edition, 1974.
Bonfil Batalla, Guillermo. 1991. *Pensar nuestra cultura: Ensayos.* México.
———. 1992. *Identidad y pluralismo cultural en América Latina.* Buenos Aires, San Juan.
Borneman, John. 1992. "State, territory, and identity formation in the postwar Berlin, 1945–1989." *Cultural Anthropology* 7 (1):45–62.
Bourdieu, Pierre. 1977. *Outline of a theory of practice.* Translated by R. Nice. Cambridge. Original edition, 1972.
———. 1990. *The logic of practice.* Translated by R. Nice. Stanford, CA. Original edition, 1980.
———. 1998. *Practical reason: On the theory of action.* Translated by R. Johnson. Stanford, CA. Original edition, 1994
Boyer, Paul S. 1992. *When time shall be no more: Prophecy belief in modern American culture.* Cambridge, MA.
Braght, Tieleman J. Van. 1982. *The bloody theater, or, martyrs mirror of the defenseless Christians, who baptized only upon confession of faith, and who suffered and died for the testimony of Jesus, their saviour, from the time of Christ to the year A.D. 1660.* Translated by J. F. Sohm. Scottdale, PA. Original edition, 1660.
Brow, James. 1990. "Notes on community, hegemony, and the uses of the past." *Anthropological Quarterly* 63 (1):1–6.
Bruce, Steve. 1996. *Religion in the modern world: From cathedrals to cults.* Oxford.
Bush, Perry. 1998. *Two kingdoms, two loyalties: Mennonite pacifism in modern America.* Baltimore, MD.
Cameron, Euan. 1991. *The European Reformation.* Oxford.
Cañás Bottos, Lorenzo. 1998. "*Christenvolk*. Historia y etnografía de una colonia menonita." Tesis de Licenciatura, Departamento de Antropología, Facultad de Filosofía y Letras, Universidad de Buenos Aires, Buenos Aires.
———. 1999. "Some aspects of kinship in a Mennonite colony." MA(econ) Dissertation, Department of Social Anthropology, University of Manchester, Manchester.
———. 2005. *Christenvolk: Historia y etnografía de una colonia menonita.* Buenos Aires.
———. 2006. "Old colony Mennonites in South America: Refractions of the 'other'." *Cambridge Anthropology* 26 (1):1–23.
Castells, Manuel. 1998. *The information age: Economy, society and culture.* Vol. III: End of Millenium. Oxford.
Chidester, David. 1991. *Salvation and suicide: An interpretation of Jim Jones, The Peoples Temple, and Jonestown.* Bloomington, IN.
Clastres, Hélène. 1995. *The land-without-evil: Tupí-guaraní prophetism.* Translated by J. Grenez Bovender. Urbana, IL. Original edition, 1975.

Clifford, James. 1997. *Routes. Travel and translation in the late twentieth century*. Cambridge, MA.
Cohen, Anthony P. 1985. *The symbolic construction of community*. London.
Cohn, Norman. 1957. *The pursuit of the millenium*. London.
———. 1993. *Cosmos, chaos and the world to come: The ancient roots of apocalyptic faith*. New Haven, CT.
Coleman, Simon. 2000. *The globalisation of charismatic Christianity: Spreading the gospel of prosperity*. Cambridge.
Collins, J. 1995. "Literacy and literacies." *Annual Review of Anthropology* 24:75–93.
Comaroff, Jean, and John L. Comaroff. 1991. *Of revelation and revolution: Christianity, colonialism and consciousness in South Africa*. 2 vols. Vol. 1. Chicago.
———. 1992. *Ethnography and the historical imagination*. Boulder, CO.
Comisión Nacional sobre la Desaparición de Personas. 1984. *Nunca más: Informe de la comisión nacional sobre la desaparición de personas*. Buenos Aires.
Consejo Nacional de Población—Fondo de Naciones Unidas para Actividades en Población. 1986. *Bases para una política de inmigración extranjera en Bolivia*. La Paz.
Cordeu, Edgardo Jorge, and Alejandra B. Siffredi. 1971. *De la algarroba al algodón. Movimientos milenaristas del Chaco Argentino. Movimiento mesiánico de los Guaycurú*. Buenos Aires.
Crummey, Robert O. 1991. "The spirituality of the Vyg Fathers." Pp. 23–37 in *Church, nation and state in Russia and Ukraine*, edited by G. Hosking. London.
Csordas, Thomas J. 1994. *The sacred self: A cultural phenomenology of charismatic healing*. Berkeley.
———. 1997. *Language, charisma, and creativity: The ritual life of a religious movement*. Berkeley.
Davidson, James West. 1977. *The logic of millennial thought. Eighteenth-century New England*. New Haven, CT.
Deiros, Pablo A. 1991. "Protestant Fundamentalism in Latin America." Pp. 142–196 in *Fundamentalisms observed*, edited by M. E. Marty and R. S. Appleby. Chicago.
Deleuze, Gilles, and Felix Guattari. 1987. *A thousand plateaus: Capitalism and schizophrenia*. Translated by B. Massumi. Minneapolis, MN. Original edition, 1980.
Derksen, Enrique. 1988. Los menonitas. Origen—dilema religioso-vivencial desafio actual. *Estudios Paraguayos* XVI (1–2):43–78.
Douglas, Mary. 1985. *Purity and danger. An analysis of the concepts of pollution and taboo*. London. Original edition, 1966.
———. 1991. "Witchcraft and leprosy—2 strategies of exclusion." *Man* 26 (4):723–736.
Driedger, Leo. 2000. *Mennonites in the global village*. Toronto.
Durkheim, Emile. 1962. *The rules of sociological method*. Glencoe. Original edition, 1893.
———. 2001. *The elementary forms of religious life*. Translated by C. Cosman and M. S. Cladis. Oxford.
Dyck, Cornelius J. 1981. "Mennonite churches in Latin America." Pp. 312–334 in *An introduction to Mennonite history. A popular history of the Anabaptists and the Mennonites*, edited by C. J. Dyck. Scottdale, PA.
Eisenstadt, S. N., and Louis Roniger. 1980. Patron—client relations as a model of structuring social exchange. *Comparative Studies in Society and History* 22 (1):42–77.
Elias, Norbert. 1982. *The civilizing process*. Oxford.
Elton, G. R. 1966. *Reformation Europe, 1517–1559*. New York.
Erikson, Kai T. 1966. *Wayward puritans: A study in the sociology of deviance*. New York.
Faubion, James D. 1999. "Deus absconditus: Waco, conspiracy (theory), millennialism and (the end of) the twentieth century." Pp. 375–404 in *Paranoia within reason: A casebook on conspiracy as explanation*, edited by G. E. Marcus. Chicago.
Feeley-Harnik, Gillian. 1994. *The Lord's table: The meaning of food in early Judaism and Christianity*. Washington, DC.
Feitlowitz, Marguerite. 1998. *A lexicon of terror: Argentina and the legacies of torture*. New York.

Ferguson, James, and Akhil Gupta. 1992. "Beyond 'Culture': Space, identity, and the politics of difference." *Cultural Anthropology* 7 (1):6–23.

Fernandez Saavedra, Gustavo. 1999. "Bolivia y sus circunstancias." Pp. 89–154 in *Bolivia en el siglo xx. La formación de la Bolivia contemporánea*, edited by F. Campero Prudencio. La Paz.

Fifer, Valerie J. 1967. Bolivia's pioneer fringe. *The Geographical Review* LVII (1):1–23.

———. 1982. "The search for a series of small successes: Frontiers of settlement in eastern Bolivia." *Journal of Latin American Studies* 14 (2):407–432.

Fix, Andrew. 1987. "Radical reformation and second reformation in Holland: The intellectual consequences of the sixteenth-century religious upheaval and the coming of a rational world view." *Sixteenth Century Journal* 18 (1):63–80.

———. 1989. "Angels, devils and evil spirits in seventeenth-century thought: Balthasar Bekker and the Collegiants." *Journal of the History of Ideas* 50 (4):527–547.

Francis, E. K. 1948. "The Russian Mennonites: From religious to ethnic group." *American Journal of Sociology* 54 (2):101–107.

Freidenberg, Judith. 2005. *Memorias de Villa Clara*. Buenos Aires.

Frigerio, Alejandro, and María Julia Carozzi. 1994. "Los estudios de la conversión a nuevos movimientos religiosos: Perspectivas, métodos y hallazgos." Pp. 17–54 in *El estudio científico de la religión a fines del siglo xx*, edited by A. Frigerio and M. J. Carozzi. Buenos Aires.

Fuller, C. J. 1992. *The camphor flame: Popular Hinduism and society in India*. Princeton, NJ.

Gaignard, Romain. 1966. "Origen y evolución de la pequeña propiedad campesina en la pampa seca Argentina (el caso de la provincia de la pampa)." *Desarrollo Económico. Revista de Ciencias Sociales* 6 (21):57–76.

Gauchet, Marcel. 1997. *The disenchantment of the world: A political history of religion*. Translated by O. Burge. Princeton, NJ. Original edition, 1985.

Gellner, Ernest. 1983. *Nations and nationalism: New perspectives on the past*. Oxford.

Giddens, Anthony. 1979. *Central problems in social theory. Action, structure and contradiction in social analysis*. Berkeley.

———. 1986. *The constitution of society. Outline of the theory of structuration*. Berkeley. Original edition, 1984.

Ginsburg, F. 1987. "Procreation stories—reproduction, nurturance, and procreation in life narratives of abortion activists." *American Ethnologist* 14 (4):623–636.

Goody, Jack. 1968a. "Introduction." Pp. 1–26 in *Literacy in traditional societies*, edited by J. Goody. Cambridge.

———. 1986. *The logic of writing and the organization of society*. Cambridge.

———, ed. 1968b. *Literacy in traditional societies*. Cambridge.

Goody, Jack, and Ian Watt. 1963. "The consequences of literacy." *Comparative Studies in Society and History* 5 (3):304–345.

Gould, Roger V, and Roberto M Fernandez. 1989. "Structures of mediation: A formal approach to brokerage in transaction networks." *Sociological Methodology* 19:89–126.

Graybill, Beth, and Linda B. Arthur. 1999. "The social control of women's bodies in two Mennonite communities." Pp. 9–30 in *Religion, dress and the body*, edited by L. B. Arthur. Oxford.

Greenfield, Sidney. 1977. "Patronage, politics, and the articulation of local community and national society in pre-1968 Brazil." *Journal of Interamerican Studies and World Affairs* 19 (2):139–172.

Gupta, Akhil, and James Ferguson. 1997. "Discipline and practice: 'The field' As site, method, and location in anthropology." Pp. 1–46 in *Anthropological locations: Boundaries and grounds of a field science*, edited by A. Gupta and J. Ferguson. Berkeley.

Habermas, Jürgen. 1996. "The European nation-state—its achievements and its limits. On the past and future of sovereignty." Pp. 281–294 in *Mapping the nation*, edited by G. Balakrishnan. London.

REFERENCES

Hack, Henk. 1978. "Indios y menonitas en el chaco paraguayo (i)." *Suplemento Antropológico* XIII (1–2):205–260.
———. 1979. "Indios y menonitas en el chaco paraguayo (ii)." *Suplemento Antropológico* XIV (1–2):201–248.
———. 1980. "Indios y menonitas en el chaco paraguayo (iii)." *Suplemento Antropológico* XV (1–2):45–137.
Hage, Ghassan. 2005. "A not so multi-sited ethnography of a not so imagined community." *Anthropological Theory* 5 (4):463–475.
Harding, Susan Friend. 1987. "Convicted by the Holy Spirit—the rhetoric of fundamental Baptist conversion." *American Ethnologist* 14 (1):167–181.
———. 2000. *The book of Jerry Falwell: Fundamentalist language and politics*. Princeton, NJ.
Harrison, Wes. 1992. "The role of women in Anabaptist thought and practice: The Hutterite experience of the sixteenth and seventeenth centuries." *Sixteenth Century Journal* 23 (1):49–69.
Harvey, David. 2000. *Spaces of hope*. Edinburgh.
Hefner, Robert W. 1993a. *Conversion to Christianity: Historical and anthropological perspectives on a great transformation*. Berkeley.
———. 1993b. "World building and the rationality of conversion." Pp. 3–44 in *Conversion to Christianity: Historical and anthropological perspectives on a great transformation*, edited by R. W. Hefner. Berkeley.
Heirich, Max. 1977. "Change of heart: A test of some widely held theories about religious conversion." *American Journal of Sociology* 83 (3):653–680.
Hermitte, Esther. 1972. *Asistencia técnica en materia de promoción y asistencia de la comunidad en la Provincia de Catamarca. Informe final*.
———. 1979. "The growth and structure of a provincial community of poncho weavers, Belén, Argentina, 1678–1869." Pp. 49–73 in *Peasants, primitives, and proletariats. The struggle for identity in south america*, edited by D. L. Browman and R. A. Schwartz.
Hermitte, Esther, and Leopoldo J. Bartolomé. 1977. "Introducción." Pp. 9–22 in *Procesos de articulación social*, edited by E. Hermitte and L. J. Bartolomé. Buenos Aires.
Hermitte, Esther, and Carlos Herrán. 1970. "¿Patronazgo o cooperativismo? Obstáculos a la modificación del sistema de interacción en una comunidad del noroeste argentino." *Revista Latinoamericana de Sociología* (2):293–317.
———. 1977. "Sistema productivo, instituciones intersticiales y formas de articulación social en una comunidad del noroeste argentino." Pp. 238–256 in *Procesos de articulación social*, edited by E. Hermitte and L. J. Bartolomé. Buenos Aires.
Hobsbawm, Eric J. 1971. *Primitive rebels: Studies in archaic forms of social movement in the 19th and 20th centuries*. Manchester. Original edition, 1959.
———. 1992. *Nations and nationalism since 1780. Programme, myth, reality*. Cambridge.
Hoerder, Dirk. 2002. *Cultures in contact: World migrations in the second millennium*. Durham, NC.
Hosking, Geoffrey. 1997. "The Russian national myth repudiated." Pp. 198–210 in *Myths and nationhood*, edited by G. Hosking and G. Schopflin. New York.
Hostetler, Beulah Stauffer. 1992. "The formation of the Old Orders." *Mennonite Quarterly Review* LXVI (1):5–25.
Hostetler, John A. 1964. The Amish use of symbols and their function in bounding the community. *Journal of the Royal Anthropological Institute of Great Britain and Ireland* 94 (1):11–22.
———. 1974. *Hutterite society*. Baltimore, MD.
———. 1983. *Mennonite life*. Scottdale, PA.
———. 1989. *Amish roots: A treasury of history, wisdom, and lore*. Baltimore, MD.
———. 1993. *Amish society*. Baltimore, MD. Original edition, 1963.
———. 1995. *The Amish*. Scottdale, PA. Original edition, 1982.
Hostetler, John A., and Gertrude E. Huntington. 1967. *The Hutterites in North America*. New York.

Huebert, Helmut. 1999. *Events and people: Events in Russian Mennonite history and the people that made them happen*. Winnipeg, MB.
Huntington, Gertrude Enders. 2003. "Health care." Pp. 163–190 in *The Amish and the state*, edited by D. B. Kraybill. Baltimore, MD.
Introvigne, Massimo. 1997. "Latter day revisited: Contemporary Mormon millenarianism." Pp. 229–245 in *Millennium, messiahs, and mayhem: Contemporary apocalyptic movements*, edited by T. Robbins and S. J. Palmer. London.
Israel, Jonathan Irvine. 2001. *Radical Enlightenment: Philosophy and the making of modernity, 1650–1750*. Oxford.
Janzen, William. 1990. *Limits on liberty: The experience of Mennonite, Hutterite, and Doukhobor communities in Canada*. Toronto.
Jefferson, Mark. 1926. *Peopling the Argentine Pampa*. New York.
Kah, Gary. 1978. *En route to global occupation*. Lafayette.
Kantorowicz, Ernst Hartwig. 1957. *The king's two bodies: A study in mediaeval political theology*. Princeton, NJ.
Kidd, Stephen W. 1995. "Land, politics and benevolent shamanism: The Enxet indians in a democratic Paraguay." *Journal of Latin American Studies* 27 (1):43–75.
Kirchner, Walther. 1974. "State and Anabaptists in the sixteenth century: An economic approach." *The Journal of Modern History* 46 (1):1–25.
Klaassen, C. F. 1955. "Canada." Pp. 501–504 in *The Mennonite Encyclopedia. A comprehensive reference work on the Anabaptist-Mennonite movement*, edited by H. S. Bender and C. H. Smith. Vol. I. Scottdale, PA.
Klaassen, Walter. 1992. *Living at the end of the ages: Apocalyptic expectation in the Radical Reformation*. Lanham, NY.
Kniss, Fred LaMar. 1997. *Disquiet in the land: Cultural conflict in American Mennonite communities*. New Brunswick, NJ.
Koselleck, Reinhart. 2004. *Futures past: On the semantics of historical time*. Translated by K. Tribe. New York. Original edition, 1979.
Krahn, Cornelius. 1957a. "Manitoba." Pp. 457–466 in *The Mennonite Encyclopedia. A comprehensive reference work on the Anabaptist-Mennonite movement*, edited by H. S. Bender and C. H. Smith. V vols. Vol. III. Scottdale, PA.
———. 1957b. "West Reserve." Pp. 926–929 in *The Mennonite Encyclopedia. A comprehensive reference work on the Anabaptist-Mennonite movement*, edited by H. S. Bender and C. H. Smith. IV vols. Vol. IV. Scottdale, PA.
———. 1959a. "Old Colony Mennonites." Pp. 38–42 in *The Mennonite Encyclopedia. A comprehensive reference work on the Anabaptist-Mennonite movement*, edited by H. S. Bender and C. H. Smith. Vol. IV. Scottdale, PA.
———. 1959b. "Russia." Pp. 381–392 in *The Mennonite Encyclopedia. A comprehensive reference work on the Anabaptist-Mennonite movement*, edited by H. S. Bender and C. H. Smith. V vols. Vol. IV. Scottdale, PA.
———. 1959c. "Villages." Pp. 821–823 in *The Mennonite Encyclopedia. A comprehensive reference work on the Anabaptist-Mennonite movement*, edited by H. S. Bender and C. H. Smith. Vol. IV. Scottdale, PA.
———. 1959d. "Wüst, Eduard." Pp. 997 in *The Mennonite Encyclopedia. A comprehensive reference work on the Anabaptist-Mennonite movement*, edited by H. S. Bender and C. H. Smith. v vols. Vol. IV. Scottdale, PA.
Kraybill, Donald B. 1989. *The riddle of Amish culture*. Baltimore, MD.
———, ed. 2003. *The Amish and the state*. Baltimore, MD.
Kraybill, Donald B., and Carl F. Bowman. 2001. *On the backroad to heaven: Old Order Hutterites, Mennonites, Amish, and brethren*. Baltimore, MD.
Kraybill, Donald B., and Steven M. Nolt. 1995. *Amish enterprise: From plows to profits*. Baltimore, MD.
Kulick, D., and C. Stroud. 1990. "Christianity, cargo and ideas of self-patterns of literacy in a Papua-New-Guinean village." *Man* 25 (2):286–304.

Kuper, Adam. 1997. *The invention of primitive society: Transformations of an illusion.* London. Original edition, 1988.
Kurtz, Lester R. 1983. "The politics of heresy." *American Journal of Sociology* 88 (6):1085–1115.
Lanning, James W. 1971. "The Old colony Mennonites of Bolivia: A case study." MA, Texas A&M University.
Latour, Bruno. 1993. *We have never been modern.* Cambridge, MA.
Lattas, Andrew. 1998. *Cultures of secrecy: Reinventing race in bush Kaliai cargo cults.* Madison, WI.
Lehmann, David. 1996. *Struggle for the spirit: Religious transformation and popular culture in Brazil and Latin America.* Cambridge.
Lehner, Beate. 1989. *El territorio de Che'iro y los Mennonitas.* Asunción.
Lerner, Robert E. 1981. "The black death and Western European eschatological mentalities." *The American Historical Review* 86 (3):533–552.
Lewis, I. M. 1999. *Arguments with ethnography: Comparative approaches to history, politics and religion.* London.
Loewen, Royden. 1993. *Family, church, and market: A Mennonite community in the old and the new worlds, 1850–1930.* Urbana, IL.
Lofland, John, and Rodney Stark. 1965. "Becoming a world-saver: A theory of conversion to a deviant perspective." *American Sociological Review* 30 (6):862–875.
Lomnitz-Adler, Claudio. 1992. *Exits from the labyrinth: Culture and ideology in the Mexican national space.* Berkeley.
Lomnitz, L. A. 1988. "Informal exchange networks in formal systems—a theoretical-model." *American Anthropologist* 90 (1):42–55.
Longhofer, Jeffrey. 1993. "Specifying the commons: Mennonites, intensive agriculture, and landlessness in nineteenth-century Russia." *Ethnohistory* 40 (3):384–409.
Malkki, Liisa H. 1992. "National Geographic—the rooting of peoples and the territorialization of national identity among scholars and refugees." *Cultural Anthropology* 7 (1):24–44.
———. 1995a. *Purity and exile: Violence, memory, and national cosmology among Hutu refugees in Tanzania.* Chicago.
———. 1995b. "Refugees and exile—from refugee studies to the national order of things." *Annual Review of Anthropology* 24:495–523.
Marcussen, A. Jan. 1983. *National sunday law.* Thompsonville, IL.
Martínez Montiel, Luz María, and Araceli Reynoso Medina. 1993. "Inmigración europea y asiática, siglos xix y xx." Pp. 245–424 in *Simbiosis de culturas. Los inmigrantes y su cultura en México,* edited by G. Bonfil Batalla. México.
Mauss, Marcel. 1950. *Sociologie et anthropologie.* Paris.
Merrill, William L. 1993. "Conversion and colonialism in Northern Mexico: The Tarahumara response to the Jesuit mission program, 1601–1767." Pp. 129–164 in *Conversion to Christianity: Historical and anthropological perspectives on a great transformation,* edited by R. W. Hefner. Berkeley.
Michaelson, Karen L. 1976. "Patronage, mediators, and the historical context of social organization in Bombay." *American Ethnologist* 3 (2):281–295.
Miller, Elmer S. 1970. "The Christian missionary, agent of secularization." *Anthropological Quarterly* 43 (1):14–22.
———. 1979. *Los Tobas Argentinos. Armonía y disonancia en una sociedad.* México.
Morgan, Edmund Sears. 1988. *Inventing the people: The rise of popular sovereignty in England and America.* New York.
Mullet, Michael A. 1980. *Radical religious movements in early modern Europe.* London.
Mullins, Mark R. 1997. "Aum Shinrikyo as an apocalyptic movement." Pp. 313–324 in *Millennium, messiahs, and mayhem: Contemporary apocalyptic movements,* edited by T. Robbins and S. J. Palmer. London.
Munck, Ronaldo. 1985. "The "Modern" Military dictatorship in Latin America: The case of Argentina (1976–1982)." *Latin American Perspectives* 12 (4):41–74.

Myovich, Sam. 1996. Review of Edmund Kizik, "Mennonites in Danzig, Elbing and the Vistula lowlands in the second half of the seventeenth century and in the eighteenth century: A study in the history of a small confessional community." *Mennonite Quarterly Review* LXX (2):215–232.

Niezen, R W. 1991. "Hot literacy in cold societies: A comparative study of the sacred value of writing." *Comparative Studies in Society and History* 33 (2):225–254.

O'Leary, Stephen D. 1994. *Arguing the apocalypse: A theory of millenial rhetoric.* Oxford.

Ochs, E., and L. Capps. 1996. "Narrating the self." *Annual Review of Anthropology* 25:19–43.

Oro, Ari Pedro, and Pablo Semán. 2000. "Pentecostalism in the southern cone countries: Recent perspectives." *International Sociology* 15 (4):605–627.

Peacock, James L., and Dorothy C. Holland. 1993. "The narrated self: Life stories in process." *Ethos* 21 (4):367–383.

Pereira de Queiroz, Maria Isaura. 1965. *O messianismo: No brasil e no mundo.* Sao Paulo.

Peter, Karl A. 1983. "The certainty of salvation: Ritualization of religion and economic rationality among Hutterites." *Comparative Studies in Society and History* 25 (2):222–240.

Pollman, Judith. 1996. "A different road to god: The protestant experience of conversion in the sixteenth century." Pp. 47–64 in *Conversion to modernities: The globalization of christianity*, edited by P. van der Veer. New York.

Powers, Nancy R. 1995. "The politics of poverty in Argentina in the 1990s." *Journal of Interamerican Studies and World Affairs* 37 (4):89–137.

Pozzi, Pablo A. 1988. "Argentina 1976–1982: Labour leadership and military government." *Journal of Latin American Studies* 20 (1):111–138.

Ranis, Peter. 1991. "View from below: Working-class consciousness in Argentina." *Latin American Research Review* 26 (2):133–156.

Redekop, Calvin Wall. 1969. *The Old colony Mennonites. Dilemmas of ethnic minority life.* Baltimore, MD.

———. 1975. "Anthropologists and anthropological reporting." *American Anthropologist* 77 (1):81–83.

Regher, Walter. 1981. "Movimientos mesiánicos entre los grupos étnicos del Chaco Paraguayo." *Suplemento Antropológico* XVI (2):105–118.

Reiling, Denise M. 2002. "The 'Simmie' Side of life. Old Order Amish youth's affective response to culturally prescribed deviance." *Youth & Society* 34 (2):146–171.

Rempel, Herman. 1995. *Kjenn jie noch plautdietsch? A Mennonite Low German dictionary.* Rosenort, MB.

Renshaw, John. 1987. "Property, resources and equality among the indians of the Paraguayan Chaco." *Man* 23 (2):334–352.

Richardson, James T., and Massimo Introvigne. 2001. "'Brainwashing' Theories in european parliamentary and administratie reports on 'Cults' And 'Sects'." *Journal for the Scientific Study of Religion* 40 (2):143–168.

Ricoeur, Paul. 1991. *From text to action: Essays in hermeneutics.* Translated by K. Blamey and J. B. Thompson. Vol. II. Evanston, IL. Original edition, 1986.

Robbins, Thomas, and Susan J. Palmer. 1997. "Introduction: Patterns of contemporary apocalypticism." Pp. 1–30 in *Millennium, messiahs, and mayhem: Contemporary apocalyptic movements*, edited by T. Robbins and S. J. Palmer. London.

Roniger, Luis. 1987. "Caciquismo and coronelismo: Contextual dimensions of patron brokerage in Mexico and Brazil." *Latin American Research Review* 22 (2):71–99.

Rothstein, Frances. 1979. "The class basis of patron-client relations." *Latin American Perspectives* 6 (2):25–35.

Saunders, G. R. 1984. "Contemporary Italian cultural-anthropology." *Annual Review of Anthropology* 13:447–466.

———. 1995. "The crisis of presence in Italian pentecostal conversion." *American Ethnologist* 22 (2):324–340.

Sawatzky, Harry Leonard. 1971. *They sought a country: Mennonite colonization in Mexico.* Berkeley.
Schmitt, Carl. 1996. *The concept of the political.* Translated by G. Schwab. Chicago. Original edition, 1932.
———. 2005. *Political theology: Four chapters on the concept of sovereignty.* Translated by G. Schwab. Chicago. Original edition, 1922
Schreiber, William I. 1962. *Our Amish neighbours.* Chicago.
Schutz, Alfred. 1967. *The phenomenology of the social world.* Translated by G. Walsh. Evanston, IL.
Schwieder, Elmer, and Dorothy Schwieder. 1975. *A peculiar people: Iowa's Old Order Amish.* Ames, IA.
Scott, James C. 1990. *Domination and the arts of resistance: Hidden transcripts.* New Haven, CT.
———. 1998. *Seeing like a state: How certain schemes to improve the human condition have failed.* New Haven, CT.
Scribner, Bob. 1994. "Practical utopias: Pre-modern communism and the Reformation." *Comparative Studies in Society and History* 36 (4):743–774.
Secretary General to the Council. 1934. "Report of the League of Nations Commission on the Chaco dispute between Bolivia and Paraguay." *American Journal of International Law* 28 (4, Official Documents):137–217.
Serulnikov, Sergio. 1994. "When looting becomes a right: Urban poverty and food riots in Argentina." *Latin American Perspectives* 21 (3):69–89.
Sherkat, Darren E., and John Wilson. 1995. "Preferences, constraints, and choices in religious markets: An experimentation of religious switching and apostasy." *Social Forces* 73 (3):993–1026.
Shumway, Nicolas. 1991. *The invention of Argentina.* Berkeley.
Siffredi, Alejandra B., and Susana Santini. 1993. "Movimiento, localización y experiencia. Una aproximación a la historia oral de los Nivaclé septentrionales en los últimos sesenta años." *Memoria Americana* 3.
Siffredi, Alejandra, and Ana María Spadafora. 1991. "Condiciones de posibilidad del movimiento de la 'Buena nueva'. Reflexiones sobre la dinámica sociorreligiosa Nivaclé (Chaco Boreal) en la década de los cincuenta." *Religiones Latinoamericanas* (2):125–148.
Simons, Menno. 1983a. *The complete works.* II vols. Vol. I. Aylmer, ON and Lagrange, IN. Original edition, 1871 John F. Funk & Brother, Elkhart.
———. 1983b. *The complete works.* II vols. Vol. II. Aylmer, ON and Lagrange, IN. Original edition, 1871 John F. Funk & Brother, Elkhart.
Smith, Anthony. 1997. "The 'golden age' and national renewal." Pp. 36–59 in *Myths and nationhood,* edited by G. Hosking and G. Schopflin. New York.
Smith, Willard H. 1957. "Paraguay." Pp. 117–119 in *The Mennonite Encyclopedia. A comprehensive reference work on the Anabaptist-Mennonite movement,* edited by H. S. Bender and C. H. Smith. IV vols. Vol. IV. Scottdale, PA.
Smith, William C. 1991. "State, market and neoliberalism in post-transition Argentina: The Menem experiment." *Journal of Interamerican Studies and World Affairs* 33 (4):45–82.
Snow, D. A., and R. Machalek. 1984. "The sociology of conversion." *Annual Review of Sociology* 10:167–190.
Sommerfeld Mennonite Church of Manitoba. 1995. *Catechism: Or a brief instruction for young people from the holy scriptures, in the form of questions and answers. New german-english edition.* Altona, MB.
Spadafora, Ana María. 1994. "Movimientos sociorreligiosos y lucha política: El movimiento de 'La buena nueva' Y la rebelión del '62 entre los Nivaclé del Chaco Boreal Paraguayo." *Runa. Archivo para las Ciencias del Hombre* (XXI):301–316.
Stark, Rodney, and William Sims Bainbridge. 1996. *A theory of religion.* New Brunswick, NJ.
Stayer, James M. 1978. "Oldeklooster and Menno." *Sixteenth Century Journal* 9 (1):50–67.

Stølen, Kristi Anne. 1996. *The decency of inequality. Gender, power and social change on the Argentine prairie*. Oslo.
Stromberg, P. G. 1990. "Ideological language in the transformation of identity." *American Anthropologist* 92 (1):42–56.
Stromberg, Peter G. 1985. "The impression point: Synthesis of symbol and self." *Ethos* 13 (1):56–74.
———. 1986. *Symbols of community: The cultural system of a Swedish church*. Tucson, AZ.
———. 1993. *Language and self-transformation: A study of the Christian conversion narrative*. Cambridge.
Suarez Vilela, Ernesto. 1967. *Breve historia de los Menonitas. Con especial referencia a su llegada a la América Latina*. Buenos Aires, Montevideo.
Susnik, Branislava, and Miguel Chase-Sardi. 1995. *Los indios del Paraguay*. Madrid.
Suzuki, Taku. 2006. "Becoming 'Japanese' in Bolivia: Okinawan-Bolivian trans(national) formations in Colonia Okinawa." *Identities: Global Studies in Culture and Power* 13 (3):455–481.
Tambiah, Stanley J. 1968. "Literacy in a Buddhist village in north-east Thailand." Pp. 85–131 in *Literacy in traditional societies*, edited by J. Goody. Cambridge.
Taylor, Charles. 2004. *Modern social imaginaries*. Durham, NC.
Taylor, Diana. 1997. *Disappearing acts: Spectacles of gender and nationalism in Argentina's "Dirty war"*. Durham, NC.
Todorov, Tzvetan. 1984. *The conquest of America: The question of the other*. Translated by R. Howard. New York.
Toews, Paul. 1989. "Mennonites in American society: Modernity and the persistence of religious community". *Mennonite Quarterly Review* LXIII (3):227–246.
Toulis, Nicole Rodriguez. 1997. *Believing identity: Pentecostalism and the mediation of Jamaican ethnicity and gender in England*. Oxford.
Turner, Victor W. 1994. *The forest of symbols. Aspects of Ndembu ritual*. Ithaca, NY.
———. 1995. *The ritual process: Structure and anti-structure*. New York.
Umble, Diane Zimmerman. 1996. *Holding the line: The telephone in Old Order Mennonite and Amish life*. Baltimore, MD.
Urquiola, Miguel. 1999. "La distribución de la población en el siglo xx." Pp. 193–218 in *Bolivia en el siglo xx. La formación de la Bolivia contemporánea*, edited by F. Campero Prudencio. La Paz.
Urry, James. 1978. "The closed and the open: Social and religious change amongst the Mennonites in Russia (1789–1889)." D.Phil Thesis, University of Oxford, Oxford.
———. 1983. "'The snares of reason'—changing Mennonite attitudes to 'Knowledge' In nineteenth-century Russia." *Comparative Studies in Society and History* 25 (2):306–322.
———. 2006. *Mennonites, politics, and peoplehood: Europe—Russia—Canada 1525 to 1980*. Winnipeg, MB.
van der Veer, Peter. 1996. "Introduction." Pp. 1–22 in *Conversion to modernities: The globalization of Christianity*, edited by P. van der Veer. New York.
Viswanathan, Gauri. 1996. "Religious conversion and the politics of dissent." Pp. 89–114 in *Conversion to modernities: The globalization of Christianity*, edited by P. van der Veer. New York.
Waite, Gary K. 1987. "The Anabaptist movement in Amsterdam and the Netherlands, 1531–1535: An initial investigation into its genesis and social dynamics." *Sixteenth Century Journal* 18 (2):249–265.
———. 1992. "The Dutch nobility and Anabaptism, 1535–1545." *Sixteenth Century Journal* 23 (3):458–485.
Walbert, David J. 2002. *Garden spot: Lancaster county, the Old Order Amish, and the selling of rural America*. Oxford.
Walker-Bynum, Caroline. 1987. *Holy feast and holy fast: The religious significance of food to medieval women*. Berkeley.
Warkentin, Abe. 1987. *Gäste und fremdlinge / strangers and pilgrims*. Steinbach, MB.

Warkentin, John. 1959. "Mennonite agricultural settlements of southern Manitoba." *Geographical Review* 49 (3):342–368.
Watson-Franke, Maria-Barbara, and Lawrence Craig Watson. 1985. *Interpreting life histories: An anthropological inquiry*. New Brunswick, NJ.
Weaver-Zercher, David. 2001. *The Amish in the American imagination*. Baltimore, MD.
Weber, Max. 1946. *From Max weber: Essays in sociology*. Translated by H. H. Gerth and C. W. Mills. New York.
———. 1978. *Economy and society: An outline of interpretive sociology*. Translated by E. Fischoff, H. Gerth, A. M. Henderson, F. Kolegar, C. Wright Mills, T. Parsons, M. Rheinstein, G. Roth, E. Shils and C. Wittich. II vols. Vol. I. Berkeley.
———. 1991. *The protestant ethic and the spirit of capitalism*. London. Original edition, 1904–5.
Weir, Peter. 1985. Witness. USA.
Werbner, Richard. 1984. "The Manchester-school in south-central Africa." *Annual Review of Anthropology* 13:157–185.
———. 1991. *Tears of the dead: The social biography of an African family*. Edinburgh, Washington DC.
———. 1997. "The suffering body: Passion and ritual allegory in Christian encounters." *Journal of Southern African Studies* 23 (2):311–324.
Wessel, Kelso L, and Judith A Wessel. 1967. "The Mennonites in Bolivia. An historical and present social-economic evaluation." Ithaca, NY.
Wiebe, Johannes. 1881. "Confessions of faith of the Mennonites in Manitoba, North America." in *Catechism: Or a brief instruction for young people from the holy scriptures, in the form of questions and answers. New german-english edition*. Altona, MB.
Will, Martina E. 1997. "The Mennonite colonization of Chihuahua: Reflections of competing visions." *The Americas* 53 (3):353–378.
Williams, George Huntston. 1962. *The Radical Reformation*. Philadelphia, PA.
Wilson, Bryan. 1981. "Time, generations, and sectarianism." Pp. 217–234 in *The social impact of new religious movements*, edited by B. Wilson. New York.
———, ed. 1967. *Patterns of sectarianism: Organisation and ideology in social and religious movements*. London.
Wilson, Kathleen M. 1975. "Mennonites in the Paraguayan Chaco: Response to Redekop and Basso." *American Anthropologist* 77 (4):881–883.
Wimmer, Andreas, and Nina Glick Schiller. 2002. "Methodological nationalism and beyond: Nation-state building, migration and the social sciences." *Global Networks* 2 (4):301–334.
Wittgenstein, Ludwig. 1967. *Philosophische untersuchungen. Philosophical investigations*. Translated by G. E. M. Anscombe. Oxford.
Wolf, Eric R. 1997. *Europe and the people without history*. Berkeley. Original edition, 1982.
Worsley, Peter. 1970. *The trumpet shall sound. A study of 'cargo' cults in Melanesia*. Aylesbury.
Wright, Stuart A. 1991. "Reconceptualizing cult coercion and witdrawal: A comparative analysis of divorce and apostasy." *Social Forces* 70 (1):125–145.
Wuthnow, Robert. 1989. *Communities of discourse: Ideology and social structure in the reformation, the enlightenment, and european socialism*. Cambridge, MA.
Yamba, C. Bawa. 1992. "Going there and getting there: The future as a legitimating charter for life in the present." Pp. 109–123 in *Contemporary futures: Perspectives from social anthropology*, edited by S. Wallman. London.
Yoder, Paton. 2003. "The Amish view of the state." Pp. 23–42 in *The Amish and the state*, edited by D. B. Kraybill. Baltimore, MD.
Zagorin, Perez. 2003. *How the idea of religious toleration came to the west*. Princeton, NJ.

INDEX*

Absolutism 18, 19
Agamben, Giorgio 3
Altkolonier Reinlaender Menonniten Gemeinde 27, 56, 76
Amish 4–6, 23
  in Bolivia 138, 139, 186
  ideology and behaviour, confussion between 6
  romantic vision of 5–6
  studies of 4
Anabaptism 1, 18–19, 20–27
  background 1
  excommunication in 23, 24
  history of 18–27, 171
Anderson, Benedict 28, 53, 69, 141n
Anderson, Perry 18–20, 51, 52, 53, 93
Angrosino, Michael 169
Argentina xi, 1, 32, 59, 76
  dictatorship 127, 128, 142
  economic situation 136, 142
  evangelism in 87, 88, 105, 106, 107, 113, 117, 123–125, 128, 139, 172
  imagination of 62, 63
  La Pampa xi, 63, 73
  Mennonite migration to 62–64
  migration to 62, 63
  religion and state in 128, 129
Argentina, Mennonite colonies in
  La Nueva Esperanza xii–xv, 31, 62–64, 92, 117, 172
  Sachayoj 76, 77t, 79, 125
  Pampa de los Guanacos 117
Asad, Talal 33, 36, 43, 69, 116, 141, 193

baptism
  experiences of 162, 172, 173, 182
  Old Colony Mennonites, among 37, 38, 87, 192
  social consequences of 37–39, 157, 193

Bateson, Gregory 110
Beckford, James A. 114, 117
Belize 67, 122
Bender, Harold S. 19, 24, 26
Bennett, John W. 4, 5, 7
Bible 33, 34, 44, *See also under* literacy
  Book of Revelation 16, 42, 146–148, 153, 160, 163, 166, 175, 183
  disputes with 101, 134, 136, 144–146, 153, 156, 161, 166, 171, 177, 187, 189, 190
  interpretations of 19, 20, 90, 101, 102, 132, 133, 144, 145, 147, 148, 152, 153, 157, 160, 161, 163, 164, 166, 172, 183
  inerrancy of 144
Bloch, Marc 28, 113, 117
Bloch, Maurice 144
Bolivia 1, 32, 59, 60–62, 65
  Amish in 138
  Charagua 179
  conditions before Mennonite arrival 60–62
  Decreto Supremo 06030 61
  Mennonite colonies in 62, 118, 138, 139, 161, 178
  Mennonite migration to 62–64
  Santa Cruz 35, 60
  Tarija 126, 127, 138, 139, 179, 186, 188
Bonfil Batalla, Guillermo 13
Bourdieu, Pierre 10, 11, 33, 57n, 69, 110, 111
Boyer, Paul S. 145, 147, 165
Braght, Tieleman J. Van. 34, 42, 43, 69
  See also Martyrs' Mirror
British Honduras 59
  See also Belize
Bush, Perry 65

---

* I thank Christopher Brennan and Carlos Moreno Romero for their assistance in compiling this index.

Cameron, Euan 1n, 18, 19, 21, 23
Canada
 conditions before Mennonite arrival 54
 Manitoba 55
 Manitoba Public Schools Act 56
 Mennonite colonies in 55, 56
 Mennonite migrations to 54–57
Capps, L. 114, 117
Catherine the Great 26, 51, 53
Chaco 60, 65
Chaco War 60
Chortitza 26, 52
Christenvolk 17, 40, 42, 59
Christianity 19, 115
 history of 19
 dissenters definition of 120–124, 126, 128, 139, 141, 146–151, 154–157, 159–163, 165, 166, 173, 176
 Old Colony Mennonite definition of 92, 100–102, 113, 115, 124, 142, 143, 147, 148, 155, 156, 159, 173, 176, 191, 192
Clifford, James 3
Cohen, Anthony P. 6, 17, 35
Cohn, Norman 19, 20n, 146n
conflict
 among Mennonites xiii–xvi, 4, 27, 39, 44, 107, 138, 160, 167, 176, 178
 between principles 105, 107, 189
 schism 15, 24, 27, 39, 56, 60, 64, 70, 75, 77t, 81, 178, 192
 with others 15, 86, 103–105, 111
 See also dissent, *and* excommunication
Consejo Nacional de Población 61
conversion
 experience of 127–132, 139, 140
 studies of 114–117, 132, 133
Csordas Thomas J. 38n, 116, 163n

d'Azeglio, Massimo 69
Deiros, Pablo A. 129
Deleuze, Gilles 3, 49, 52, 53, 68
Derksen, Enrique 26, 65, 66
deviance
 definition 146, 170
 as methodological strategy 145, 170
 See also dissent, *and* excommunication
Die Mennonitische Post 79, 94
dissent
 externalization of 124, 135, 165, 169, 171, 177, 178, 180, 189, 190, 196

 internal ostracism 138, 174, 178, 180, 189, 190
 isolation of 171, 180, 190, 192
Donnadach xiii, 30
Douglas, Mary 86, 186, 188
Durkheim, Emile 57n, 170, 193
Dutch Patriot Movement 22
Dyck, Cornelius J. 66, 67

Elias, Norbert 18
Elton, G. R. 18, 19
Erikson, Kai 145, 170
exception *See* state of exception
excommunication 30, 40, 118, 138, 154, 162, 169–171, 178, 179, 190, 192
 avoidance of 138, 169–171, 179, 190
 experiences of 178
 Menno Simons, according to 23
 ritual of obedience, as 118, 154, 162, 190, 192
 social consequences of 40, 41, 118, 138, 171, 192

Faubion, James D. 110, 165
Feeley-Harnik, Gillian 39
Feitlowitz, Marguerite 127, 158n
Ferguson, James 3, 51
Fibel 28
fieldwork conditions xv, xvi
Fix, Andrew 22, 50, 68
Francis, E. K. 24–26
Fuller, Chris 34

Giddens, Anthony 11, 116
Glick Schiller, Nina 4, 70
Goody, Jack 20, 34, 35, 143, 144, 153, 169
Grebel, Conrad 19, 20
Guatraché Land Co. xi
Guattari, Felix 3, 49, 52, 53, 68
Gupta, Akhil 3, 51

Habermas, Jürgen 20, 51, 53, 70
Hack, Henk 65, 66
Hage, Ghassan 49
Harding, Susan Friend 116, 132, 172
Harvey, David 10
Heavy metal 127–131, 133
Hefner, Robert 116
Heirich, Max 114, 116
Hermitte, Esther 85, 86
Hobsbawm, Eric J. 19, 20, 53, 59
Hoerder, Dirk 24, 51, 52, 54
Hoffman, Melchior 21

Holland, Dorothy C.   114
Holy Roman Empire   18
Holy Spirit   99, 130–133, 135,
  140–142, 152, 157, 161
Hostetler, Beulah Stauffer   7, 23n
Hostetler, John A.   4–7, 46n
Huebert, Helmut   26, 27, 52
Huntington, Gertrude E.   5, 7, 103n

imagination of the future
  alternative   35, 36, 113, 120, 121,
    123, 124, 126, 146–160, 170, 173,
    174, 175–179, 183, 187–189, 194,
    195
  concept of   2–13
  conflicts on   3, 69, 70, 180–187
  dominant   7, 8, 35, 36, 85, 137, 170,
    171, 180, 184, 186, 187, 189, 192,
    194, 195
  and moral order   7, 8, 11, 12, 14, 18,
    33, 149, 152, 171, 191, 192, 194

Janzen, William   55, 56, 61n
Jehova's Witnesses
  conversion to   186, 189
  Mennonite labeling as   186–188, 192

Kantorowicz, Ernst Hartwig   55, 68
Kirchner, Walther   24, 26
Klaassen, C. F.   5, 55–57
Kleine Gemeinde   27
Kniss, Fred LaMar   1, 4–6, 39, 65, 171
Koselleck, Reinhart   19
Krahn, Cornelius   5, 25–27, 52, 56–58
Kraybill, Donald B.   4–8
Kurtz, Lester R.   169

La Nueva Esperanza   xii–xv, 31, 62, 64
  formation of   62–64
  layout   xii
  location of   xii
  property regime   31
Lanning, James W.   59, 60
Latour, Bruno   21, 22, 50, 193
Liminality   178, 190
Literacy   105, 143, 144, 153, 179
Loewen, Royden   5, 65
Longhofer, Jeffrey   26, 52, 53
Lord's Supper
  according to Menno Simons   39
  among Old Colony Mennonites   40,
    136, 173, 192
  social consequences of   40, 41, 136
Luther, Martin   18–21, 23

Malkki, Liisa H.   4, 51, 53, 195
Manz, Felix   19, 20
Marginality   xvi, 145, 170
Martyrs' Mirror   33, 42, 140, 141, 152,
  157, 174
Marx, Karl   9
Mauss, Marcel   33
Mennonite Central Committee (Centro
  Menno)   89, 182
Mennonites
  history   18–26, 51–67
  history, at the end of their   8
  ideology and behaviour, confussion
    of   6
  demographic trends   80–83
  early moderns, as   47, 22, 50, 193
  modernity, relationship with   2, 5,
    10, 48, 59, 67, 99, 120, 134, 145,
    146, 149, 172, 193
  perception of the world   87, 88, 99,
    104, 121, 137
  perfect community, examples of   2
  persecution of   18–26
  representations of, *See under*
    representations of Mennonites
  self-definition   87, 92, 95, 102,
    103, 106, 107, 123, 157, 174,
    176, 182, 193, 194
  social transformation of   14
  time, attitudes to   24, 25, 151, 194,
    See also under time
Mennonites, internal organization of
  134, 138, 142, 144, 169
  administrative structure   25, 27–31,
    97, 104, 109, 177, 184, 185, 191
  educational structure   28–30, 110,
    179, 196
  religious organization   xiii, 16,
    28–31, 33, 37, 40, 47, 37, 74, 90,
    91, 101, 107, 109, 192, 196
Mennonites, relationship with
  nation-states   50–70, *See also under*
    nation-state *and* Privilegia
  Argentine government   63, 64, 104,
    105, 124
  Canadian nationalism, rejection of
    56, 57
  Mexico, irrigation issues in   59, 60
  migration to Argentina   62–64
  migration to Belize   67
  migration to Bolivia   62–64
  migration to Brazil   67
  migration to Canada   54–57
  migration to Mexico   57–59

migration to Paraguay 65–67
migration to Ukraine 51, 53, 54
migration to Uruguay 67
public schooling 50, 53, 55–57, 59, 63, 64, 66, 67, 69, 75, 83, 99, 103–106, 137, 150, 174, 177
Russification, rejection of 53
sovereignty 15, 41, 50, 52–54, 65, 68
territorialization of states 52–56
Mennonites, transformations of
Leardeenst becoming a state 18, 31, 33, 47, 80, 109, 120, 145, 146, 152–157, 171, 176, 190, 192, 194, 196
nation, becoming a 25, 79, 105, 124, 134–138, 166, 167, 191–193, 196
Mennonites, practices
anointing with oil 182, 188
articulation 85–111,
attire xii, 45, 46, 121, 152, 153
authoritative texts 33–35, *See also* Bible; literacy; *Martyrs' Mirror*; Simons, Menno
automobile restrictions 44, 45
baptism 37–39
burial 43
economic activities 32, 33, 58, 72, 92
electricity, usage of 45
excommunication 40, 118, 138, 154, 169–171, 178, 179, 190, 192
feet-washing 162, 173, 182, 188
inter-colony dynamics 71–83
land acquisition 72–74
Lord's Supper 39, 40
marriage practices 88, 89, 96, 121, 136, 137
music, restrictions 45
parish records 80–83
prayers of the elders 182
property regime 31
secularization 33, 194
separation from the world 24–26, 68–70
Mennonite colonies
cross-border practices 77
formation of 27, 72–74, 77
layout of 28
movement between 78, 79, 82
transformation of 46–48
Mexico
conditions before Mennonite arrival 58

Mennonite colonies in 58
Mennonite migrations to 57–59
millennialism 165
modernity
constitution of 21, 22, 193
structural differentiation of domains 33, 195
narrative of 2, 7, 8, 10
and religion 114–116, 142, 190, 191, 193–196
rejection of 2, 5, 134, 145, 146, 151, 159, 166, 193
social order of 50, 51, 166, 182
See also under national order of things
moral order *See under* imagination of the future
Morgan, Edmund Sears 11, 12, 20, 53, 55, 68, 111
Mullet, Michael A. 19–21, 24
Munster 20
Murillo, Father Julio 60, 61

national order of things 4, 83, 165, 195
nation-state
citizenship and nationality 2, 15, 49, 50, 53, 63, 68–70, 166, 195, 196
conflicts with 57, 70, 86, 103–106, 111
formation of 2, 3, 18, 50, 51, 53, 68–70, 191
loyalty to 57, 69, 70, 196
legitimation of 11, 20, 52–55, 61, 69, 195, 196, *See also under* sovereignty
negotiation with 54, 57, 62, 64, 68, 137, 195, 196, *See also under* Privilegia
public schooling, Mennonite rejection of 104–106, 137, 155
rejection of the nation 56, 57, 106
soverreignty of *See under* sovereignty
territorialization of 52, 53, 55, 56
unreadability of states 110
Nolt, Steven 8

O'Leary, Stephen D. 19, 145
Obregón, Álvaro 58
Ochs, E. 114, 117
Ordninj 30, 42–46, 74, 78, 79

Paraguay River 60
Paraguay 59, 60, 65–67
Peacock, James L. 114

persecution
  as mark of true Christian   40, 42, 69, 76
  of Mennonites   18–27, 38, 47, 48, 65, 110, 111, 141, 154, 155, 165, 174
  within Old Colony Mennonites   120, 152, 155, 174
Peter, Karl A.   144, 156
Pilgrim's Progress   34
Poland   24–26
politics and religion
  political absorption and concealment of the religious   54, 55, 70, 196
  political externalization of the religious   21, 50,
  religious absorption and concealment of the political   14, 18, 41, 194, 196
  religious externalization of the political   14, 41
  separation of church and state   21, 41, 196
Pollman, Judith   140
Potemkin, Grigori Aleksandrovich   26, 51, 52
Poverty   120, 121, 128, 154, 162
Privilegia
  as state of exception   3, 41, 68, 196
  in Argentina   63
  in Bolivia   62, 123
  in Canada   55
  in Mexico   58
  in Ukraine   51–53

Redekop, Calvin Wall   4, 6–8, 39, 52n, 54–59, 66n, 75
  cultural vs. structural assimilation   7, 8
  on Mennonite migration   59, 75
Reformation   18–21
religion and politics
  political absorption and concealment of the religious   54, 55, 70, 196
  political externalization of the religious   21, 50,
  religious absorption and concealment of the political   14, 18, 41, 194, 196
  religious externalization of the political   14, 41
  separation of church and state   21, 41, 196
religion as total social fact   33, 194, 195

religious experience
  cold   154, 155, 174, 189, 195
  faith in humans vs. faith in God   124, 148, 149, 152–154, 156, 174, 187
  fear of God   142, 150–152, 161
  hot   99, 101, 129, 130–133, 135, 140, 157, 173, 182–187, 189, 195
  natural   126, 140–142, 152, 157, 193, 194, 195
  supernatural   129–133, 136, 140–142, 157, 173, 183, 184, 193–195
representations of Mennonites   1, 7
  academic   1, 93
  confussion of ideology and reality   7, 154
  popular   1, 93, 98, 103

Santa Cruz   35, 60
Saunders, G. R.   114–116
Sawatzky, Harry Leonard   31, 55–59
schism   15, 24, 27, 39, 56, 60, 64, 70, 75, 77t, 81, 178, 192
Schmitt, Carl   42, 50, 55, 57, 68
Schutz, Alfred   10
Scott, James C.   41, 49, 53, 61, 190
Siffredi, Alejandra B.   65, 66
Simons, Menno   1, 18, 20–23, 33–35, 36–42
  baptism   22
  breaking with Catholic church   22
  life and background   21
  Lord's Supper   39
  separation from the world   40–42, 141
  signs for identifying the Church of Christ   36–42
  spreading of Anabaptism   23
  writings   35, 33, 151
sovereignty   11, 20
  and nationality   69
  changes of   68
  Mennonite contribution to   15, 50, 52–54, 65, 68
  popular   11, 20, 54, 55
state of exception   3, 41, 68, 196
Stayer, James M.   21, 22
Stromberg, Peter G.   17, 116, 140
suffering   *See also Martyrs' Mirror*
  and knowledge   xiv, 115, 126, 154, 157
  and morality   41–43, 115, 133, 141, 162
Swiss Brethren   19, 21

Taylor, Charles 11, 39, 50
Taylor, Diana 127, 129
time
  and history 113, 115
  and modernity 2, 5, 8, 151, 194
  end of 10, 19, 155, 157
  Mennonite attitudes to 24, 25, 151, 194
  sacred 45, 194
Todorov, Tzvetan 6
Trappe, George van 26
Turner, Victor W. 86, 178

Ukraine 14, 26, 27
  Chortitza 26, 52
  conditions before Mennonite
    arrival 26, 51, 52
  Mennonite migration to 26, 51, 52
Umble, Diane Zimmerman 4–6
Urquiola, Miguel 60, 61
Urry, James 1n, 22–27, 51–55, 65, 68n

Waite, Gary K. 21
Warkentin, Abe 58, 62, 66–68
Warkentin, John 28n, 32, 55, 56
Watt, Ian 35, 143
Weber, Max 10, 25, 156, 171n
Weltmensch 42, 87, 88, 114, 137, 176, 192
Werbner, Richard 114, 115, 117n, 85
West Prussia 24
Wiebe, Johannes 55, 66
Williams, John Huntston 1n, 18, 19, 21–24
Wimmer, Andreas 4, 70
Wüst, Eduard 27

Yoder, Paton 41, 50, 147n

Zagorin, Perez 20, 23, 40
Zurich 19
Zwingli, Ulrich 19, 20